THE
MOTIVATED
JOB SEARCH

A PROVEN SYSTEM TO
HELP YOU STAND OUT

BRIAN E. HOWARD, JD, CCMC, CJSS, CPRW

CERTIFIED CAREER MANAGEMENT COACH
CERTIFIED JOB SEARCH STRATEGIST
CERTIFIED PROFESSIONAL RESUME WRITER

Virginia

The Motivated Job Search - A Proven System to Help You Stand Out, Second Edition
© 2018 Brian E. Howard. All rights reserved.

The external links are being provided as a convenience and for informational purposes only; they do not constitute an endorsement or an approval by WriteLife Publishing of any of the products, services or opinions of the corporation or organization or individual. WriteLife Publishing bears no responsibility for the accuracy, legality or content of the external site or for that of subsequent links. Contact the external site for answers to questions regarding its content.

Published in the United States by WriteLife Publishing
(An imprint of Boutique of Quality Books Publishing Company)
www.writelife.com

Printed in the United States of America

978-1-60808-191-2 (p)
978-1-60808-192-9 (e)

Library of Congress Control Number: 2018938200
Book design by Robin Krauss, www.bookformatters.com
Cover design by Ellis Dixon, ellisdixon.com

LinkedIn, the LinkedIn logo, the IN logo and InMail are registered trademarks of LinkedIn Corporation and its affiliates in the United States and / or other countries. Screenshots contained in this book are used for informational and educational purposes.

The Certified Career Management Coach (CCMC) and the Certified Job Search Strategist (CJSS) designations are sanctioned by The Academies, as approved by the International Coach Foundation (ICF).

The Certified Professional Resume Writer (CPRW) designation is sanctioned by the Professional Association of Resume Writers.

Praise for *The Motivated Job Search*

If you're conducting a job search for a professional position or considering such a job search, you should read this book. Brian Howard provides a thorough, approachable guide to each of the components of a job search that will help you be the selected candidate.

Vice President Human Resources

From my 30 years in recruiting and helping recruit or hire over 1,000 employees, The Motivated Job Search *is comprehensive, inspiring and thorough from beginning to end and guides you through the challenges and complexities facing job seekers today. You will learn new ways to look at old problems such as resumes and cover letters, and gain the upper hand in navigating through the employment process by discovering ways to differentiate yourself from the pack. From professional networking to the power of social media, Brian Howard covers it all!*

Corporate Recruiting Manager

I received an advanced copy of The Motivated Job Search. As a seasoned professional with many years of experience I was a bit skeptical of finding something new. I soon discovered however, that The Motivated Job Search *offered many new strategies supported by detailed examples to further drive home the points! I especially appreciated the need to establish a brand and seek alternatives to the stale resume format I was using. In addition, the book offered numerous strategies to help differentiate me as a job seeker. This useful resource changed my approach to the job search. I look forward to buying a copy that I can notate, dog-ear, and refer to over and over. Thank you and well done Brian!*

Operations professional in the technology and telecommunications industries

As a job seeker, I found **The Motivated Job Search** *extremely helpful! The book is a complete A to Z guide to conducting an effective job search. The topics on creating differentiation, resumes, networking, interviewing, and negotiating job offers were particularly impactful for me. It contained ideas and strategies I did not know about or ever considered. It is the complete job search book!*

Sales representative in the wellness and
healthcare industry

The book is OUTSTANDING *and a must-read/must-have!* The Motivated Job Search *is a culmination of Brian Howard's 20+ years as a highly successful executive recruiter, career coach, and advocate. The book provides a step-by-step road map to help you proactively land the right opportunity or career change at the right time, no matter where you are in your life. Brian Howard speaks to the reader from an authentic, sincere, yet practical perspective and provides all of the tools to help you differentiate yourself in a competitive marketplace and get the job you want.*

As a sales executive who has read many books, hands down, this is the best and most effective that I have ever read. I will continue to use the tools and information in this book and apply them to my work and life. Thank you Brian Howard for this game-changing job search book.

Sales Executive

Other Books by Brian E. Howard

The *Motivated* Networker
Over 50 and *Motivated!*
The *Motivated* Job Search Workbook
Motivated Resumes & LinkedIn Profiles

This book is dedicated to my wife Kathy and our three wonderful children Tucker, Justin, and Taylor.

The Top Ten Things You Can Do to Shorten Your Job Search

1. **Get emotionally prepared to start your job search.** There will be successes and disappointments during your search. When the disappointments occur, they will not stall your efforts and defeat your positive attitude.

2. **Treat your job search as a job.**
   A. If you are unemployed—it's a full-time job.
   B. If you are employed—it's a part-time job.

3. **Mentally prepare for it to take longer than you think.** This book will help shorten the process, but don't get discouraged when things don't happen as fast as you'd like. Perseverance is the key!

4. **Start organized and stay organized.** Keep track of what you are doing. Being organized will streamline your efforts and prevent embarrassing situations with potential employers and networking contacts.

5. **Create an impactful resume.** Having a well-designed and informative resume is a direct reflection of you as a professional.

6. **Create a complete LinkedIn profile.** Your LinkedIn profile must be optimized for maximum impact. Your profile is how many HR recruiters and hiring executives will find you.

7. **Set up job alerts.** Use Indeed.com or Simplyhired.com, LinkedIn, Twitter, and company websites. Get a flow of job openings coming to you.

8. **Research.** Devote the necessary time and effort to research companies, people, positions, and the industry, among other topics.

9. **Network timely and professionally.** Most jobs are a result of some form of networking. It's imperative that you do it right.

10. **Proactively market your professional credentials.** Marketing your professional credentials directly to employers will get you into the Hidden Job Market.

Message from the Author

For over twenty-five years I have been helping people find new jobs. It is remarkable to me to this day how many don't know how to do it well. Many think they do, but once quizzed on what they are doing and how they are going about things, they realize their efforts are not as effective as they believe. I've heard the ineffective approaches repeated many times over. It would take me two hours, or in some cases two days, to undo the way some people approach a job search.

The process of a job search is reasonably simple. Anyone can understand the overarching concepts. First, you must understand what to do (knowledge). This is understanding what the action steps are that comprise a job search. Then, learn to effectively do it (action). This is executing the steps of a job search. And finally, in the process of execution, you differentiate yourself from other job seekers to get the job you want (uniqueness). This is vitally important because the ultimate decision to hire is the result of a selection process.

The key to be selected and offered a job is having strategic insight regarding the job search process and presenting yourself as unique at every step along the way. This book was written to teach you the steps of a successful job search, but more importantly the strategy and insight that other job seekers simply will not know that will make you stand out from the crowd.

This book is the culmination of a career's worth of experience. I wrote it to be the most comprehensive and effective job search book possible so your search will be short and successful!

— Brian E. Howard

Table of Contents

Introduction

Don't bunt. Aim out of the ballpark.
Aim for the company of immortals.
— David Ogilvy[1]

This job search book is written for the career-minded professional or executive who wants quick and direct answers on how to effectively conduct a job search in today's competitive marketplace.

The approach is simple: each chapter is designed to tell you what you need to know and what you need to do to get a job. The book is written in straightforward language, assuming that the reader already has a basic understanding of hiring practices in the business world.

The Advantages of a Self-Motivated Job Search

There are two ways to conduct a job search: by being self-motivated or passive. Being passive in a job search is similar to using a saw to do a hammer's work—it's ineffective, makes the job (your search) longer, and may result in failure. The passive search bases all sense of direction on jobs posted on the Internet. In contrast, the self-motivated method is both effective and efficient, making it the best way to conduct a job search. Why? This method is

---

1 "David Ogilvy Quotable Quote," Goodreads, http://www.goodreads.com/quotes/262108-don-t-bunt-aim-out-of-the-ballpark-aim-for-the (accessed May 28, 2015).

proactive—the job seeker actively engages the job market to discover opportunities where their skills and competencies bring the greatest value to an employer. There are several distinct advantages of conducting a self-motivated job search that help you get a job more effectively.[2]

These advantages can also help you get the job offer you want. These advantages include:

Access to the Hidden Job Market

A self-motivated job search will tap the Hidden Job Market, uncovering unadvertised positions. Statistically speaking, 75 to 80 percent of all open jobs are not advertised.[3] Instead of passively searching, you'll engage the job market proactively by networking and contacting target companies to create your own pipeline of opportunities with as many leads as your well-planned efforts can produce.

Being Able to Present Yourself as a Solution/Value Proposition

Your professional value proposition is the totality of your education, experience, and other intangible factors that an employer views as valuable to the company. When you present yourself as a solution to a hiring need, this professional picture of you sparks the employer's interest and motivates them to evaluate the benefits and costs of making you an employee of the company. You will discover how to transform information about the company, products, services, executives, industry, company news releases, and so on into messages to the hiring executive of how you can prevent, solve, or divert a business problem.

In the end, your value proposition must make or save the company money beyond the costs of hiring you and keeping you as an employee (leading to a positive return on investment, or ROI).

Improved Attitude/Confidence

A self-motivated job search puts you in control. Rather than being at the whim of posted job openings, you make things happen. This will keep your attitude about your job

---

2 Joyce, Susan P. "Job Search Success Strategy: PROactive vs. REactive Job Search," Job-Hunt.org, http://www.job-hunt.org/article_proactive_job_search.shtml (accessed July 14, 2015).

3 Kaufman, Wendy. "A Successful Job Search: It's All About Networking," National Public Radio, February 3, 2011, http://www.npr.org/2011/02/08/133474431/a-successful-job-search-its-all-about-networking (accessed June 2, 2015); "Developing Job Search Strategies," University of Wisconsin, https://www.uwgb.edu/careers/PDF-Files/Job-Search-Strategies.pdf (accessed June 3, 2015).

search positive, helping build your confidence and self image. Believe it—maintaining a positive attitude and showing confidence is a big deal and being proactive will keep things moving forward.[4] It's likely you won't fall victim to the negative emotions a stale job search may bring if you're feeling good about how your search is progressing.

Direct Contact with Hiring Executives

One of the keys to landing job offers is getting hiring executive(s) inspired about your background and the benefits you can bring to the company. Enlisting a champion for your cause will significantly increase your odds of more interviews and job offers.[5]

Increased Networking Opportunities

Networking is proactively reaching out to others in your professional and personal database, both online and face-to-face, offering yourself as a resource to help others, and knowing that they will do what they can to help you in return. Networking keeps you engaged with others and with the events, news, and emerging trends in your industry. Networking will include reaching out to your contacts in a variety of settings including LinkedIn, your local Chamber of Commerce, professional associations, and civic and philanthropic organizations, among others. Networking creates relationships. Your next job will likely be as a result of "people, talking to people, about people." It's estimated that from 60 to 80 percent of jobs are filled by networking.[6]

Referrals

As your networking expands and your relationships mature, you will receive a steady

4 Kanfer, Ruth, and Charles L. Hulin. "Individual Differences in Job Searches Following Lay-off." Abstract. Person-nel Psychology 38, no. 4 (December 1985): 835–847, http://www.researchgate.net/publication/227749499_INDIVIDUAL_DIFFERENCES_IN_SUCCESSFUL_JOB_SEARCHES_FOLLOWING_LAYOFF (accessed July 9, 2015); Moynihan, Lisa M., Mark V. Roehling, Marcie A. LePine, and Wendy R. Boswell "A Longitudinal Study of the Relationships Among Job Search Self-Efficacy, Job Interviews, and Employment Outcomes." Abstract. Journal of Business and Psychology 18, no. 2 (2003): 201–233, http://link.springer.com/article/10.1023%2FA%3A1027349115277 (accessed July 3, 2015).

5 Kurtzberg, Terri R., and Charles E. Naquin. The Essentials of Job Negotiations: Proven Strategies for Getting What You Want. (Santa Barbara, CA: Praeger, 2011), p. 18.

6 "Using LinkedIn to Find a Job or Internship," LinkedIn, https://university.linkedin.com/content/dam/university/global/en_US/site/pdf/TipSheet_FindingaJoborInternship.pdf (accessed June 7, 2015); Kimberly Beatty, "The Math Behind the Networking Claim," Jobfully Blog, July 1, 2010, http://blog.jobfully.com/2010/07/the-math-behind-the-networking-claim/ (accessed June 11, 2015); Steven Rothberg, "80% of Job Openings are Unadvertised," College Recruiter (blog), March 28, 2013, https://www.collegerecruiter.com/blog/2013/03/28/80-of-job-openings-are-unadvertised/ (accessed June 11, 2015).

flow of referrals and recommendations from colleagues, insider-employees, former bosses, and others. Your reputation and sphere of influence will grow and you will gain the inside track regarding open positions.

Reduced Competition

It's no secret that in today's market, open job positions teem with competing job seekers, all with the same goal: to be hired. However, in a self-motivated search, you could become one of just a handful of referred or recommended candidates, or in some cases the only job seeker under consideration, minimizing competition.

Access to Direct Insider Information

When you use a self-motivated job search strategy, you will quickly learn what the hiring executive wants from the person filling a position. This invaluable information allows you to focus your background and achievements to fulfill those needs.

Rapport Building

A self-motivated job search encourages building rapport. If you are introduced to a hiring executive by referral from your network, you may be able to speak with others who know the individual. They can give you valuable insight on personality, hot buttons, and so on. And if the executive is the decision maker for hiring, you avoid Human Resources, sometimes until after you're hired.

A self-motivated job search is an effective and efficient approach. It gets you moving, thinking, reaching out to others, and working toward your future. It puts you in control and boosts your attitude and job-search confidence. It's generally accepted that hiring executives view the self-motivated approach favorably because they see you taking action.

The Psychology of Persuasion and Your Job Search

Before we dive into the steps and techniques for conducting a job search, it's beneficial to talk briefly about the psychology of persuasion and how it will affect your job search.

What follows are some very important concepts woven throughout the rest of this book. Knowing them will help you maximize your job-search success because they combine so effectively with the self-motivated approach.

According to Robert Cialdini, a leader in the field of psychology and persuasion, there are six principles that persuade others to think and act as they do. They are:

- Scarcity
- Authority
- Liking (and Personal Chemistry)
- Social Proof
- Commitment and Consistency
- Reciprocity / Reciprocation[7]

Scarcity

If a job seeker is viewed to be unique or special, he or she is seen as valuable.[8] How do you capitalize upon the persuasion principle of scarcity? Answer: differentiation.

Much of this book is about creating differentiation (separation) between you and other job seekers. During the course of the interviewing process, seemingly small and isolated thoughts of differentiation compound upon themselves in the mind of the hiring executive, such as if he/she dresses well, is knowledgeable on industry trends, has a professional designation, and so on. All of this affects your perceived value and motivates the hiring executive to continue the interviewing process with you, hopefully ending in an employment offer.

The more uniquely you can justifiably portray yourself, the more you are using the persuasion principle of scarcity.

Authority

Most people respond to and respect authority, whether it is a title, position, professional designation, experience, or station in life.[9]

A good example of creating intangible authority is appropriate interview attire: A starched white shirt or stylish blouse, pressed suit, polished hard-soled shoes, the pen you use, or even the watch you wear can all convey authority that others may react to favorably.

Any job-search technique or information that triggers professional respect (or elevation) with the hiring executive is using the persuasion principle of authority.

---

7 Cialdini, Robert B. Influence: Science and Practice, 4th ed. (Needham Heights, MA: Allyn & Bacon, 2001), quoted in Kurtzberg and Naquin, Essentials, chapter 5, p. 94–101.

8 Cialdini, Influence, p. 204–205, and chapter 7, "Scarcity: The Rule of the Few," quoted in Kurtzberg and Naquin, Essentials, p. 94–101.

9 Cialdini, Influence, p. 180–185, and chapter 9, "Authority: Directed Deference," quoted in Kurtzberg and Naquin, Essentials, p. 94–101.

Liking (and Personal Chemistry)

Sixty percent of most hires are based on personal chemistry.[10] In other words, hiring executives are persuaded to hire job seekers they personally like. Getting others to like you is often based on similarity or common interests. We tend to like other people similar to ourselves.[11]

There are several ways to lay the foundation for similarity and personal chemistry. Here are a few ideas:

1. Common industry associations or groups

2. Common personal interests or experiences

3. Common former employers

4. A sincere compliment

5. Name dropping (identifying common friends or professional colleagues that the hiring executive feels good about)

6. Being employed (perhaps formerly employed) by an industry-leading or innovative company

Any job-search technique that creates a positive impression on the hiring executive based on association or personal chemistry is using the persuasion principle of liking (and personal chemistry).

Social Proof

What others say about you is more persuasive than what you say about yourself. That's the power of social proof.

Psychologically, social proof is more influential and persuasive when decisions are shrouded in uncertainty. A hiring executive may be thinking: Which candidate is better qualified? Who would fit in best? What about compensation? (And so on.) This is why recommendations, references, or any form of affirmation from a trusted source can impact the hiring decision.

Any job-search technique that contains a recommendation or positive affirmation of you as a job seeker is using the persuasion principle of social proof.

---

10 Diane DiResta, interview by Christina Canters, "Episode 29—How to Blitz Your Job Interview—Secrets of Execu-tive Speech Coach Diane Diresta," DesignDrawSpeak, podcast audio, June 12, 2014.

11 Byrne, Donn Erwin. The Attraction Paradigm. (New York: Academic Press, 1971), quoted in Kurtzberg and Naquin, Essentials, p. 35.

Consistency and Commitment

People desire a reputation of upholding their own commitment and generally do not like to go back on their word.[12] It's that simple.

An example of this principle in action is when you close an interview by asking if you will be proceeding in the process. If the hiring executive indicates that you will, it will be more difficult to retreat from that answer due to the persuasion principle of consistency and commitment.

Any job-search technique that tends to bind a hiring executive to a self-imposed course of action is using the persuasion principle of consistency and commitment.

Reciprocity/Reciprocation

There is a strong psychological motivation to return favors and not to feel indebted to others. People feel the compulsion to repay another. This can be especially true if the item (of whatever nature) was given for free.[13]

An example of using this persuasion technique in a job search is providing a free sales lead, nonproprietary industry information, or information to the hiring executive about the whereabouts of a colleague. To be most effective, the gesture should be done with the expectation of receiving nothing in return, but with the awareness that the psychology of reciprocity is present.

Any job-search technique that endears you to a hiring executive by doing something for him or her (especially for free) is using the persuasion principle of reciprocity.

By raising your awareness to these persuasion principles, you will be on the alert for opportunities to capitalize upon them when opportunities present themselves. You can use the psychology to advance your candidacy.

Now that you have a basic understanding of many of the principles of persuasion, you understand the reasons for (and persuasive power of) many of the job-search techniques presented throughout this book—the same techniques used by many others, to their success. As you go along, try to identify the persuasion principle (there could be more than one) that makes a technique useful. Occasional reference is made to these persuasion principles to help your job search be more effective.

---

12 Cialdini, Influence, p. 53, and chapter 3, "Commitment and Consistency: Hobgoblins of the Mind," quoted in Kurtzberg and Naquin, Essentials, p. 94–101.

13 Cialdini, Influence, p. 144, 161, and chapter 5, "Liking: The Friendly Thief," quoted in Kurtzberg and Naquin, Essentials, p. 94–101.

How to Use This Book

This book is designed for professionals and executives who desire to take control of their job search and are committed to the work necessary to succeed.

As you read this book, have a highlighter and a pen available. Highlight concepts you want to remember. Write in the margins. Dog-ear pages. Use a notepad to write down thoughts and to-do's as they occur to you. Then, after your job search is underway, review this book to stay motivated and on track. Be careful! There are several things during a job search that can cross the line from being productive to just doing busywork disguised as being productive. Ask yourself: am I being productive with my time and effort, or am I just doing busywork, thinking that I am being productive? You'll know the answer.

Pay particular attention to the star ★ throughout the book. These useful, powerful job-search concepts or techniques will differentiate you from other job seekers, shorten your job search, and enhance your professional reputation and network.

Remember that a successful job search is about presenting yourself in a professional manner, engaging in conversations with those who can help and hire you, and providing real-life examples of your skills and accomplishments.

Chapter 1

Things to Know about Your Job Search

In the end, what we regret most are the chances we never took.
—Frasier Crane[14]

Your Job-Search Arsenal: Considerations, Tools, and Tactics

The following is a reasonably comprehensive, though not necessarily an exhaustive list of considerations, tools, and tactics for a self-motivated job search. The checklist is designed as a visual reminder of the tools and tactics at your disposal during your job search. Use it as you prepare for your search and to identify action items as you proceed through your search. Read the other chapters in this book for in-depth information.

It's recommended that you review this list every once in a while as a reminder of what you should be doing or can be doing to advance your job search.

---

14 Frasier. "Goodnight, Seattle: Part 2," first broadcast 13 May 2004 by NBC. Directed by David Lee and written by Christopher Lloyd and Joe Keenan.

Item	Comments	Check-off √
Covenant-not-to-compete Non-solicitation agreement	Adjust your job search if you have either of these	
Cleanse all social media sites	All inappropriate pictures and comments must be deleted	
Emotions – positive attitude	Stay away from negative thoughts / feelings. Positive attitude. Gratitude list.	
Resume	Appealing to the eye. Impactful.	
LinkedIn profile	Optimized	
Business cards • Traditional • Networking • Resume • Infographic	Select the one(s) you will use in your search	
Exit statement	Explanation of unemployment or why you are looking for a new job. Script for social events and one for interviews	
Target opportunity profile	Know what job(s) you're looking for	
Keywords	Know the keywords that apply for you, especially for your LinkedIn profile and resume	
Job alerts	Indeed, SimplyHired, LinkedIn, job boards, Twitter, others	
Master job description	Doing this helps you think like the hiring executive	
Accomplishments	Know what accomplishments differentiate you	
Transferrable skills and professional qualities	Those skills and qualities that make you truly unique and are often sought after by employers	
Success stories	Pre-write three. Helps in interviews and answering behavior-based questions	
Branding	Those words and statements that announce to the market who you are and what you offer	
Elevator speech	Who you are, what you do, accomplishments, start a conversation, scripted and practiced.	
Cover letter	Write a template then modify. Similar to a marketing email	
List target employers	Create a list. Add new employers when they are discovered	
Short-list of networking contacts	Your Cabinet (your inner-circle), plus others	
Networking • Local events • National conferences • Online • Research interviews	A high percentage of all jobs are found through some form of networking.	
Icebreaker questions	Prepared in advance of networking events. Having them reduces anxiety for networking events	

Item	Comments	Check-off ✓
Search firms/recruiters	Identified and contacted	
Proactively marketing your professional credentials by phone • Script marketing call • Voice mail script • Responses to objections • Script for handling the gatekeeper	This approach drives straight into the heart of the hidden job market. It is the most direct method for getting interviews and job leads.	
Proactively marketing your professional credentials by email (InMail) • Write email message • Script follow-up call	Another effective approach that works to discover jobs in the hidden job market. Always follow up with a phone call.	
Drip marketing	Used to stay in touch with a hiring executive with new information	
Last ditch effort email	Last email contact to a hiring executive that is not responding	
Interviewing • Scripted answers to common questions • Scripted answers for anticipated questions • Research	A lot of information about interviewing. Prepare for common or anticipated questions. Do research before every interview	
References	Wisely chosen and listed. Unsolicited third-party affirmation technique	
Brag book	Differentiation tactic	
Career summary sheet	Differentiation tactic	
Testimonial sheet	Differentiation tactic	
Action plan	Differentiation tactic	
Personal website	Differentiation tactic	
Blog	Differentiation tactic	
Infographic resume	Differentiation tactic	
Direct US Mail contact to hiring executives	Traditional approach. Can be useful for hard-to-reach hiring executives or as a last ditch effort.	
Career fairs	Useful for some levels of positions	
Emotion – rejection	Disappointments will happen. Continue to move forward. Don't get stuck!	
Career transition coach	For in-depth job search advice, accountability, insight	

Item	Comments	Check-off √
Effort	Stay busy! Thirty plus hours/week if unemployed, six to eight hours/week if employed	
Avoid busywork	Focus on those tasks that truly advance your search. Your heart will know the difference.	
Volunteering, consulting	If unemployed, volunteer or do paid consulting projects. Some employers view volunteering equal to work experience.	
Relying on posted job openings	Relying solely on posted job openings will significantly lengthen your job search and tear down your self-confidence	**X – No!**

★ Getting off to a Successful Start

Beyond "I need to update my resume," many job seekers don't know what to do, let alone in what order to do it, especially if they are starting their job search from scratch. It can easily be overwhelming, especially if you didn't expect to become unemployed, haven't looked for a job in a long time, or need to find a new job. Relax and take a deep breath. In this topic we will list, then briefly discuss, the A-1 priorities to successfully launch your job search and reduce any feelings of anxiety. They are:

1. **Get (and keep) your emotions in check.** This is the first order of business. If you need a day or a weekend to work through the emotions of losing your job before starting your job search, that's fine, but no more than that. You don't have time for a pity party. Now here comes the big secret: the moment you start taking real steps to begin your job search, the sooner the feelings of anxiety, fear, and even anger will fade. Not dwelling on the past moves you forward to your future and your next job.

2. **Identify your keywords.** What words apply to you? Start simple. What titles have you held? What industries have you worked in? What knowledge do you have? These concepts and others will form the messaging behind who you are and how you present yourself to the job market. There will be much more on keywords as you progress through the book.

3. **Get organized.** You will need to make lists—of companies, people, and to-do lists. Think through how you will keep track of everything. Relying on your memory

or sticky notes in a shotgun fashion is a recipe for disaster. In the thick of your job search, you won't be able to keep track of what you're doing without a system. Excel spreadsheets are highly recommended for creating lists of companies and people. Only create columns for the information you will really need (name of contact, company, company website, email address, phone number, date contacted). Don't get carried away recording non-useful information. There are commercial services that can help you stay organized in your job search. Check out JibberJobber (www.jibberjobber.com) and CareerShift (www.careershift.com). Microsoft Outlook's calendar feature can also help. You can record tasks to be done, schedule follow-up calls, and so on.

4. **Create a short list of target employers you would be interested in working for.** It may be only three, five, or ten companies to start with. Add to the list as you discover new companies. The point here is to start the list that gets you thinking. Now, look up the companies on LinkedIn. Follow them by setting up alerts for news, press releases, and job postings. Google Alerts may also be used. If you have Twitter, follow the companies. This starts the flow of information from these companies (and others you'll add), including jobs and industry trends, which will benefit your job search. Add this information to your Excel spreadsheets to create a complete picture of each company before moving ahead, to eliminate needless backtracking for additional research.

5. **Create a short list of networking contacts.** This one is like the list of companies from the last step. Make a list of close professional colleagues you feel comfortable speaking to about your circumstances and job search. As you think of more, add to the list. This list likely will not exceed twenty to twenty-five names to begin with (although it could be more). After you make out the list, do not contact them. You are not ready (even though you may think you are). Regardless of your business or personal relationships, don't "blow it" by not being properly prepared. Be patient. Read the Professional Networking section in this book, and do things right the first time. Just like with your target companies, be sure to include all relevant information before moving on.

6. **Update your resume.** Read the Impactful Resumes section, and either prepare one yourself, or seek professional services (which will free your time for other job-search activities). Having your resume professionally prepared could be a good investment.

7. **Update your LinkedIn profile and expand your network.** Consult the LinkedIn section and optimize your LinkedIn profile. Make sure your resume and LinkedIn profile are in sync with each other (especially the names of former employers and dates of employment). After you look over the Networking chapter, expand your network by adding one hundred new connections (it's not as hard as you may think). These have to be the right kind of high-value connections (explained later) that will significantly advance your job search.

8. **Create job alerts.** Use websites like Indeed.com and SimplyHired.com. You can choose to be alerted about titles, locations, specific companies (from your short list), and so on. Set up job alerts on LinkedIn too. Companies (and recruiters) post jobs on LinkedIn and you can receive notifications when they do. Are there any industry-specific or niche job boards you could search? Check out http://airsdirectory.com to research them, as well as recruiters, and then set up alerts. Get a sense of the job market, and start the flow of opportunities you are looking for. If a position pops up, and you're interested, do not apply for it through the website. Research the likely hiring executive(s) and contact them directly. Much more on this strategy later.

More about Job Alerts

The number of job openings you receive from your job alerts can be an indication of the market demand for someone with your skill set or whether your target market is broad enough. There are a host of factors that can influence the number of jobs that pop up from your job alerts. As you evaluate them, here are some general guidelines:

Eight or fewer job openings per month. If the trend indicates that you are getting eight or fewer job openings per month (two or fewer per week), it could be an indication that the demand for your specific skill set may not be strong enough to drive your job search, or your target market is too limited. Broaden the parameters of your job alerts to capture more openings.

Nine to thirty-six job openings per month. This range is likely healthy—you are being alerted to three to four and upward to nine openings a week. There is demand for your skill set, and your target market is large enough. As you screen the openings, the number you choose to pursue is manageable.

Thirty-seven or more openings per month. In this case, you may want to consider tightening the parameters of your job alerts. You are being notified about eight or more openings a week. Depending upon the quality of the openings, they could become unmanageable to effectively evaluate and pursue.

Resentment and Bitterness

We need to talk about emotions, because having the right frame of mind is crucial to a successful job search. If you happened to lose your job unexpectedly, you know that it means more than just losing your paycheck. There's the loss of identity, self-esteem, friendships with those at work, possible embarrassment, feelings of no longer being productive, loss of a sense of purpose, loss of a sense of control, and emptiness, not to mention the change in your daily routine. It's a jolt and there's a lot to process, especially emotions. It's okay to cry . . . more than once if you feel the need to do so. Let the emotions out, don't internalize them and bottle them up.

Harboring negative feelings (including holding grudges) about your employment situation, *will* negatively impact your job search. A poor attitude or an unintended slip-of-the-tongue in an interview will dissuade any employer from hiring you. Employers will not knowingly hire a person with an attitude problem that can poison company culture. As difficult as it is, you must take steps to "let it go."

Setting aside clinical psychology, holding a grudge will harm you mentally and physically, and will harm your job search. Here is some layman's advice to get you thinking and moving in the right direction.

Releasing your feelings of resentment and bitterness is a process, not an event. But, you must begin by intellectually and emotionally moving from the pain that has been inflicted to the future of a fulfilling new career position. The longer you wallow in self-pity, the longer you will obsess and continue to have intense negative feelings. It's fine to take time to vent; in fact, it's healthy to do so. But don't get stuck and dwell on the past. Focus on moving yourself forward.

One helpful technique is to write about your feelings. Don't hold back. Write what you wish you would have said to your former boss and others. Write about anything that bothers you. Do this repeatedly if you feel the need. That's okay. Getting it down on paper releases the mental pressure inside you and helps relieve the obsessive thoughts in your head.

You are an adult, and you should know that holding on and obsessing only continues to force out good feelings and the joys of life, and clouds your thinking about your future career fulfillment. When you're thinking "bad," you can't be thinking "good." Open your mind and your heart to the value of releasing the resentment and bitterness. Ask yourself, "What will I gain by letting go of these bad feelings?" (The answer is "plenty!") Once you do, you will begin to feel lighter, more optimistic, and energized about the tasks of your job search.

Actively choose a new way of thinking. Choose a new outlook. Choose a new attitude. Do what you can to think differently. Try to fill your mind with thoughts that are positive.

Take active steps in your job search. There are a lot of things you can do to move your job search forward. Start doing them. Getting active with your search will help lessen the feelings of resentment and move you to optimism about your future. "Act yourself to right thinking," as the saying goes.

Do not view yourself as a victim. That is a defeatist attitude. Instead, see your situation as an opportunity . . . a blessing. You've been given the opportunity to write the next chapter in your life. What's the story going to be? You can control much of what happens but you will diminish your career fulfillment (your story) if you cling to resentment and bitterness.

Besides the mental torture resentment and bitterness can bring, there are very real physical harms that come from harboring resentments. According to Carsten Wrosch, professor of psychology at Concordia University, "studies have shown that bitter, angry people have higher blood pressure and heart rates and are more likely to die of heart disease and other illnesses."[15] Why invite physical ailments into life?

Here's the best way to put it: "Resentment is like taking poison and waiting for the other person [such as a former employer] to die."[16] As hard as it is, you must move on.

If you believe that you have significant emotional feelings about your situation that are holding you back and a professional therapist would be helpful, by all means seek help. There's no shame it that. In fact, it's smart. Getting over these emotional hurdles is important and the sooner you can clear them, the sooner you can meaningfully pursue your job search.

---

15 See also, Cohen, Elizabeth, Blaming others can ruin your health, The Empowered Patient , August 18, 2011 http://edition.cnn.com/2011/HEALTH/08/17/bitter.resentful.ep/index.html (accessed March 28, 2017).

16 "Malachy McCourt Quotes," Goodreads, http://www.goodreads.com/author/quotes/3373.Malachy_McCourt (ac-cessed February 5, 2016).

Keeping a Positive Attitude

Always bear in mind that your own resolution to succeed is more important than any other one thing.
—Abraham Lincoln[17]

Looking for a job is work . . . at times, very hard work, both physically and emotionally.

Despite the best job-search strategies, it's disheartening not to receive a job offer after making networking contacts, sending resumes, and going on interviews. The process can take a toll on your self-image and self-worth. And, of course, if you are unemployed, the financial hardship of little or no income and bills to pay can be difficult as well.

We've talked about how to get bad feelings out of your life so you can move forward with your job search. Now let's talk inspiration. Stacey A. Thompson is a certified career coach and marketing professional with more than twenty years of experience in marketing communications, public relations, and business writing. She is also the founder of Virtues for Life, a website designed to inspire and coach people in the daily practice of virtues. She has written about insightful virtues to practice during a job search.

---

17 "Lincoln's Advice to Lawyers," Abraham Lincoln's letter to Isham Reavis, November 5, 1855, Abraham Lincoln Online, http://www.abrahamlincolnonline.org/lincoln/speeches/law.htm (accessed May 27, 2015).

The following tips can be found on her website:

1. **Faith.** Having faith that you will find a job and really believing this in your heart—even when there is no evidence that this is true—is an enlightened way of thinking. Part of such faith is the understanding that whatever happens, there is a good reason for it, even if you don't know it at the time. As the saying goes, "Everything happens for a reason." Who would have thought that when you got laid off from your last job it would lead to a more fulfilling and joyful career? It can happen. Or it can catapult you into your own business. That happens more often than you might think. No matter how much you may dislike something that happened to you, having faith in the journey of life and what it may hold will help you to free yourself from worry and fear.

2. **Perseverance.** As weeks or even months pass, job searching may take a toll on your willpower. You also may feel that you can't look at one more job posting, make one more phone call, type one more cover letter, or attend one more networking event. But the mindset it takes for a runner to finish a marathon—uphill in the rain—is what it takes to land a job. Keeping your eye on the goal and becoming unstoppable in the quest for professionally satisfying employment can mean the difference between success and failure. No matter how many times you get rejected, how much you are suffering financially, or how fed up you become, persevering *will* get you a job.

3. **Courage.** It takes great courage to keep trying and sticking your neck out there to find a job even when the results seem futile. But practicing courage helps you to press on as you market yourself, write cover letters, attend networking functions (where you know no one), and face interview after interview to eventually achieve your career goals.

4. **Confidence.** While the job search continues and more rejection follows, your confidence can suffer even more. But understanding that rejection is part of the process and is not personal can make you stronger and more resilient. It's easy to lose sight of your talents, strengths, and experiences when you receive little validation or acknowledgment. Focusing on your abilities and the value you will add to potential employers will boost and maintain your confidence. Posting daily reminders or repeating affirmations to yourself relating to your abilities and your value as a person, or visualizing yourself happy and fulfilled in your next job can help you stay motivated and confident.

5. **Gratitude.** The practice of gratitude can have a significant impact on a person's well-being. There is always something to be grateful for in life. It isn't always easy to see this, especially during hard times, but being thankful for the many blessings and simple pleasures of life will make you happier. Grateful people—according to scientific research—experience higher levels of positive emotions, cope better with stress, recover more quickly from illness, and benefit from greater physical health. Having an attitude of gratitude shifts our mental focus from negative to positive. Positive thinking, as we well know, has transformative powers. Practicing gratitude in life and during the job search is a powerful tool we can use to help prevent negative emotions, focus our thoughts on what is working in life, and make positive change. There may come a time or a day when you feel all is lost in regard to your job search. Before this happens, write a gratitude list of all the things that you have, including all the experiences, all the people, and everything in your life that you are grateful for. Write this list, review it, and continue adding to it. You will be surprised how it will lift your spirits and actually motivate you to persevere. Remember, "This too shall pass."

6. **Hope.** Without hope, finding a job would be next to impossible. Hope is the fuel to keep you going in the darkest of times, the feeling that your next job is right around the corner and it's just a matter of time until you find the right position. Remain hopeful by thinking about what's possible for you and your career, and not on what's not happening for you. Every part of the job search has value, even if it doesn't feel that way. Through the practice of hope, our journey becomes lighter as we shift our focus from hardships to wishes.[18]

Being mindful of these virtues will help you stay emotionally centered during the ups and downs of your job search. They can inspire and motivate you. However, a job search always requires action. It has been written, "faith without action is dead."[19]

Throughout your job search, there are ultimately three things in your control: effort, attitude, and beliefs. This includes how many hours/days per week you devote to your search, how many times you will network per day or week (whether calling or emailing), and more. Be productive with your effort, stay positive, and believe in yourself.

---

18 Thompson, Stacey A. "6 Virtues to Practice for Job Search Success," Virtues for Life, http://www.virtuesforlife.com/6-virtues-to-practice-for-job-search-success/ (accessed June 1, 2015).

19 "In the same way, faith by itself, if it is not accompanied by action, is dead" (James 2:17, NIV).

Your Career . . . Your Responsibility

What is a career? Setting aside the dictionary definition, a career is a series of experiences in your professional working life, which could last forty to fifty years. This career longevity is especially true as our population grows older and we choose to work longer.[20] It is your responsibility to make your career as fulfilling as possible.

Sadly, too many people set out on a career path just to have the wind blow them in directions they really did not want to go, or perhaps had no choice but to go. They had the best of intentions, only to have circumstances dictate their career direction, leading to a disappointing and unfulfilling career experience.

As you move forward, here are some perspectives to consider adopting that will add clarity, understanding, and perception to your job search. These viewpoints will benefit you now and throughout your entire career by creating a fulfilling experience and reinforcing that your decisions are entirely within your control. These perspectives are:

1. **I am solely responsible for my career success.** You took the initiative and put in the hard work to get the necessary education and experience that qualifies you for your chosen career. Own that career by guiding and directing your job-search pursuits.[21]

2. **It is my responsibility to enhance my professional value proposition.** All industries and all functions within industries evolve, advance, and change. Falling out of touch can have serious and negative career ramifications. It is your responsibility to your career to stay up-to-date and enhance your skills.

3. **I must deliver an ROI (Return on Investment) to my employer.** Staying in a job where you do not deliver value is not fair to your employer, you, or your career. It puts you at risk of demotions, pay decreases, and job termination. It can also be a sign that your career is stalling. It is your responsibility to bring value to your employer.

4. **I am responsible for my work-life balance.** Your work-life balance will likely change. For many, there is intense focus early in a career to get established. Then, at some point, as marriage, children, aging parents, and a host of other life dynamics come along, the intensity shifts for a period. It is common for career intensity to resume

---

20 Woods, Jennifer. "Working Longer—Whether You Want to or Not," CNBC.com, December 23, 2014, http://www.cnbc.com/id/102264601 (accessed June 9, 2015).

21 "Proactive Career Planning at Any Age," Aequus Wealth Management Resources, http://www.aequuswealth.com/newsletter/article/proactive_career_planning_at_any_age (accessed July 10, 2015).

(e.g., after kids are out of the house), but regardless, you control where you place your priorities.

5. **It is my responsibility to stay informed about the financial health and well-being of my employer and the industry in which I work.** Be informed and be aware of how your employer is doing. Look around. Is your employer investing in the company, technology, people, and other resources? Are people leaving? Is the company expanding and hiring? Is your industry contracting or expanding? Are there new competitors (a possible sign of a healthy industry)? How are other competitors doing? Read about your company (for publicly traded companies, take a look at the annual report). Ask a stockbroker to assess your company or industry. Do your best to stay ahead of possible negative career events.

6. **Change is inevitable in my career. How I respond to change is completely within my control.** Unforeseen things will happen in your career. Mergers. Acquisitions. Reorganization. Layoffs. Downsizing. Promotions. Change often creates opportunities that can be capitalized upon if given perspective, knowledge, a positive attitude, and focused effort. Change often comes with a natural level of discomfort, uncertainty, and a dose of anxiety. But change frequently accompanies growth, which is the gift of change.

In addition, each part of your job search, from profiling and preparing your resume, to interviewing and professionally negotiating an offer, are up to you as well. Conducting a professional job search is also your responsibility to your career.

How Long Will Your Job Search Take?

Over the years, an easy formula has evolved regarding the length of time it takes to successfully conduct a job search: one month for every $10,000 of income.[22] If you were earning $80,000, your search will take eight months.

To the best we can determine, this formula is not supported by much (or any) credible, empirical data. It may have been developed by job seekers as an easy measure to track their search efforts against the calendar—which in the end is fine; the formula can create a level of urgency because it is time relevant.

---

22 Elaine Varelas, "How Long Will My Job Search Take?" The Job Doc (blog), The Boston Globe, June 12, 2013, http://www.boston.com/jobs/news/jobdoc/2013/06/how_long_will_my_job_search_ta.html   (accessed June 4, 2015).

For this book's objectives, your challenge and goal is to beat the formula—by a wide margin. For example, if you make $80,000, your goal is to land a professionally satisfying job in less than an eight-month time frame.

Factors unique to your personal situation will influence the amount of time it takes to find a new job. Here are some common factors that tend to influence a job search's time line:

Factor 1: Your Skill Set and Track Record

Do you have the skills—those professional value propositions—or something of value in your background and experience to benefit an employer? Transferable job skills? Do your skills and experience make or save an employer money? For sales professionals, product knowledge and distribution channels would be relevant here. How many other job seekers have similar skills? Supply and demand can have a huge impact on the length of your search. Do you have a track record of success utilizing your skill set which demonstrates ROI? This will help to differentiate you from other job seekers.

Factor 2: Education and Experience Level

Most companies require a certain level of education consistent with the position being filled, as well as minimum experience. Do you have both of these? If many others do, you'll need to differentiate yourself.

Factor 3: Sales, Account Management, or Other Customer-Facing Roles

- Relationships—Do you have the right kinds of business relationships? The right distribution channel?
- Location—Are you located in or near an open territory?
- Product Knowledge—Are you familiar with the requisite product knowledge of the employer (i.e., less training, quicker ROI for you)?

Factor 4: Relocation and Travel

How do you feel about moving? Would a new location for the right job lead to a better future, with better compensation? Remember that cost of living differs throughout the country. How about the effect on immediate family? Do you have children in high school? Are you an empty nester? Would extended family be affected? Some positions require frequent travel. Your search will probably be longer if you can't or won't travel as the position demands.

Factor 5: Compensation

Do your compensation parameters match market conditions and the prevailing wage for the position? If your previous employer overpaid compared to competitors, you'll have to adjust. It's not fun, but it may shorten your search.

Factor 6: The Strength of Your Network and Online Visibility

Networking is the most effective mechanism to land your next position. Most estimate that 60 to 80 percent of jobs are found by networking.[23] The size, depth, and effective use of your professional and social network(s) will affect your job search's duration. This is also why you need a robust profile on LinkedIn for your job search. Without it, recruiters will pass you over as invisible—especially if information about your qualifications is weak or missing.

Factor 7: Job Search Strategy and Your Effort

Have you profiled your desired position, industry, and target companies? Will you conduct a passive or self-motivated job search? Developing a sound strategy will positively affect the job search time line. Taking a casual, shotgun approach will significantly lengthen your job search. Work hard and work smart—even if that means thirty to forty hours per week if you're unemployed, or six to eight if employed—to get a new job. Your effort can yield success with companies on and under the radar if you focus, show courage, and persist.

Factor 8: Your Economic Environment and Personal Life

External economic factors can adversely affect a job search. Hiring does occur, even in an economic downturn. Stick to your plan, put in the effort with a positive attitude, and you will succeed. Remember: the economy is not standing in your way . . . you are.

Life does have its seasons, which tend to bring new joys, challenges, and distractions (some are simply annoying while others can be debilitating). Is the personal life issue you are facing honestly preventing you from pursuing your job search? Or is it an excuse to put off your search? Your heart will know the answer.

Answering Questions about Your Unemployment: Your Exit Statement

If you are unemployed, it is inevitable that you will be asked questions like: "What happened?" "Why you are looking for a job?" "Why are you unemployed?" These kinds of questions can create an awkward moment unless you are prepared with a professional,

23 Elaine Varelas, "How Long Will My Job Search Take?" The Job Doc (blog), The Boston Globe, June 12, 2013, http://www.boston.com/jobs/news/jobdoc/2013/06/how_long_will_my_job_search_ta.html (accessed June 4, 2015).

honest response. That response needs to be fit for social gatherings, colleagues, and potential employers, and be fair to your former employer. Write down your explanation, and commit it to memory. Remember these concepts to help you formulate your response about your unemployment:

1. **Keep it aligned.** Make sure your statement reflects what happened and what your former employer may say.

2. **Keep it positive.** Do not make any negative statements about your former company, boss, and colleagues.

3. **Keep it factual.** Do not unload emotions into your explanation.

4. **Keep it short.** Do not get into an extended explanation. Make your statement and be done.

Some poor explanations would be:

- "Those jerks over at XYZ can't find their butts with both hands! Yet they fired *me*!"

- "It's all politics! I got great job reviews and what did it get me? A ticket in the unemployment line, that's what!"

Often your explanation can be as brief as:

- "The company went through a reorganization."

- "The company was purchased."

- "The company had to make budget cuts and there were departmental layoffs. I was a casualty."

- "Based on company direction, we mutually agreed to part ways."

If you follow this advice, you will reduce the probability of additional probing questions regarding the circumstances regarding your unemployment.

There will be times, though, when a short one- or two-sentence response simply does not fit the circumstances, such as in an interview with a senior executive. For those situations, you must be able to provide additional information while still adhering to the general rules (aligned, positive, factual, and short). Below is an example of one such exit statement:

I was hired four years ago to build the sales structure and process to put Up-and-Comer, Inc. on a solid growth trajectory. I was responsible for driving the strategies that generated a 40+% increase in software revenue and a robust client base increase from 92 to over 650 clients including an increase from 2 to 9 Fortune 50 clients. In 20XX, we achieved 101% client revenue retention.

Our current CEO is the founder of the company. He is a brilliant man with a passionate vision for Up-and-Comer's position in the market and society. It has been a delight and a privilege to be his partner in achieving the company's status as a proven, transformative solution for employers.

I am still invested in Up-and-Comer's success, however, over the course of the last [a time frame] the CEO and I reached a conclusion that we had different visions regarding the direction of the company. Together we agreed that it was time I move on. So the CEO and I amicably agreed to a severance arrangement from the company.

Note that the first paragraph of the exit statement showcases accomplishments. You want to emphasize achievements up front. The statement is positive in tone and is written in a factual way. The length is about 175 words and should be delivered in a little over one minute (given a normal rate of speech of 150 words per minute). That is short given the level of content.

Once you have written your exit statement, memorize it. Read it over and over. Then, create "talking points" for the statement. These are the major points you want to make in your statement. Use them as guides as you rehearse your speech. This will help make your statement come across as conversational when delivered.

Searching for a Job While Employed—The Confidential Job Search

Conducting a job search while employed poses notable challenges.[24] You've concluded that it is time to find a new opportunity. To ensure that your confidential job search does not raise red flags with your current employer, follow the suggestions below.

Be aware of your behavior. You may have intellectually and emotionally "turned the corner" at your current employer. But do things just like before and go out of your way to defuse suspicion. Keep your current job a priority (you owe that to your employer)

24 See also, Beshara, Tony. The Job Search Solution: The Ultimate System for Finding a Great Job Now! 2nd ed. (New York: AMACOM, 2012), Chapter 13, "Looking for a Job When You Have a Job."

and finish strong. Resist the urge to tell coworkers of your intentions (which may not be easy), and do not use your employer's computer equipment or email for your job search (use your personal email, even if you have to create one). When you network (as you will and should), let your contacts know about the confidential nature of your search—they'll understand, but they must be made aware first. You should arrange similar confidentiality with recruiters at search firms; they can be great eyes and ears for new opportunities, and they are trained to keep dealings confidential.

Update your LinkedIn profile. Depending on the changes you make to your LinkedIn profile, they could be broadcast to your network connections and raise suspicion. To hide your changes on LinkedIn, go to your Profile page and turn off "sharing profile edits." That is done through the Settings & Privacy tab of your account.

Be careful about asking for employment documents. Requesting copies of past performance reviews, covenants-not-to-compete, and the like are unusual requests. Some larger employers have policies to keep requests confidential when Human Resources' channels and protocols are used. Hopefully you kept copies of these documents and you do not need to ask for them.

Be aware of telephone communications. Avoid having job-search telephone (or cell phone) conversations in the office, especially in open spaces. Go to a conference room and close the door (keep your voice down), out into the hallway, outside, or to your car. And keep conversations brief. The wrong set of words overheard by the wrong person will blow your cover.

Inform employers that your search is confidential. In your first conversation with a potential employer (HR or the actual hiring executive), state that you are currently employed and your search is confidential. This puts the topic on the table, and every employer will understand. Do what you can to schedule interviews (of whatever nature) early in the day, during lunchtime, or after working hours. If you happen to be a remote employee, you have more flexibility, but don't take advantage of your flexibility to conduct a job search on company time (and dime). As your search progresses, you will likely need to take a day off (PTO or paid vacation) for longer, more involved interviews. Try not to take too many PTO days too close together. Your sudden disappearances from the office may create suspicion.

Be aware of your attire. If your office dress code leans more toward business casual, showing up in interview attire is a sure tip-off. This may require you to change clothes before returning to the office after an interview.

Anticipate that your confidential job search will eventually become known. Plan on your confidential job-search efforts being discovered by your coworkers, boss, or others, despite your efforts. Think about what you will say if a coworker or boss confronts you. Be honest. Get a short answer together and memorize it. Getting caught by surprise and stumbling through an explanation is the embarrassing alternative. You could say: "Yes. I have been approached with another opportunity, and I thought I needed to explore it, just as you would if the circumstances were reversed." The phrase "if the circumstances were reversed" often squelches a detailed conversation on the topic.

Searching for a job while employed is similar to having a second job. Stay organized and understand the time commitment necessary to succeed.

Life Rewards Action!
— Chris Widener[25]

---

25 Widener, Chris. "Life Rewards Action," http://chriswidener.com/life-rewards-action/ (accessed May 27, 2015).

Chapter 2

Profiling Your Next Career Opportunity—
The Target Opportunity Profile

You've got to be very careful if you don't know where you are going
because you might not get there.
— Yogi Berra[26]

The most important part of a successful search is figuring out what you really want. Your journey to your next career position is about to begin. How will you know you have arrived if you have no ideas or sense of direction? You will need to create a Target Opportunity Profile.

For most professional-level job seekers, there are five options to their career path. These choices are really quite logical. They are:

- Keep your job and industry the same.
- Change jobs, but stay in your industry.

26 "Yogi Berra Quotes," Baseball Almanac, http://www.baseball-almanac.com/quotes/quoberra.shtml (accessed May 27, 2015).

- Keep your job and move to another industry.
- Change both your job and industry.[27]
- Start your own business.[28]

We'll briefly discuss the considerations for each choice.

The first option is to pursue the same job in the same industry. Factors in pursuing this path include:

- You like what you do because it fulfills your career passions and goals.
- You are willing to relocate or work remotely, depending upon the local market.
- You are able to identify new employers more easily due to your familiarity with the industry.
- Networking is easier, too, for the same reason.

The second option is a different job in the same industry. Considerations for this one are:

- Your industry appeals to you, and there are available opportunities.
- You think it is time to repurpose your experience in a new role.
- Your interest in your job function has changed. Perhaps you're bored.
- You feel a need to grow and expand your horizons.

The third option is the same job in a different industry. You may be thinking the following:

- The position and its function fulfill your passion and career goals.
- It may be time for a change due to events and market trends in your previous industry.
- Your interests have changed.

The fourth option is a different job in a different industry. Things you'll need to consider are:

- This is a complete career transition.
- Making this a successful transition will require research into new industries and an evaluation and assessment of career interests.

---

27 Whitcomb, Job Search Magic, p. 34.

28 Claycomb, Heather, and Karl Dinse. Career Pathways—Interactive Workbook. (1995), Part 1, "Career Assessment"; Whitcomb, Job Search Magic, p. 478.

The fifth option is starting your own business (including consulting in your area of expertise and a franchise). This can be an intriguing idea, filled with excitement and rewards, for those with an entrepreneurial spirit and a strong work ethic. However, it also holds formidable obstacles, challenges, and financial risk. Research this option fully before venturing very far down this path, especially regarding risks and other factors involved (e.g., timing in your life, timing in your career, family issues and concerns, financial resources to pay your bills during the start-up period, the consumer market for your business venture, and so many others). Seek the advice of an attorney, accountant, and/or business consultant(s). Read one of the many books on starting your own business.

A Passions Inventory

For job seekers wanting to explore an entirely new career path, those wanting to launch a second career, or those curious about other positions that would be a good match, there is an insightful exercise that can help identify possible career paths by capitalizing upon passions, interests, and/or skills. This exercise can lead to entrepreneurial ventures and exciting new career directions.

In concept, a passions inventory is a reasonably simple exercise, though it could require some deep thought. When you start this exercise, begin by taking all practicality out of the equation, including an amount of money or education level needed. Let's start. List what you enjoy doing. What captures and holds your attention? What do you find fulfilling or interesting? Ponder what you read, listen to, or watch. Hobbies can be a great source of insight for your list. What are you particularly good at? Make this list before moving to the next step.

Once you have your list compiled, look it over and see if there are any closely related items that could be grouped together. There may be some items that stand alone. That's okay too. From this "grouping" step, you may see one or two interests that stand out, with many closely related items. Take note of these groupings—the things that interest you the most.

Now, let's shift gears a bit. What skills have you used in the past that you enjoy using? Perhaps these are the ones you are good at and you know it. These include both your technical skills (your expertise) as well as your soft skills. Sales, listening, and writing are examples.[29] This list could include any number of skills. Write them down.

---

29 See also, Yate, Martin John. Knock 'em Dead—The Ultimate Job Search Guide. (Avon, MA: Adams Media, 2014), p. 23–25.

Now cross-reference the two lists. This is where the fun (but also the work) begins as you make discoveries. Are there any interests, passions, or skills that, in combination or standing alone, you can "commercialize?" In other words, can you use your interests or proven skills and have someone pay you for it, either as an independent consultant, contractor, or employee?

Do research about what you discover about yourself, your skills, and your passions. Are they marketable? Don't be too quick to dismiss any possibilities. You could be surprised and have your mind opened to new career avenues.

For example, let's assume you have an interest in writing. You've always seemed to have a knack for it, and over the course of time others have commented that you write well. Further, let's say you have an inherent interest in employment, the unemployment rate, the labor participation rate, and the news commentaries on employment. You read about job hunting, resumes, LinkedIn, and so on. Pulling these passions and skills together equates to becoming an author of job-search books. (By the way, now you know how this author used his passions inventory to open a new career direction in addition to being an executive recruiter.) There could be (and likely is) more than one avenue to pursue as a result of this exercise.

Once you have completed the exercise and have a sense of your passions and applicable skills, you might consider contacting people who may help you evaluate the practicality of your intended pursuit(s). This could take the form of a research interview (more on that later in this book). Set up appointments (informational interviews) with professionals who are doing what you think you would like to do. Ask them about what it is like to be in that role or do what they do. Can you see yourself being happy doing their job? Is it financially viable for you?

In addition to the passions inventory, there are several proven tools available that, combined with the inventory, can provide you with an empirical read on your options. These online career-assessment tools include:

Myers-Briggs	www.mbticomplete.com/en/index.aspx
Keirsey Campbell	www.keirsey.com/advisorteam/KTS-CISS_bundle.aspx
Career Liftoff	www.careerliftoff.com
Golden Personality	www.goldenllc.com
Structure of Intellect	www.soisystems.com
Strong Interest Inventory	www.cpp.com/products/strong/index.aspx

This discovery process can bring up fascinating things to think about, but be cautious about getting too dreamy. The pursuit of these options may need to be prioritized against more pressing and urgent needs (e.g., income to pay the mortgage). But they should not be dismissed either. It might come down to a matter of timing.

Creating Your Target Opportunity Profile

Using a Target Opportunity Profile to find your next opportunity will help eliminate that "go with your gut feeling" approach to a job search that could lead you astray. Replace that potential derailer with a clearer understanding of what you require from your next opportunity.

A Target Opportunity Profile will:

- Clarify what you are looking for
- Target opportunities that meet your needs and criteria
- Allow you to evaluate opportunities by measuring them against it
- Assist you in preparing various job-search materials such as your brand, elevator speech, resume, cover letters, and LinkedIn profile

The following brainstorming exercise will identify, prioritize, and profile the important elements of your next career opportunity. The results will affect your career satisfaction, employment longevity, and personal happiness in your next position. Your Target Opportunity Profile will also encourage rational decisions about your career based on a thorough, factual self-evaluation.

Step One—Consider Your Career Wish List

As you begin formulating your Target Opportunity Profile, reflect on your current and past positions. A technique to add tremendous clarity and spark your thinking is a Career Wish List.

On a piece of paper list everything you like about your current and past jobs. This can be anything from the kind of work, environment, and people, to the company's product(s), service(s), company culture, and so on.

Once you have listed the likes, consider the flip side. List those things you dislike about your current and past jobs. And if you have poor feelings about your current or former employer, writing down the negatives may have some added psychological benefits.

For every dislike you list, contrast it with the opposite. In other words, turn that dislike into a like.

Finally, toward the bottom of the page (or on a separate piece of paper), list what you want in your next career position.

The point of this brainstorming exercise is to articulate your likes, dislikes, and desires so you can keep your likes, remove your dislikes, and move toward what you want in your next career opportunity.

Many job seekers find this to be an eye-opening exercise. They have not taken the time over the course of their careers to deeply consider their likes, dislikes, and desires. They've been busy doing their jobs and concentrating on what's familiar, which is perfectly understandable. But now could be the time for introspection. The conclusion might be to continue on the same path, or maybe change course. Either way, you'll know how to move forward.

Step Two—Identify and Evaluate the Factors

Step Two of creating your Target Opportunity Profile includes consideration of significant categories. For each category listed, write down everything that comes to mind—don't worry about ranking your thoughts in order of importance. This exercise will stimulate thinking about the various considerations affecting your profile. Some—though not necessarily all—of the items you listed in your Career Wish List from Step One could appear here.

Equally important, as you think through these considerations, are the knock-out factors for each consideration. These could be: the skills, duties, and responsibilities that you dislike or don't want to use; an industry you don't want to be in; functions you don't want to do; a type of company you don't want to be aligned with; and so on. As you profile your next career opportunity, knowing what you don't want is equally as important as what you do want. Based on these knock-out factors, you can better focus your efforts on those opportunities that align with what you are looking for. Here are the categories to consider:

Skills/Strengths
What skills (or strengths) of yours give you energy and fulfillment, or make you feel intellectually alive? Think about the results of your passions inventory. You may lose track

of time when using these skills. Psychologists refer to this as "flow."[30] There are a handful of online tools that can help you explore and identify your strengths. Two helpful ones are StrengthsFinder 2.0 (www.gallupstrengthscenter.com/) and Dependable Strengths (dependablestrengths.org).

Weaknesses/Disinterest

This part of the profiling process is the opposite and has two parts: identifying weaknesses for the purpose of improvement and those weaknesses that are a disinterest to you.

Your weaknesses that you want to improve upon are the skills in a particular area that you can strengthen in order to strategically position yourself for those opportunities you want to pursue.

On the other hand, areas of weakness that are a disinterest to you are the skills or job functions that are pure drudgery for you. The ones that make your skin crawl and you would just as soon get up and walk a mile on broken glass rather than do them. With this awareness, you can filter and avoid opportunities that require you to use a skill you are disinterested in using. The point here is it is as important to know as much about what you don't want as it is what you do want.

Industry

In what industry do you want to work? For many professionals and executives, it is the same industry in which they have the most experience. The key issue is the future viability or health of the industry of interest. A few things to consider: Is there growth? Are there new companies entering the market? What are the legislative/legal considerations, both positive and negative? Are there new innovations or products/services to propel those companies ahead of the competition?

Normally there is a host of disciplines that comprise any industry. As an example, the insurance industry has a plethora of distinct disciplines: property and casualty, life and health, group or individual, and workers' compensation. Inside that, there are carriers, health plans, brokers, consultants, third-party administrators, cost containment, networks, wellness, care management, stop loss, technology, and more.

The point? Feel good about your selected industry's future. Just as you want to grow and prosper, you want that industry to grow and prosper.

---

30 Cherry, Kendra. "What Is Flow? Understanding the Psychology of Flow," Verywell.com, last updated May 6, 2016, https://www.verywell.com/what-is-flow-2794768 (accessed May 10, 2016).

Function

What do you want to do in your chosen industry? Your function or role ties into what your unique set of qualifications and overall skill set are.

Based on your qualifications, identify positions that interest you. Does your experience transfer to different positions you have had before? For example, if insurance is your target industry, could your proven skills move you to consider working in account management, auditing, a call center, finance, human resources, management, marketing, public relations, risk management, operations, network development, sales, underwriting, and so on?

Feel comfortable—if not downright passionate—about your function or role.

Company

What does your next employer look like? There are many factors that may or may not be of any consequence to you, such as:

- Publicly held
- Privately held
- Large
- Small
- Start-up
- Venture-capital backed
- Aggressive growth strategy
- Standing in the industry
- Products—innovative or commoditized

There is a very informative website you can use to identify growing companies and companies potentially gearing up to hire. CrunchBase (www.crunchbase.com) tracks companies that have received venture capital and other investment capital. It's generally accepted that when a company receives funding, there is often a correlation to hiring.

Location

Where do you want to work? List the cities, states, or countries where you are willing to live and work. If you are not willing to relocate, simply list the name of your current town or city.

If you are willing to move, consider these factors:

- What areas of the country would interest you?
- Are there particular cities you would like to live in?
- Are there family motivations to stay or move?
- What areas of the country would you not relocate to?
- Are international locations a possibility?
- Do you have limitations on commuting time?

Title

How important is a title to you? For some, it has limited importance. For others, it matters more. A title can reflect authority and career progression. Here are some things to consider:

- What titles would be acceptable to you?
- Is there a minimum title level you want?
- Is there a titling concept you prefer (e.g., business development versus sales)?
- What about a titling "prefix" (*senior* account manager, *executive* vice president)?

Work Setting

What type of working environment is best for you? List the characteristics of the environment you would like. For example:

- Do you want an office environment?
- Are you comfortable working from a home-based office?
- Are you willing to travel? If so, how much?
- Do you prefer a larger corporate environment?
- Do you like smaller, more entrepreneurial companies?

Compensation and Employee Benefits

What would you (realistically) like to be paid? What benefits are important to you? Some issues to consider include:

- What is your minimum salary requirement?
- If variable compensation is a component to your overall compensation package, at what level or potential additional earnings?
- Will variable compensation affect your minimum salary requirement?

- Will your family be added to your employee benefits?
- Do you need specific benefits based on a loved one's needs?
- How many weeks of vacation will you want?
- Are retirement programs available (401(k), pension, or another type)?
- Are perks such as a company car, health club membership, country club membership, paid parking, and so on, a realistic expectation for your desired position?
- What is your overall threshold? Are you willing to be reasonable?

Reward System

How do you want to be rewarded for positive performance? What kind of reward system would be motivating for you to perform? Compensation immediately comes to mind, but there are other considerations you may want to think about that could apply to you.

- Increase in salary
- Bonuses
- Stock options or equity
- Private recognition from management, peers, vendors, customers
- Public recognition – awards banquets
- Increase of vacation and PTO in lieu of compensation increases
- Flexibility to work remotely – not having to be in the office
- Any other motivational factors that could be woven into a professional setting

Career Purpose

What role will this next position play in your overall career? Is it an advancement? Or, is it potentially your last stop? Contemplate what you want this next position to accomplish. Here are some suggestions:

- What is the career goal for the position?
- What skills do you want to continue to utilize?
- What skills do you want to improve or learn?
- How important is stability (a company's size may influence your decision)?
- Could this next position be a bridge or stepping-stone position?

• What role could this position play regarding your overall career?

Other Considerations

These previous categories are by no means exhaustive. In fact, you have likely thought of a few considerations unique to your situation. Add all of those considerations or aspirations that truly matter to you to your list.

Step Three—Complete Your Profile

It is now time to compile your completed profile. Prioritize your responses in terms of importance. The list will likely contain points from both Steps One and Two. For example, your top priority may be to move to Charlotte (from the *Location* section). Your number two priority might be to work for a smaller entrepreneurial company (from the *Company* section). Your third priority may be to earn $100,000 (from the *Compensation/Benefits* section). And your final goal might be to have your kids attend a private school with a reputation for high academic achievement (from the *Other Considerations* section).

Pull it all together. Create your Target Opportunity Profile by listing your job priorities in order of importance.

Another technique to help you prioritize is a point system. Start with one hundred points and assign a value to each item on your priority list. This method helps clarify the importance of each item.

Your Target Opportunity will likely undergo revisions as your job search progresses—take the time to do that when necessary.

Use your Target Opportunity Profile to evaluate potential opportunities. Next, you'll figure out how to use your Profile to formulate questions for potential employers, based on your career priorities.

Questions to Ask in Interviews

Once you have created your Target Opportunity Profile, use it to formulate questions to ask employers to ensure the position aligns with your criteria, needs, and priorities. For example, if you determine that you prefer to work remotely, you may ask an employer, "Does this position require me to be in the office, or can I work from my home office?"

For some job seekers, setting up a Target Opportunity Profile can involve serious reflection and it can take a while. That's fine—but be careful not to get stuck. For others, the process is reasonably quick.

The true purpose for your Target Opportunity Profile is to know what you are looking for. You will be making more rational career and job-related decisions by consciously comparing opportunities to your Target Opportunity Profile.

Chapter 3

Essential Job-Search Topics and Tools

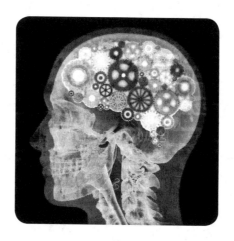

There isn't a ruler, a yard stick, or a measuring tape in the entire world long enough to compute the strength and capabilities inside you.
—Paul Meyer[31]

Understanding the Employer's Mindset

There are a variety of reasons that motivate an employer in the commercial market to hire. However, the true essence underlying each motivation comes down to two reasons: to make or save the company money.

The sole reason a job exists in a company is to contribute to the profitability. The level of your performance in your job must add value. Depending upon the job, you can help an employer's bottom line by:

1. **Making the company money (generating new revenue)**—This can be achieved

---

31 "Unleashing Your Genius," Quotes from the Masters, http://finsecurity.com/finsecurity/quotes/qm121.html (accessed May 27, 2015).

through sales, client retention, product development, and so on. You make money for the company by generating new revenue and keeping the revenue the company has.

2. **Saving the company money (productivity improvements)**—This is achieved by increasing productivity, increasing or creating operational efficiency, saving time, making others' jobs easier (more efficient or effective), and so on.

There are many ways to generate revenue or save money for a company. Revealing them to an employer establishes or increases your value (ROI). Here is a short list to get you thinking:

- Translate your duties and responsibilities from previous positions to this position's ROI.
- Implement an improvement that saves time, increases efficiency, and streamlines workflow.
- Improve company image and branding.
- Open new sales distribution channels.
- Improve a current product, or develop a new one.
- Expand business/sales through existing accounts.
- Enhance competitiveness through best practices, innovation, and so on.
- Improve client retention.
- Improve company culture, morale, and employee retention.

Whatever value you bring to the table will be directly related to your professional brand, skill set, and value proposition (which we'll discuss in later chapters).

Knowing What an Employer Wants in an Open Position

Since an employer's purpose when hiring is to make or save money, how can you get inside an employer's mind and determine what he or she is looking for in the position (or position types) you want? The answer is simple, but you'll need to do a little research, as follows:

1. **Gather job postings.** Go online and collect some well-written job postings for a

job you are qualified for and would enjoy. Websites such as www.indeed.com and www.simplyhired.com are rich resources.

2. **Create your own master job description.** Create a document. Call it your "Master Job Description" (or anything else creative you want, i.e., "My Dream Job").

   a. **Title.** Start with titles. What words do employers use? These titles will likely reflect jobs you target when you search. The key is to use these same words— or very similar ones—on your resume, business cards, LinkedIn profile, cover letters, elevator speech, and so on.

   b. **Skills, duties, and responsibilities.** Examine the job postings for skills, duties, and responsibilities that are common or frequently mentioned. Identify these skills and note how often they are used.

   c. **Match.** Tie these skills to your experience. When you use the keywords from the skills and titles in your written communications (including your resume), the higher your chances are of getting noticed because you make yourself directly relevant to an open job position.

Once it's done, familiarize yourself with your Master Job Description. Think about it. What would you look for to fill this position if you were the hiring executive? Congratulations— you are now thinking like an employer!

Now, **relate** or **match** how you have generated or saved money with former employers, while keeping your Master Job Description in mind. This is a crucial step, because you'll be tying an executive's hiring needs to your own experience and accomplishments. As you create other communication tools (resume, LinkedIn profile, cover letters, emails, and so on), refer to the insights you've discovered.

Matching Experience and "Word Clouds"

There is a very clever way to match your experience with what an employer is looking for in a position(s). "Word clouds" are images made out of large words interspersed with smaller ones (you may have seen them). Some websites that create word clouds include www.wordle.net, www.tagcrowd.com, and www.worditout.com. Here's how you use this concept to your advantage:

Copy a job description electronically, go to one of these sites, and put (copy and paste) the job description into the space provided. Give it a second and *voilà*, you have a word cloud. Pay particular attention to the larger words. Those are the words that are mentioned most frequently or deemed more important by the website's programming. Write down these larger words, and make sure they appear on your resume, LinkedIn profile, and other communications. For example, let's say you see terms like "customer experience" or "client success" in the word cloud. You reread the full job description you used to make the cloud and conclude that these terms mean account management (to you). Therefore, you need to change your terminology to match the language employers are using (at least for that employer).

This technique works especially well when you have an actual job description on a position you are pursuing (We'll reference this as the "word cloud technique" later on).

Transferable Job Skills and Professional Qualities

Start by doing what's necessary, then what's possible,
and suddenly you are doing the impossible.
— St. Francis of Assisi[32]

Transferable job skills come in two forms. First are the technical skills (expertise or ability) of your profession. If you are an engineer, you know engineering things. An accountant has skills related to accounting, and so on. We will refer to these skills as your "hard" skills.

Hard skills can be transferable by convincing an employer that your skills can be

---

32 "Doing What's Necessary, What's Possible, and What Seems to be Impossible," The Recovery Ranch, http://www.recoveryranch.com/articles/necessary-possible-impossible/ (accessed May 27, 2015).

easily repurposed and still be valuable to the employer. An oversimplified example is an accountant using math skills in a new role.

The second type of transferable job skills used in most professional-level positions is "soft." They are in addition to your technical expertise. Here is a list of some sought-after soft transferable job skills (not listed in any order of preference):

- **Communication** (writing, listening, and speaking)—This is the most frequently mentioned skill employers desire.[33]

- **Analytical Ability** (problem solving)—This is your ability to view a situation, identify issues, evaluate relevant information, and implement a plan.

- **Time Management** (prioritizing)—This is your ability to prioritize and devote the appropriate amount of time to a task.

- **Innovation** (out-of-the-box thinking)—This involves harnessing creativity, reasoning, and what you've learned in life to solve problems.

- **Collaboration** (teamwork)—This means working with others toward a shared goal.

- **Management** (people leadership)—This is your ability to gain buy-in or respect from a team, lead by defining goals and methods, and manage and guide a group toward shared goals or production targets.

- **Customer Focus** (customer service)—This is understanding that your employer must please and serve customers to be successful.

- **Business Understanding** (business acumen)—This is your ability to understand the business realities and the influences in the market and how they affect your employer.[34]

Closely aligned with the concept of transferable job skills are **professional qualities or character traits** that are sought after by employers. Here is a list:

- **Honesty**—This is the foundation of every employment relationship. An employer must

33 Hansen, Randall S., PhD, and Katharine Hansen, PhD. "What Do Employers Really Want? Top Skills and Values Employers Seek from Job-Seekers," Quintessential Careers, http://www.quintcareers.com/job_skills_values.html (accessed May 27, 2015).

34 Grant Tilus, "Top 10 Human Resources Job Skills Employers Want to See," (blog), Rasmussen College, July 29, 2013, http://www.rasmussen.edu/degrees/business/blog/human-resources-job-skills-employers-want-to-see/ (accessed July 10, 2015).

be able to trust you and respect you as a professional for the employment relationship to last and flourish.[35]

- **Positive Attitude**—Make no mistake—this is a big deal. Employers gravitate to people who show enthusiasm, energy, and a positive outlook.[36] As you will read later in this book, displaying a positive attitude will give you a competitive advantage in interviews and is a career management strategy. A positive attitude is *that* important.

- **Interpersonal Relationships**—Employers want employees who can get along with other coworkers. They avoid those that "rock the boat" and do not fit the culture.

- **Work Ethic**—Employers seek employees who put forth their best efforts at all times. They seek out employees who are motivated, internally driven, and stick with the job at hand. They want employees who are persistent and passionate about their jobs.[37]

- **Dependable**—Employers seek out employees who will show up on time. They want to rest assured you will "be there" for the company. If you are a remote employee, they want to know you are working even though you are out of sight.

- **Willingness to Learn**—This is your intellectual flexibility, curiosity, and your ability not to get stuck in your own ways. Regardless of your tenure, be willing to learn about new technology and improve your skills (and discover new ones). Markets change.[38] Business changes. Your industry changes. You must be open and pursue opportunities to learn and change. Doing so increases your value and marketability as a professional. **As a professional, you never want to stop learning and growing.**

These skills are the "bigger" ones. Other transferable skills and professional qualities include: accountability, accuracy, ambitious, assertive, autonomous, competitive, consensus building, decision making, enthusiastic, goal oriented, initiative, motivated, organized,

---

35 Hansen and Hansen, "What Do Employers Really Want?"

36 Victoria Andrew, "The Power of a Positive Attitude," (blog), Kavaliro Employment Agency, May 23, 2013, http://www.kavaliro.com/the-power-of-a-positive-attitude (accessed June 8, 2015). See also, Jobvite Recruiter Na-tion Report 2016, http://www.jobvite.com/wp-content/uploads/2016/09/RecruiterNation2016.pdf (78% of recruiters cite enthusiasm as most likely to influence a hiring decision), accessed March 15, 2017.

37 Hansen and Hansen, "What Do Employers Really Want?"

38 Ibid.

presentation skills, quality management/improvement, tactful, working well under pressure, among many others.

Some job seekers have difficulty identifying transferable skills and professional qualities because they have been doing their jobs and not thinking about the skills they've been using to succeed. That's normal. There are a couple of ideas that can help expand upon your transferable skills (and perhaps your professional qualities). Think about your last position or two. What skills did you use? Now, think how you can break down those skills into smaller elements. For example, let's say you were in sales. What does that skill really entail? What's really going on there? Plenty.

- Research on target industries
- Cold Calling
- Persuasive verbal skills
- Presentation skills
- Closing
- Follow-up

- Identifying decision makers
- Email marketing
- Articulation of value proposition
- Overcoming objections
- Negotiating

And so much more . . .

By identifying these skills you can open yourself to other opportunities and employers that are searching for job seekers with these skills.

Once you have identified your transferable job skills and professional qualities (character traits), there are several things you can do with this valuable information. Your skills and qualities could be:

- A component of your branding message
- Woven into the summary section of your resume and LinkedIn profile
- Mentioned in a core skills, experience, or accomplishments section of your resume
- Used to write success stories
- Used in cover letters and emails
- Used as a part of your elevator speech
- Used in networking conversations
- Used in interviews

The key to using your skills and unique professional qualities in your job search is to translate them as valuable and demonstrate how they solve an employer's need. For the most impact, use your accomplishments as evidence of your skills and qualities in action by providing success stories. Making this connection is crucial when you are changing career paths.

Transferable soft skills and professional qualities cut across industry lines. An employer will always value an employee with a strong work ethic whether they are an accountant or a zookeeper.

The Sum Total

Here is the magic formula for becoming a sought-after job seeker:

Your Technical Skills (your ability)
+ Your Transferable Job Skills/Professional Qualities
+ <u>Your Track Record of Success</u>
= A Qualified Candidate

Once you are a qualified candidate, you must then differentiate yourself from other qualified candidates. Much of this book is designed and written to do just that, and enable you to land the job you want.

★ Success Stories

There is no passion to be found playing small—in settling for a life that is less than the one you are capable of living.
— Nelson Mandela[39]

A success story is a description of a career-related event that provides evidence to the hiring executive regarding your skills, abilities, competencies, professional qualities, and motivation to succeed at the job for which you are interviewing. In a business context, success stories are your case studies supporting your professional value proposition (what you're good at).

Writing success stories is often a walk down your professional memory lane. Think about projects, challenges, and problems you have dealt with over your career, or even during a normal workweek. Think in terms of identifying, preventing, and solving a problem. How did you do it? What was the positive result of your efforts?

It's highly recommended to compose several success stories as a part of your job search. By writing them down and reviewing them, you will be able to more easily remember them, have ready responses to interview questions (especially for behavior-based or performance-based interviews), and use them in written communication. These success stories will support your brand and qualifications.

---

39 Nsehe, Mfonobong. "19 Inspirational Quotes From Nelson Mandela," Forbes.com, December 6, 2013, http://www.forbes.com/sites/mfonobongnsehe/2013/12/06/20-inspirational-quotes-from-nelson-mandela/ (accessed May 27, 2015).

Writing success stories is an easy and fun exercise of self-discovery. There is a simple formula that seems to work well for most job seekers:

    C. Challenge (Situation, Task)

    A. Action

    R. Result[40]

Describe the challenge you faced or task you were assigned. Describe the plan of action you took and the positive result. Try to quantify the results with numbers or percentages whenever possible. A positive recommendation, letter of commendation, or email from your boss will work too.

When you write your success stories, do so with different skills and competencies in mind (transferable job skills and professional qualities). For example, stories that reflect true technical ability, analytical thinking, communication skills, leadership, and so on, including complementary combinations of skills and competencies within a single story.

When preparing for interviews, read the job description (if you have one) and think about what the employer is looking for (in terms of hard skills, soft skills, and professional qualities). Then create some success stories that align with what you believe will be asked of you in the interview.

Having success stories pre-written, rehearsed, and at your disposal will help differentiate you from other job seekers and give you a competitive advantage. You will be able to provide a succinct and well-thought response as opposed to those that have to wing it. The Appendix has a Success Story Worksheet and samples success stories.

---

40 Safani, Barbara. "Tell a Story Interviewers Can't Forget," TheLadders, http://www.theladders.com/career-advice/tell-story-interviewers-cant-forget (accessed May 29, 2015).

★ Branding

*Always remember: a brand is the most valuable piece of real estate
in the world; a corner of someone's mind.*
— John Hegarty[41]

It is imperative that you craft a professional brand that announces your distinct talents and what you represent to the marketplace. The process of branding is discovering who you are, what you are, what are your unique abilities, and communicating them through various mediums to your network or target market.

There are numerous benefits of creating an impactful brand, including:

1. You will differentiate yourself from other job seekers, and gain a huge advantage.

2. You create the initial impression the employer has of you.

3. You can more quickly convey your value to the employer.

4. You can more easily match your skills and value proposition to the employer's needs.

5. You can better determine which opportunities to pursue.

The drawback of not having a professional brand is simple: you are an unknown or you become a commodity. Employers will determine for themselves what they want to see in you. They will cast you in a light based on their own conclusions, which may not be the message you want to communicate.[42]

---

41 "10 Ways You're Building a Fantastic Brand," Design Aglow (blog), February 3, 2015, http://designaglow. com/blogs/design-aglow/16728432-10-ways-youre-building-a-fantastic-brand (accessed May 28, 2015).

42 Ibid.

There is no perceived differentiation from other job seekers. And, you cannot command a premium, and have reduced leverage when it comes to compensation.

Perhaps the biggest benefit of creating a professional brand is the self-awareness of your unique skills and experience, and recognition of how they work together to create an impact. You will project the value of your abilities more clearly, resulting in a job that's a good match for your skill set. Branding can also help you set your sights on what you want your future career to be.

Additionally, when your networking contacts know your brand, they are much more likely to advance it for you through referrals, recommendations, and so on. When the right opportunities come along, you become top of mind (because of your brand).

The professional-branding process requires introspection and thoughtful reflection. In some cases, thinking through your branding can be both an emotional and a professionally enlightening event.

Think of it this way: as a job seeker, your goal is to connect with employers both intellectually (you can do the job) and emotionally (you're a good fit). Having a well-crafted, professional brand helps on both levels. You must be perceived as the right candidate, and through branding you are better able to align yourself to an open job position.

Keep in mind that the effectiveness of your brand is determined by the connection that exists between what the brand claims and what it can actually deliver. In other words, you must be able to prove and quantify your professional brand. Failing to do so will have disastrous results. Don't oversell your brand and capabilities.

Create a succinct brand. Think of it, in analogous terms, as a tagline or a theme that will be the foundation for your job search.

To help determine your brand, ask yourself some questions:

1. What am I good at or an expert in?
2. What have I been recognized for?
3. What is my reputation with others (subordinates, peers, senior management)?
4. What have been my strong points in past job reviews (if applicable)?
5. What differentiates me from others with the same job?
6. What professional qualities do I have that make me good at my job?
7. What are the professional achievements I am most proud of?

The answers to these questions and the thoughts they provoke are essential to forming your brand. Now, synthesize the answers and thoughts into single words or short phrases that capture the concept of your responses. Here are some examples:

Sales

Award-winning sales executive with experience in workers' compensation, pain management, consistently exceeding sales goals.

Operations Management

Operations executive dedicated to improving operational efficiency through effective leadership.

Account Management

Client-focused account manager focused on client satisfaction and retention.

ERISA[43] Lawyer

Experienced attorney protecting ERISA fiduciaries from the Department of Labor.

A branding statement could also be a few separate descriptive words or phrases:

Process Improvement ▪ Lean Six Sigma[44]
▪ Turn-around Specialist
Marketing ▪ Advertising ▪ Public Relations

When you come to this book's resume and LinkedIn chapters, you will see a few examples of branding in action.

Branding Is Important

Creating and deciding on a brand is extremely important. Take the necessary time to reflect on this. What you decide your brand is (which will vary from person to person) will form the foundation for much of what will follow in your job search.

You may discover several skills and abilities to showcase in your brand. But, for the purposes of your job search and networking, focus on promoting your top one or two choices only. Mention other skills, which will happen naturally, during networking conversations and interviews.

The purpose of branding is to get you known for the value you offer, get you in the door, and differentiate you from other job seekers.

---

43 Employee Retirement Income Security Act; see "Frequently Asked Questions About Retirement Plans and ERISA," US Department of Labor, http://www.dol.gov/ebsa/faqs/faq_consumer_pension.html (accessed July 8, 2015).

44 A process that resolves problems while reducing costs; see "What is Lean Six Sigma?" Go Lean Six Sigma, https://goleansixsigma.com/what-is-lean-six-sigma/ (accessed July 8, 2015).

Elevator Speech

The only people who don't need elevator pitches
are elevator salesmen.
— Jarod Kintz[45]

The elevator speech is a critical component to your job search. By definition, an elevator speech is "the 30-second speech that summarizes who you are, what you do, and why you'd be a perfect candidate."[46] In essence, it is your job-search commercial.

The purpose of your elevator speech is to grab the listener's attention, quickly provide relevant information, and initiate conversation. A crisply delivered elevator speech is a differentiator from other job seekers. While others may struggle and stumble, you will be able to concisely inform the listener about your professional value proposition (brand).

Take some time and develop a handful of variations for different situations, including all forms of networking, interviews, association and industry conferences, and strictly social gatherings.

Here are some tips on crafting your elevator speech (some examples can be found at the end of this chapter):

1. Know your target audience.

This single factor will give your speech the most impact. For example, if you're targeting a CEO position and you will be speaking to members of the board of directors, you want your elevator speech to include statements of vision, direction, strategy, profitability, and

---

45 "Jarod Kintz Quotable Quote," Goodreads, http://www.goodreads.com/quotes/1234580-the-only-people-who-don-t-need-elevator-pitches-are-elevator (accessed May 28, 2015).

46 Collamer, Nancy. "The Perfect Elevator Pitch To Land A Job," Forbes, February 4, 2013, http://www.forbes.com/sites/nextavenue/2013/02/04/the-perfect-elevator-pitch-to-land-a-job/ (accessed May 28, 2015).

shareholder value (especially for publicly traded companies).

If your target position is in operations and the hiring executive is the COO, you want your elevator speech to include concepts such as efficiency and operational savings.

Finally, if your target position is in sales and the hiring executive will be the director or vice president of sales, you want your elevator speech to contain information about new business sales and sales-goal attainment.

2. Know what your value proposition is.

This is where your branding comes into full play. Identify as precisely as possible what you offer, what problems you can solve, and what benefits you bring to an employer.

3. Outline your speech.

Give yourself some time to ponder the ideas and concepts you may include—it isn't necessary to start drafting the speech immediately, but begin with notes reminding you of your bottom-line message. Don't worry about proper grammar and complete sentences yet. The objective is to gather concepts and ideas first, so be careful not to edit yourself. Refer back to the concepts you used to form your brand.

4. Write your speech.

Now that you have ideas and concepts about yourself to promote, begin drafting your speech's initial version. Here are some steps to guide you:

a. Identify yourself by function.

b. Make a statement regarding your value proposition as a professional.

c. Include accomplishments or a proof statement that supports your value proposition as a professional.

d. Create a call to action in the form of a subtle invitation to have a conversation.

5. Tailor the speech to them, not you.

As a rule, people are tuned into WIIFM (What's In It For Me?). So, refer to what you have written to ensure your message addresses *their* potential needs.

Instead of: "I am a talent-acquisition professional with ten years of experience working for financial services companies," you could say: "I am a talent-acquisition professional with a demonstrable history of identifying and recruiting top-level sales talent." Hear how much more impactful that is—and how much more effective the branding would be?

Using terminology that focuses on the benefits you bring will get the listener's attention. Benefit-focused terminology persuades the listener that you have the skills and track record of success necessary for the job.

6. Practice, practice, practice—and solicit feedback.

Read your speech aloud. Then tinker with the words (the goal is to have a speech that sounds authentic and confident). Now, memorize the speech and rehearse it. Consider practicing in front of a mirror and recording it on your smartphone. This could feel odd, but with practice, your delivery will be conversational (one of the keys to making it effective). Smiling while saying the words will increase the impact of the speech. Project your voice so those listening will clearly hear and understand.

When you are ready, try the speech out with a spouse or close friends. Make eye contact, smile, and deliver your message with confidence. Afterward, ask them what they think. If their response doesn't line up with the reaction you want from your speech, the speech still needs work.

7. Prepare a few variations.

You'll want to have a different speech for a colleague than for a personal friend at a social gathering. Sometimes you'll have just fifteen seconds for your speech, and in other situations you might have a full minute.

With your key points in mind, create different forms of your speech, depending on the situation. Much of this will happen naturally as you speak with people (as long as you remember your talking points).

Set up shorter and longer versions with your computer's word-count function. It's generally accepted that you can comfortably say about 150 words in sixty seconds.[47]

Remember, the purpose of an elevator speech is to quickly inform the listener of your value proposition as a professional and begin a conversation. Putting these tips into action is the real trick. Check out these websites that contain scores of elevator speeches (not all are designed for job seekers) for a variety of industries: www.improvandy.com and www.yourelevatorpitch.net.

Examples

Employee Benefits Sales Professional

"I am an employee benefits sales professional that helps businesses control their health care and insurance costs. My expertise is in medical self-funding and population health management. I have a documented track record of exceeded sales goals; in fact, over the

---

47 Walters, *Secrets of Successful Speakers*, p. 59.

last five years I have exceeded goals by an average of 21 percent. I want to make a career move to an organization looking to expand its market share in the self-funded arena."

Sales Management Executive: Focus on Mentorship

"I am a sales management executive and my forte is training and mentoring sales professionals to achieve higher sales production. During my twenty-year career I have turned around underperforming sales professionals and trained and mentored several award-winning sales reps. On average, over the course of my career, my sales teams have met or exceeded their group production goals more than 85 percent of the time. I'm looking to make a career move to an organization that needs sales leadership to grow sales and market share."

Operations Professional: Focus on Efficiency

"I am an operations professional and I specialize in improving efficiencies and expense reduction. In fact, during my last position I decreased customer response time by more than 65 percent and reduced departmental expenses by 18 percent by realigning personnel to positions that better fit their skills. I want to make a career move to an organization that desires to save money by making operations more efficient."

Accounting: Focus on Cost Savings

"I am a CPA who specializes in identifying cost-saving opportunities in manufacturing. With my former employer, I saved more than $750,000 over five years by negotiating return credits with vendors, increasing cash flow through accounts receivables, and decreasing collections. I want to make a job change to a manufacturing organization that can benefit from my abilities to identify cost-saving opportunities."

Elevator speeches can emphasize different value propositions. If you discover a particular skill is in demand with a prospective employer and you have it, change your speech to focus on that skill.

Business Cards

High expectations are the key to everything. — Sam Walton[48]

Having a business card during a job search is a necessity. Circumstances will present themselves where providing a resume is awkward or inappropriate.[49] Getting a business card should be toward the top of your to-do list, in order to make your job search a success.

There are four different approaches to the standard three-and-a-half-inch by two-inch business card for a job search: traditional business cards, networking business cards, resume business cards, and infographic business cards.

To determine the best business-card approach for your needs, consider this key factor: which would be best received by a networking contact or the hiring executive for your level of position?

It's easy to get sidetracked when creating business cards, especially the networking, resume, and infographic versions. Resist that urge. Don't overanalyze. Also remember: the messaging behind your brand and elevator speech and the information on your card must match.

A solid case can be made for getting two sets of cards to use in different settings: traditional for truly social events, and a networking or resume card for job-networking events.

Here are examples for each kind of job-search business card:

48 Bergdahl, Michael. What I Learned From Sam Walton: How to Compete and Thrive in a Wal-Mart World. (Hoboken, New Jersey: John Wiley & Sons, 2004), p. 39.

49 Leslie Ayres, "Why You Need a Resume Business Card," Notes from the Job Search Guru: A Career Advice Blog, March 16, 2009, http://www.thejobsearchguru.com/notesfrom/why-you-need-a-resume-business-card/ (accessed November 4, 2015).

Traditional Business Cards

This business card is simple in design. It contains only your name, city of residence, (street address is optional), telephone number(s), email address, and LinkedIn profile address. It is used for contact information-exchange purposes.

Bob Johnson, CSFS®

1340 Main Street
Blue Springs, MO 64015
(816) 123-4567 (H)

(816) 987-6543 (C)
bob.johnson1340@gmail.com
www.linkedin.com/in/bobjohnson

Networking Business Cards

Networking business cards contain the same key contact information as a traditional card, except this variety also has a title and a concise statement regarding your career focus and unique value proposition or brand.[50] Remember to keep the messaging consistent among your networking card, elevator speech, LinkedIn profile, resume, and so on. There is some room for variation, but the theme of these job-seeking tools must align.

Award-Winning Population Health Management
Sales Professional
Bob Johnson, CSFS®
National Sales Executive

1340 Main Street
Blue Springs, MO 64015
(816) 123-4567 (H)

(816) 987-6543 (C)
bob.johnson1340@gmail.com
www.linkedin.com/in/bobjohnson

---

50 Hansen, Randall S., PhD. "Networking Business Cards: An Essential Job-Search Tool for Job-Seekers, Career Changers, and College Students When a Resume Just Won't Do." Quintessential Careers, http://www.quintcareers.com/networking-business-cards/ (accessed November 4, 2015).

Resume Business Cards

A resume business card takes the networking card one step further. Here you may expand descriptive information on the front of the card and put key qualifications and accomplishments on the back. Focus on your top two or three strong achievements (or qualities), instead of responsibilities or titles.

This next point is optional, but leave a little white space at the bottom of the back of the card, allowing the recipient room to jot a note about you. Hopefully the note will read, "Need to call."[51]

Bob Johnson, CSFS®

National Sales Executive

Award-winning population health management sales professional with 5+ years of consistent goal achievemenet

1340 Main Street
Blue Springs, MO 64015
(816) 123-4567 (H)

(816) 987-6543 (C)
bob.johnson1340@gmail.com
www.linkedin.com/in/bobjohnson

Qualifications Summary

• #1 Sales Producer last three years
• Presidents Club Qualifier 20XX to present
• Consistently produces over $4M annually

---

[52]   *Front*   *Back*

It's fine to mix and match the concepts from any of the three types. For example, you may determine that it would be best received by your target audience that the front of the card has a traditional look. But on the back you may choose to put a branding statement and a couple of achievements. That's fine. Exercise your best judgment.

Business cards can be printed at most office supply stores and are reasonably inexpensive for a few hundred cards. In addition, many online companies produce business cards inexpensively. And if you're technology savvy, you can print your own cards using special paper and a template that is already loaded on most computers.

When creating your job-search business cards, keep the design simple. Use traditional fonts and conservative, business-appropriate color schemes. If you are pursuing jobs in advertising, media marketing, or other creative fields, you have more latitude with design and use of colors.

---

51 Ayres, "Resume Business Card."

52 Adapted from ibid.

Infographic Business Cards

An infographic business card is a very unique concept. It is not a business card in the traditional sense. Instead, it is more of a "networking handbill." In concept, an infographic business card is a colorful, high-resolution document containing impactful and persuasive background information and accomplishments presented through creatively designed pie charts and bar graphs.

Conceptually, an infographic business card is larger than the standard-size business card. Although there is no hard-and-fast rule, a four-by-six-inch card is a good starting point.

The infographic business card is ideal for networking events, especially for association gatherings and conventions. Printed on business-card-grade paper, with colorful graphics, it is a clear differentiator. If it's not too large, it can still easily slip into the inside jacket pocket or portfolio of a networking contact or hiring executive.

If this infographic-card idea appeals to you, it is highly recommended that you use the services of a professional with experience creating infographic resumes, as this experience translates well to creating infographic cards. You may also fast-forward to the infographic resume discussion later in this book (under Unique Tactics That Create Differentiation). Or you can check out Piktochart (www.piktochart.com) if you want to try your hand at creating your own infographic document. There are advantages and disadvantages that need to be carefully considered before you pursue this job-search tactic.

Chapter 4

Impactful Resumes

Great works are performed, not by strength, but by perseverance.
— Prince Imlac, character from Samuel Johnson's *Rasselas*[53]

Do Job Seekers Still Need a Resume if They Have a LinkedIn Profile?

The question is: Are resumes dead? The answer is, no.

With the worldwide acceptance of LinkedIn, many job seekers ask whether there is still a need for a traditional resume. Has the LinkedIn profile replaced the need for a traditional resume? No. You must have a well-written resume in your job-search arsenal. A LinkedIn profile does not replace your need for a resume. Let's briefly discuss the uses of both as they relate to your job search.

Purpose of a LinkedIn Profile – Discoverability and Information.
Your LinkedIn profile is your ever-present digital presence and digital footprint. When

---

53 "Quotes on Perseverance," *The Samuel Johnson Sound Bite Page,* http://www.samueljohnson.com/persever. html (accessed June 2, 2015); "Rasselas: A Word of Caution," *The Samuel Johnson Sound Bite Page,* http://www. samueljohnson.com/rasselas.html (accessed June 2, 2015).

complete, optimized, and compelling, it can get you noticed. It can get you discovered by a hiring executive or recruiter. This is its function in a job search. However, it has limitations. A LinkedIn profile is a one-size-fits-all template. Although the contents differ from person to person, the format is the same for everyone.

LinkedIn does have features that allow for customization such as attaching media, links, slide shares, and so on. These can heighten the interest of a hiring executive or HR recruiter, if they should take the time to watch (presuming it is not your current employer's information). This is all good. But, this is still a function of creating interest and getting you discovered.

In addition, the programming on LinkedIn requires a HR recruiter or hiring executive to go through a series of clicks to view certain areas of your profile. The information does not lay out in an easy-to-read or flowing way. Reading the information on your profile can be a cumbersome process at times.

The Tactical Uses of a Resume.

A resume is a completely customizable document. It can, and should be, tailored to specific positions and for particular companies. It allows you to present yourself in a creative way apart from the format limitations of a LinkedIn profile. You can format your resume to showcase your achievements, skills, knowledge, and competencies in a way that appeals to a hiring executive. When done properly, a customized resume can more easily be used by the hiring executive as a guide for the interview. This is a tactical advantage. Your customized resume plays to your strengths because you designed the format and strategically placed the information to differentiate you from other job seekers.

Resumes Still Required.

Most employers, either by direct request of the hiring executive or through the HR department, still require job seekers to submit resumes via online applications or by email. It is an accepted tool and business practice to submit a resume. This begs the question: if resumes are passé, why are they still a requirement in the application and interviewing process? Truth is: they are not passé and therefore required. This is not to say that there could be pockets in some industries that are moving away from the use of resumes. However, for the vast and overwhelming number of industries, and for the vast and overwhelming positions within those industries, the need for a well-written resume lives on.

What a Resume Is Not

You are not writing an autobiography![54] Too many job seekers put too much historical information on a resume. It's easy to have that happen. You start writing and remembering, and all of a sudden, you have a resume that is a blizzard of words. Hiring executives refuse to read resumes like that. It's too much work. A resume must be an informative marketing piece—easy on the eyes with plenty of white space.

So, What Is a Resume?

A resume is a unique form of written communication designed to quickly gain the attention of the hiring executive, inform them about you, sell you as a qualified candidate, and differentiate you from other job seekers. You have complete control of the appearance and content, and should feel comfortable about how it represents you, but (as previously stated) it is not your autobiography.

★ Time Is of the Essence

Most hiring executives spend between five and twenty seconds when first looking at a resume. So assume your resume will not have much time to make a positive impression. If you're perceived as valuable to the company, you're in. If not, you're out. An employer must be able to quickly determine your potential value to the organization. This is another reason to use the word cloud technique so key words and phrases appear on your resume and speak to the hiring executive.

How can you make the most of those precious seconds? Showcase your most impactful qualifications and accomplishments in the top half of the first page of your resume. The title of your resume, branding words/phrases/statement, the first sentence of your summary, and the first bullet point or two of your first showcase section create the biggest impact. By then, time's up. (More on showcase sections in a moment.) If these grab the interest of the employer, you get the next few seconds and perhaps more. This is why titling and branding are so important on a resume. And, the reason why showcase resumes have become so popular. Once you have created initial interest, then the hiring executive will generally look at your current/previous employer, your position/function, length of employment, and successes.

---

54 Claycomb and Dinse, *Career Pathways*, Part 3.

Your Resume Is Your Marketing Brochure

Your elevator speech is your commercial. Your success stories are your case studies. Your resume is your marketing brochure.

Your resume is frequently the first formal presentation of your professional credentials to a hiring executive. Take the time to write an impactful resume. In order for your resume to provide that positive first impression, make sure that it:

- **Has a clean, professional appearance.** Develop a document that is easy on the eyes, with plenty of white space, and plain, simple language. Also be sure that the use of font size, bold print, lines, headings, spacing, bullet points, and so on, is consistent throughout. Any graphics and shading must be readable. Your resume must have a wow factor.

- **Has a title.** A title announces the professional qualifications to follow in the resume's body.

- **Has branding words or a branding statement.** Either of these will help present your value proposition.

- **Contains accurate contact information.** Review to ensure your contact information is up-to-date.

- **Features a concise, professional summary.** This should highlight your background and give information to support your professional value proposition.

- **Lists core competencies or qualifications.** Showcase your strongest skills, abilities, experience, education, and special knowledge.

- **Lists achievements.** State what separates you from the pack.

- **Honestly represents your background.** It is estimated that "more than 80 percent of resumes contain some stretch of the truth."[55] Be honest about your background and achievements. If an embellishment is discovered, you lose your integrity and credibility, and it will be extremely difficult to regain it. Your employer (whether current or prospective) won't trust you. And if others find out you embellished your information, that will make it harder still on your reputation.

---

55 Bucknell Career Development Center, "Creating an Effective Resume," Bucknell University, http://www.bucknell.edu/documents/CDC/Creating_An_Effective_Resume.pdf (accessed February 19, 2016).

It is perfectly acceptable, and encouraged, to write a generic form of your resume. From this generic resume, you can modify it for specific opportunities that you pursue. Just remember what form of your resume you use with specific employers!

Use of Keywords

Keywords are specific words or phrases that reflect your experiences and abilities, and are frequently buzzwords, or terms-of-art. Examples include P&L, and ROI for commerce; others include "pull through strategies" for sales and marketing, or are specific to a particular industry (like a professional designation). Your resume must contain certain keywords to get the employer's attention and communicate that you are qualified for a particular position. The importance of keywords on your resume cannot be overstated.

Keywords can include the following:

- Position title
- Professional designation
- Skills, knowledge, core competencies
- Industry terms-of-art (and abbreviations)
- Employer names (past or present)
- Licenses, certifications
- Location (state, city)
- Software and technologies you're familiar with
- Education (school names and degrees)

It can be persuasive to connect a keyword to an accomplishment, whenever possible. For example, *Client Retention—maintained a client retention rate of 94 percent for the last four years.*

You are likely familiar with the keywords of your industry (terms-of-art) and abilities. Make sure they appear prominently on your resume.

When pursuing a particular opening, use the word cloud technique to capture buzzwords used by that employer. Strategically placing those words on your resume is using the "language of the employer," can be persuasive, and can enhance your candidacy for the position.

Resume Formats

There are three fundamental variations to resumes: Chronological, Functional, and Showcase.

The **Chronological** format is the most traditionally used resume format. A job seeker's experience in the work world is listed in reverse chronological order. This format emphasizes duties and responsibilities with accomplishments listed under each employer. Jobs, as well as managerial and other responsibilities, are grouped by title and company, with dates of employment. This is a common format frequently used by tenured professionals with consistent work experience in one field or position type.[56]

The **Functional** format emphasizes skills and qualifications to strategically sell experience that may align to the needs of the employer. A job seeker's experience is divided into a skill-based section that demonstrates qualifications, training, education, and specific accomplishments, and a reverse chronological listing of employment including company name, title, and dates (toward the end of the resume). This format works well for those with gaps in employment and those whose career has involved several employers.[57] Most job seekers should be careful when considering the Functional format since employers strongly favor a Chronological or Showcase resume.

The **Showcase** resume is a growing trend that has developed over the last several years and combines the best features of the Chronological and Functional formats. For most experienced professionals and executives (whether they have a more diverse employment background or not), this format is worth serious consideration. The concept is to showcase your best professional selling points—qualifications, industry knowledge, and achievements—immediately in the top half or top two-thirds of the resume's first page. Work and education is then listed in reverse chronological order just like a traditional chronological resume. Using this format, you are allowed to be selectively repetitive. Some of your showcase items can appear again in the chronological section of your resume. This way, the hiring executive knows where and when you learned or achieved your showcase qualifications.

---

56 Yate, *Knock 'em Dead*, p. 45–46.

57 Ibid., p. 46.

There is an additional kind of resume called an Infographic resume. It is a colorful, high-resolution document that visually presents your background and accomplishments by using pie charts, bar graphs, and time lines in creative ways. The use of an Infographic resume is discussed in the chapter, Unique Tactics That Create Differentiation.

Parts of a Resume

No matter what form of resume you choose (setting aside the Infographic resume), each has certain parts in common that appear in the same places, or serve the same function. These are:

Identification/Contact Information

This section appears at the top of your resume and includes your name (with notable professional designations), address, telephone numbers (home and/or cell phone), and email address. Including your LinkedIn profile address is optional. A new trend is omitting your residential address. This is acceptable, but still include city and state.

No photos should appear on your resume (unless it is required in your industry). If they want to know what you look like they can check out your LinkedIn profile.

Email Addresses

Your email address must be professional. Some advocate that you create an email account tailored for your job search and the email address should be supportive of your branding, i.e., engineeringexpert@xyz.net. **Avoid this.** Many hiring executives view this technique with chagrin.

There are several professional formats you can use:

- jsmith@xyz.com
- john.smith@xyz.com
- smithj@xyz.com
- john@xyz.com
- johns@xyz.com
- johnsmith@xyz.com

If you need to, add your lucky number, area code, ZIP code, or other number prior to the @ symbol, but not your date or year of birth. Be absolutely sure the address is professional.

Title

By titling your resume, it announces what the resume is going to describe so the reader doesn't have to scan the entire resume to determine your professional background. Be reasonably specific with your title. For example, "Senior Healthcare Sales Representative," "Casualty Field Claims Professional," "Vice President of Operations."

The title of your resume should be nearly identical to the titles on your Master Job Description. The title should also align with your LinkedIn profile, networking or resume business card, and at least share a theme similar to your elevator speech.

Branding Statement

Your branding statement should appear under your resume's title. This could be either a statement or a few descriptive words that relate to or support your brand. Some examples include:

Dedicated to improving sales through effective leadership.

▪ Process Improvement ▪   Manufacturing Efficiency ▪   Strategy

Objective Statement

The objective statement has fallen out of favor for seasoned professionals and should not be used except for special circumstances (a significant change in career path, industry sabbaticals, and so on).

When using the objective statement, ensure it clearly states your purpose for pursuing a position with the employer. The resume material following should support, as much as possible, that you are able to perform the objective.

If you choose to use an objective statement, keep it short. Avoid such nebulous phrases as:

- "Opportunity for advancement" or "Advance my career"
- "Challenging opportunity"
- "Utilizing my experience"
- "Professional growth"
- "Increase in compensation"

Summary

The summary brings together the experiences of your career into the present. It is a recommended section for seasoned professionals and should be a concise paragraph(s) summarizing experience, areas of expertise, technical or professional skills, traits, and accomplishments.

A summary section can have several different names, including:

- Career Description
- Career Summary
- Professional Qualifications
- Profile
- Qualifications
- Summary of Qualifications

The summary could contain some of the following information: level of responsibility, skills and responsibilities, potential contributions (as seen from the employer's perspective), and highlights of top strengths and accomplishments. It emphasizes key information detailed in the body of the resume and should also include information such as languages, special degrees, and team and communication skills. The summary acts much like an executive summary section of a long document or white paper.

A simple three-part formula to help you create the foundation for an impactful summary is:

1. A statement regarding your function or title, possibly including a reference to tenure.

2. A statement identifying your technical abilities and qualifications. Accomplishments can be included here as well.

3. A statement regarding your transferable job skills and/or professional traits.

For example:

Position: Senior Accountant

Statement regarding function or title: A detail-oriented CPA with twenty-two years of experience.

Statement regarding technical ability or qualifications: Proven ability in financial forecasting and analysis, audit, reconciliation, tax law, and evaluating and consulting with clients regarding business investments and opportunities.

Statement regarding transferable job skills/professional qualities: Conscientious, self-motivated, and service-oriented professional who enjoys client interaction.

Complete Summary:

A detailed-oriented CPA with twenty-two years of experience. Proven ability in financial forecasting and analysis, audit, reconciliation, tax law, and evaluating and consulting with clients regarding business investments and opportunities. Conscientious, self-motivated and service-oriented professional who enjoys client interaction.

An effective summary section should be concise and to the point. Many professionals make the mistake of making a summary too long. By using the three-part formula you will built the foundation for a solid summary.

Core Competencies

Almost all resumes for experienced professionals and executives should have a Core Competencies section. Although there are likely hundreds of competencies and skills that could be listed, as a rule keep it to no more than three columns of five, totaling fifteen.

Your competencies should fall into one of the following major areas: technical ability (what you are good at), communication skills, leadership, analytical thinking, teamwork, and time management. These tend to be the broad skills most employers seek. When listing your core competencies, match those identified in the job description to those you have.

This section can have other titles, such as:

- Abilities
- Core Strengths and Expertise
- Key Skills
- Skills
- Signature Strengths

Showcase Section(s)

If you elect to use a Showcase resume, the next section (or two, depending upon your circumstances) can be your showcase section. Although you have a lot of discretion on titling and content, the key to this section is to make it substantive and impressive. Use lists and bullet points to make the information in these sections easier to read.

Possible titles for showcase sections include:

- Achievement summaries
- High-Impact Contributions
- Notable Performance Highlights
- Distribution or Vendor Partners
- Expertise
- Languages (Foreign or IT)
- Marquee Clients
- Product Knowledge
- Recommendations
- Sales Awards

Employment History

The employment history section is a summary of work experience and accomplishments that cover the past fifteen years or so. Begin with your current job first and work backward. Work experience older than fifteen years may be summarized at the end of this section in a single sentence. Describe experiences in a coherent and continuous manner.

Begin with details on the most important items: current company/employer's name, job title, job function, and dates (in years). List the current name of the company even if you started working with a company that was bought or merged with the current company, e.g., "GlobalOutlook (formerly Global SpyGlass)." Use the official name of the company. Because many companies have names or initials that may make it difficult to identify what kind of a company it is, use a short tagline to describe each company: industry position, dollar volume, customer base, products, and/or recognition. For example, NAME OF COMPANY: *"An international manufacturer of professional and retail personal care products with $134M in annual sales."*

Most times, be sure to list the company name first, and only once. This reduces the likelihood employers will think you have job-hopped when you have not.

Next, follow the company name with your title. If this title is in-house and hard to understand, include a translation or generic job title. For example, you can substitute "Purchasing Agent" with "Product Specialist/Purchasing Representative" if that makes things easier for those who aren't a part of your industry or company. Providing a functional title educates the hiring executive about your actual function and role. If you held multiple titles with the same employer, mention a date next to each to show promotions or advancement within an organization.

Job Scope Description

For each position, write a four- to six-sentence description of your duties and responsibilities. This could include information regarding the dimension and scope of the position, function, staff size, geographical reach, budget, reporting relationships, departments, and so on. In essence, describe what you did and your responsibilities. Here's an example:

Professional Experience

GlobalOutlook (formerly Global SpyGlass), Anytown, Anywhere 20XX–Present

Regional Sales Executive
Promoted to revitalize underperforming northeast sales territory. Developed new business channels on a regional and national basis. Reestablished relationships with client base. Products include enrollment technology, analytics, and predictive modeling, among others.
   This section can have other titles, such as:

- Career Experience
- Employment Background
- Experience
- Professional Experience
- Relevant Experience
- Work Experience
- Career Narrative

Accomplishments

An accomplishment is a specific example of success involving a key element or most important aspect of your job. The specific results of your actions should be immediately clear to the hiring executive.

An important message about accomplishments. Accomplishments are vitally important to your job search. It has been said that qualifications often get you an interview, but accomplishments get you the job.[58] Identify and quantify your accomplishments, and use bullet points for easy reading.

Accomplishments:

- Clearly demonstrate past ability to contribute to the productivity and/or profitability of the employer

- Emphasize past achievements and successes by using quantifiable and measurable information

- Highlight the value, benefits, and contributions that you bring to the organization

- Substantiate the strengths included in your summary with results produced in similar situations

Accomplishments focus on quantities, improvements, and results from an organization's perspective. How did you make or save the employer money?[59] Or how did your actions lead to a beneficial result?[60] Highlight accomplishments with $, %, or # as applicable to enhance credibility (as long as it's true).

Accomplishments can be a separate showcase section on your resume. Or, especially for Chronological resumes, they can be a subsection to each position you have held.

What Accomplishments Get Employers' Attention?

Remember that employers generally hire with two main goals: to make or save money.[61] The more obvious your accomplishments appear to achieve either goal, the more powerful the accomplishment is. The following list of accomplishments can help spark ideas as you contemplate your own (refer back to Understanding the Employer's Mindset):

Accomplishments

1. Increased revenue
2. Awards, rankings against your peers, production numbers

---

58 Guest Author (Bob Bozorgi), "Qualifications Will Get You an Interview, But They Won't Get You Hired," *The Undercover Recruiter* (blog), http://theundercoverrecruiter.com/qualifications-will-get-interview-wont-get-hired/ (accessed May 29, 2015).

59 Whitcomb, Job Search Magic, p. 274.

60 See also, Safani, "Tell a Story."

61 Whitcomb, *Job Search Magic*, p. 274.

3. Process improvement that saves money or time, increases efficiency, makes work easier
4. Improved company image, branding
5. New distribution channels opened for sales
6. Product improvements, product development
7. Business/sales expanded through existing accounts
8. Anything that enhances competitiveness
9. Improved client retention
10. Improved company culture, morale, employee retention

The following is a short list of positions. Under each are ideas from which accomplishment statements can be created. Although a particular position type may not apply to you, adopt this mindset when considering your accomplishments.

Accounting
- Design and implementation of cost controls and quantifiable results
- Optimization of business output through software or other technology
- Application of tax laws

Account Management
- Client retention
- Contribution to sales growth (upselling)
- Key account responsibilities

Engineering
- Financial outcomes from new designs or products
- Patents awarded or pending
- Projects managed and financial results

Executive-Level Management
- Measurable increases in revenue, profits, EBITDA,[62] and/or ROI
- Leadership regarding strategic planning, long-term business development
- Mergers, acquisitions, joint ventures

---

62 "Earnings before interest, taxes, depreciation, and amortization"; see Arline, Katherine. "What is EBITDA?" *Business News Daily*, February 25, 2015, http://www.businessnewsdaily.com/4461-ebitda-formula-definition.html (accessed February 19, 2016).

Healthcare
- Increase in quality of patient care, with detailed results
- Increased impact of outreach services, with their results
- Attainment and maintenance of stringent regulatory requirements
- Reduction in re-admittance

Human Resources
- Success in recruiting personnel
- Employee retention
- Improvements in employee benefits and cost reduction

Manufacturing
- Increases in production and worker productivity
- Improvements in safety
- Reductions in operating costs and overhead expenses

Retail
- Increases in gross revenue, profit margins, and market impact
- Improvements in inventory turnover, speed to market
- Reductions in inventory, operating, and personnel costs

Sales
- Sales honors, awards, percentages over quota, rankings against peers
- Increases in revenue, profits, and market share
- New national accounts sales
- Expansion into previously undeveloped territories and markets

Technology
- Development of new technologies and their financial results
- Detailed results of implementation (e.g., revenue increases, cost reductions)
- Patents awarded
- Timely systems conversion, integration

Education
Provide educational background starting with your most advanced degree, major, and listed by the university or college name. Abbreviations are fine: BS, BA, MS, MBA, and PhD. Give school names the same font treatment as company names. If you do not have a full degree, include those details by mentioning what degree you

pursued and the number of years or semesters attended (or percentage completed, if available). Include your education at the bottom of your resume unless you feel there is grounds to move it up or it is customary in your industry to have it appear early on a resume.

Other Credentials

The following sections can add depth to your resume. You may not need every section below—just those representing strong qualifications for you.

1. Affiliations/Associations

Affiliations and associations can be persuasive on a resume by indicating your involvement in your industry and the community. Include groups you are a member of. An Affiliations section may look like this:

American Marketing Association

Society for Human Resource Management

Health Care Administrators Association

American Red Cross

2. Appointments

Appointments are offices you held (generally in the last five years) and demonstrate involvement in professional and civic organizations. Include only professional or significant charitable organizations—Middle School Bake Sale Organizer doesn't count. An Appointments section may look like this:

Chairperson, American Management Association, 20XX–20XX

Paul Harris Fellow, Rotary International, 20XX–20XX

Regional Director—Rapid Response, American Red Cross, 20XX–20XX

3. Awards/Honors

This section reveals achievements, awards, and honors not connected to your career. Include accolades from college activities, professional service organizations, volunteer work, and so on. Examples include:

Team Captain, Central Minnesota University Softball Team

Up and Comer Award, Rotary International

Volunteer of the Year, American Red Cross

3. **Languages**

The world is getting smaller. Being fluent or proficient in a foreign language can be a significant differentiator, depending on the kind of positions you are pursuing. A Language section generally appears this way:

Fluent in Portuguese

Proficient in Italian

4. **Licenses**

List all licenses relevant or required in your industry or the job description for your desired position. Don't list a real estate license if you aren't seeking a position in that industry.

5. **Professional Training and Designations**

If you have achieved an industry designation or significant certification, list it along with the date of achievement. This is a clear indication that you stay current and are enhancing your skills and knowledge. Professional Training sections generally appear this way:

Dale Carnegie Corporate Strategy—20XX

Managing for Excellence, sponsored by the American Management Association—20XX

Selling!, a five-day program sponsored by Kaufman and Gentry Sales Training—20XX

If you've completed more than five courses, just note the types along with who sponsored them, such as:

Completed sales, management, and computer skills programs sponsored by the American Management Association

6. **Technical**

Understanding technology is becoming indispensable in today's world. As applicable to the positions you are pursuing, include your proficiencies with technology here. A Technical section generally appears this way:

C++, Cisco UCS, Commvault, VMWare, Windows Servers, Microsoft Active Directory, WordPerfect, PowerPoint, Microsoft Office, Microsoft Outlook, Adobe Acrobat

Use of Recommendations on a Resume

When properly used, recommendations, testimonials, and endorsements appearing on a resume can be impactful. These affirmations capitalize upon the persuasion principle of social proof mentioned earlier in the book.

Due to a resume's limited space, a statement of recommendation (appearing in quotes, italics, or both) must be short, relevant, and direct. Testimonials and endorsements from others are more powerful than what you say about yourself.

To be effective, the person providing the recommendation must be identified by name and title. Get permission from the individual offering the recommendation prior to including it on your resume.

Example:

"Increased average profit on special orders by 17 percent, resulting in thousands of dollars in new revenue."
—Letter of Appreciation from Elizabeth Jones, VP of Sales

"We are proud to have Jessica on our team. Her knowledge of cost accounting and financial strategy has contributed significantly to our bottom line."
—Elizabeth Jones, VP of Sales

You can also close a resume with a recommendation:
"Katy was clearly the most client-focused account manager we had on our team!"
—Bob Johnson, Vice President of Account Management

Again, for effect, consider putting the recommendation in italics. Identify the source of the recommendation by name and title and get permission. Remember, since it is a recommendation, this technique is using the persuasion principle of social proof.

Information NOT to be Included on a Resume

- Never put "References Upon Request" at the end of your resume. It is naturally assumed that you will furnish references if asked.

- Don't include the reasons for leaving your different jobs.

- Don't include salary history on your resume.
- Avoid putting personal or legally protected characteristics such as age, marital status, race, state of health, social security number, height, weight, and so forth on your resume.

Testing the Impact of Your Resume

After your resume is complete, see if it makes the initial impression you want. Give your resume to two or three objective colleagues that you trust. Ideally, you want colleagues from the business world that hire as a part of their job. Ask them to take ten to fifteen seconds to look at your resume. What do they remember?

If the "impact" points of your resume are not what you want them to remember, you may need to revise it. On the other hand, if your review group remembers what you want to communicate with your resume, it's ready for use. Have your quality control group do the same for your other job-search documents or online profiles, as well.

Attaching Your Resume to Your Online Profile

When it comes to attaching your resume to your online profile (we'll discuss profiles in detail later), you have some decisions to make. If you are currently employed, it is recommended that you not attach your resume. Doing so opens you up to some awkward questions from your current employer or informs your employer that you are always on the market for other opportunities. Having a complete online profile should be sufficient to inform a hiring executive or recruiter about your professional qualifications.

If you are unemployed, it is entirely permissible to attach your resume. The potential exists that your resume could be printed off or electronically forwarded to a hiring executive by an internal company recruiter or any other source. However, you may want to skip attaching your resume to your profile, as a conscious strategy. Remember, communicating with hiring executives is pivotal to your job-search success, and the desired goal. A well-constructed online profile creates interest on its own, triggering the hiring executive to communicate with you. After communication starts, then send your resume directly to the recruiter or executive. Not attaching your resume could help you generate more inquiries, emails, and conversations.

Dealing with Employment Gaps on a Resume

Employment gaps on a resume can create anxiety for job seekers. Fortunately, most employers understand the difficulties of the job market, the negative employment dynamics of a particular industry, or have experienced a gap in employment themselves.

Judgments regarding employment gaps have eased. According to a study conducted by CareerBuilder, 85 percent of hiring executives and human resource professionals "are more understanding of employment gaps" than they once were.[63] While there is an understanding that bad things can happen to good people, there are limits. If your gap is reasonably short and you have been productive in some way using or enhancing your skills, the gap is generally overlooked. But the longer the gap, the more negatively an employer views that gap.

Studies indicate that once your employment gap exceeds six months, your job search can become precipitously more difficult.[64] The unstated reasoning is if you have been unemployed for over six months nobody wants to hire you (especially when you have been actively looking for a job).

So, how can you get around this potential judgment and frightening statistic? Take comfort—there are ways:

- On your resume, list your dates of employment in years only, not month and year. It is honest and can cover your gap. However, be forthright if asked about actual dates of employment.

- Use a Showcase resume. Do what you can to emphasize your strongest selling points up front on your resume. Hopefully, this will focus the employer on your skills, knowledge, and achievements and not on the employment gap.

- Become a consultant. You obviously have ability, so try to secure paid opportunities to advise companies in your area(s) of expertise. Show that you have remained active and are using your skills.

- Volunteer for a worthy cause or association. It may not be complicated work, but it is

---

63 CareerBuilder, "Employers Share Encouraging Perspectives and Tips for the Unemployed in New CareerBuilder Survey," news release, March 21, 2012, http://www.careerbuilder.com/share/aboutus/pressreleasesdetail.aspx?id=pr684&sd=3/21/2012&ed=12/31/2012&siteid=cbpr&sc_cmp1=cb_pr684_ (accessed February 19, 2016).

64 O'Brien, Matthew. "The Terrifying Reality of Long-Term Unemployment," *The Atlantic*, April 13, 2013, http://www.theatlantic.com/business/archive/2013/04/the-terrifying-reality-of-long-term-unemployment/274957/ (accessed February 19, 2016).

using your skills in some capacity. Examples: As an accountant, do the bookkeeping for a nonprofit you are passionate about. As a sales professional, volunteer to do fund-raising.

- Continue your education. This does not necessarily mean getting an MBA (although, clearly, that would be advantageous), but begin working toward a substantive industry designation.

- Be very cautious of the word "sabbatical" on a resume. It is an unusual word to the commercial private business sector, and raises the suspicion of long-term unemployment.

- Depending upon the circumstances, briefly address the employment gap in your cover letter. It could be that you chose not to look for a job, but you must have a very good reason. This information would come under the "Additional Information" section. (See Cover Letters and Other Written Communications.) Keep it brief.

As a last resort, use the Functional resume format. Above all, never sacrifice your integrity.

Creating Your Own Resume

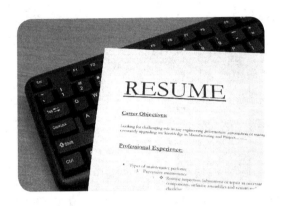

To grow, you must be willing to let your present and future
be totally unlike your past. Your history is not your destiny.
— Alan Cohen[65]

Although an employer reads a resume for content, they also draw conclusions based on its appearance. If you are comfortable with your word-processing skills, create your own resume. There are resume-writing books on the market with examples to help you with construction, style, and content. One you should check out is *Motivated Resumes and LinkedIn Profiles.* This book contains advice and insight from some of the most experienced, credentialed, and award-winning resume writers in the country. There are over eighty sample resumes presented in a portfolio format by each resume writer. There is biographical information for each writer and contact information should you be interested in having the resume writer create a resume for you.

If you decide to hire a resume writer, it is recommended you find a resume writer who is certified by a resume credentialing organization such as:

- CPRW (Certified Professional Resume Writer), designation sanctioned by the Professional Association of Resume Writers (www.parw.com).

- NCRW (Nationally Certified Resume Writer), designation sanctioned by The National Resume Writer's Association (www.thenrwa.com/).

- CARW (Certified Advanced Resume Writer) and CMRW (Certified Master Re-

---

65 "Self-Limiting Beliefs," *Quotes from the Masters,* http://finsecurity.com/finsecurity/quotes/qm103.html (accessed May 28, 2015).

sume Writer), designations provided by Career Directors International (www. careerdirectors.com). They also have awards for resume writers.

Websites for these organizations provide a listing of resume writers by location. Designations of some kind (there are others) offer some assurance that the writer has the prerequisite level of expertise to create a resume to your satisfaction.

There are other talented resume writers who do not have a designation. Simply ask to see samples of their work.

Most professional- and executive-level resumes cost from $250 to $1,000, or more. A well-written, professional resume is one of the best investments to make in yourself. The Appendix of this book contains a few sample resumes for your review.

A resume is vitally important to a job search, and it must be well-constructed and impactful. However, it will not get you a job. It can only help you get noticed, help you get an interview, and then operate as a guide for hiring executives to ask questions during an interview. Don't overemphasize its role.

Too many job seekers erroneously believe that a great resume is the ticket to a great job. It's not. A resume is a tool . . . one of several.

Spend the appropriate amount of time building your resume, but don't grind over its creation. Normally four to six hours spent on a resume, if you do it yourself, is adequate. Any more than that may be busywork disguised as being productive. Don't make this mistake. You have other important things to do. Once your resume is satisfactorily written, move on to other important tasks that can move your job search forward, such as networking, proactively marketing your professional credentials, and getting interviews. These tasks will shorten your search more than grinding over a resume's tiny details.

Chapter 5

LinkedIn

Active participation on LinkedIn is the best way to say,
'Look at me!' without saying 'Look at me!'
— Bobby Darnell[66]

Please Note: LinkedIn changes its format, features, appearance, and functionality regularly and without notice. These changes enhance the LinkedIn experience as well as restrict some of its uses. Some of the instructions included here could be slightly different due to changes made by LinkedIn and influenced by the level and kind of the LinkedIn account of the user.

This topic on LinkedIn is as current as possible at the time of writing.

---

66 Knyszweski, Jerome. "How to Use LinkedIn as a Student—And Nail That Dream Job," *LinkedIn Pulse*, April 28, 2015, https://www.linkedin.com/pulse/how-use-linkedin-student-nail-dream-job-jerome-knyszewski (accessed May 28, 2015).

LinkedIn is the most used and effective professional networking website on the planet, with more than 500 million members in two hundred countries and growing.[67] In the United States alone there are more than 128 million members. At present, LinkedIn adds "more than two new members every second."[68] "Over 25 million profiles are viewed on LinkedIn daily."[69]

In today's job market, it is imperative to have a complete and robust LinkedIn profile. In a recent survey of HR professionals and recruiters, 65 percent cite a lack of skilled candidates in the market as the largest obstacle to hiring.[70] Human talent is the lifeblood for every company, but there is a war for talent in the market due to the lack of well-qualified candidates in many industries.

Being in a candidate-driven job market is a good environment when you are looking for a job (should you be fortunate enough to be in that environment when searching for a job). But how can you maximize being discovered for open opportunities? Answer: your LinkedIn profile. LinkedIn is the overwhelming resource (87 percent) most frequently used by HR recruiters to identify and evaluate candidates.[71] By having a complete LinkedIn profile, you significantly increase your chances of being contacted by a HR recruiter. In fact, "Users with complete profiles are 40 times more likely to receive opportunities through LinkedIn."[72]

What makes your profile complete? Generally speaking, your profile is complete when it has the following:

---

67 Smith, Craig. "133 Amazing LinkedIn Statistics." Last updated November 17, 2016, http://expandedramblings.com/index.php/by-the-numbers-a-few-important-linkedin-stats/. (accessed November 28, 2016). *See also*, Smith, Craig, DMR, "200+ Amazing LinkedIn Stats" (Last Checked/Updated October 2016) http://expandedramblings.com/index.php/by-the-numbers-a-few-important-linkedin-stats/. (downloaded November 28, 2016).

68 "About LinkedIn," *LinkedIn Newsroom*, https://press.linkedin.com/about-linkedin (accessed May 29, 2015).

69 Geoff, "Top LinkedIn Facts and Stats [Infographic]," (blog), *We Are Social Media*, July 25, 2014, http://wersm.com/top-linkedin-facts-and-stats-infographic/ (accessed May 29, 2015).

70 Jobvite 2016 Recruiter National Survey www.jobvite.com (accessed November 17, 2016).

71 Ibid. *See also*, Smith, Craig, DMR, "200+ Amazing LinkedIn Stats" (Last Checked/Updated October 2016) http://expandedramblings.com/index.php/by-the-numbers-a-few-important-linkedin-stats/. (downloaded November 28, 2016). This source indicates that 94% of recruiters use LinkedIn to vet candidates.

72 Foote, Andy, Why You Should Complete Your LinkedIn Profile, (December 7, 2015). https://www.linkedinsights.com/why-you-should-complete-your-linkedin-profile/ (accessed November 22, 2016).

- Location and industry
- Summary
- Current position
- Two past positions (best practice)
- Education
- Skills (minimum of three)
- Profile photo
- At least fifty connections[73] (best practice)

Once your profile is complete, it should register as an "All-Star."

If your profile is incomplete, it won't register as high in searches as those that are more robust.[74] It cannot be overemphasized. LinkedIn should be your primary online professional networking and job-search tool.

In many cases, your LinkedIn profile could be the first impression a hiring executive has of you. A strong profile is a must. It gives you credibility.

Before we begin discussions on specific LinkedIn topics, and if you already have a profile, it is recommended that you turn off the network notification function until you have completed making all changes to your profile. Here's how:

---

73 Ibid.

74 Reynolds, Marci. "How to Be Found More Easily in LinkedIn (LinkedIn SEO)," *Job-Hunt.org*, http://www.job-hunt.org/social-networking/be-found-on-linkedin.shtml (accessed June 4, 2015).

Go to your Profile page. Click on the "Me" icon at the top and from the drop down menu, select "Settings and Privacy."

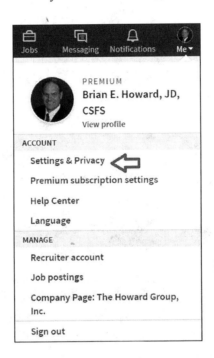

Then, select the Privacy option.

Scroll down and click on the "Sharing profile edits." Turn off Sharing profile edits.

By doing this, your network (those you are connected to) will not be alerted regarding changes you may be making. You can reactivate the announcements later if you choose.

Use of Keywords

It is estimated that there are more than a billion searches annually on LinkedIn.[75] Companies and recruiters search keywords to find candidates (in addition to people who search for a particular company or person).

Let's take a quick review of keywords. As you know, keywords are specific words or phrases that reflect your experiences and abilities, and are frequently buzzwords, or terms-of-art that are applicable to you professionally. Like your resume, your profile must contain certain keywords to get attention and communicate that you are qualified for a particular position.

Keywords can include the following:

- Position title
- Industries
- Professional designation
- Skills, knowledge, core competencies
- Industry terms-of-art (and abbreviations)
- Employer names (past or present)
- Licenses, certifications
- Location (state, city)
- Software and technologies you're familiar with
- Education (school names and degrees)

We will have an extended discussion about the use of keywords when we talk about optimization.

Your LinkedIn Profile - Sections

Before we discuss building an impactful profile (optimization), let's briefly introduce the major components of your profile.

---

75 Stephanie Frasco, "11 Tips To Help Optimize Your LinkedIn Profile For Maximum Exposure and Engagement," *Convert with Content* (blog), https://www.convertwithcontent.com/11-tips-optimize-linkedin-profile-maximum-exposure-engagement/ (accessed June 10, 2015).

1. Photo

Your photo is important.[76] It shows that you are a real person. Since LinkedIn has a professional focus—and you are looking for a job—it is recommended to have a photo taken at a studio by a professional or, at a minimum, a close-up photograph of you professionally dressed. According to experts, "profiles with a photo are fourteen times more likely to be viewed."[77] Moreover, having a photo makes you thirty-six times more likely to receive a message on LinkedIn.[78]

Here are some dos and don'ts when it comes to your LinkedIn photo. Many of these have been cited in a study by PhotoFeeler[79], while others should be common sense considering that LinkedIn is a professional networking site.

Do:

Be professionally dressed
The photo should be of your head and shoulders
Look directly into the camera; make eye contact
Smile

Don't:

No sunglasses (clear eyeglasses are fine)
No fishing photos
No pets
No golf course photos
No family portraits
No kids or grandchildren
No Glamour Shots

---

76 Jobvite Recruiter Nation Report 2016, http://www.jobvite.com/wp-content/uploads/2016/09/RecruiterNation2016.pdf (41% of recruiters believe that seeing a picture of a candidate before meeting them influences their first impression) (accessed March 15, 2017).

77 Smith, Jacquelyn. "The Complete Guide To Crafting A Perfect LinkedIn Profile," *Business Insider*, January 21, 2015, http://www.businessinsider.com/guide-to-perfect-linkedin-profile-2015-1 (accessed June 4, 2015).

78 Smith, Craig, DMR, "200+ Amazing LinkedIn Stats" (Last Checked/Updated October 2016) http://expandedramblings.com/index.php/by-the-numbers-a-few-important-linkedin-stats/. (downloaded No-vember 28, 2016).

79 PhotoFeeler. "New Research Study Breaks Down The Perfect Profile Photo," PhotoFeeler, May 13, 2014 https://blog.photofeeler.com/perfect-photo/. (accessed November 7, 2016).

2. Name

Use the name you commonly go by. If your given name is Richard, but you go by Rich, use Rich. It is permissible to put both your given name and the name you use in quotation marks or parentheses. If you have a common name, you may want to add your middle initial.

Professional designations appearing in the name field. There is a difference of opinion among commentators on this topic.[80] However, it can be to your advantage to put one (maybe two) notable professional designations behind your name. Designations should be significant to your industry, add to your credibility, or create a competitive advantage in the job market. Using one notable designation could increase the odds of having your profile viewed.

3. Headline

Under your name is your Headline area. It is the first thing someone reads about you.

You have 120 character spaces in your headline. Make it informative (which will increase the number of views you receive) by describing yourself with keywords or short phrases

80 Isaacson, Nate. "Professional Designations Are Great But They Are Not A Part of Your Name," *LinkedIn Pulse*, April 14, 2014, https://www.linkedin.com/pulse/20140414223601-23236063-professional-designations-are-great-but-they-are-not-a-part-of-your-name (accessed July 16, 2015); Hanson, Arik. "Should You Put MBA Behind Your Name on Your LinkedIn Profile?" *LinkedIn Pulse*, May 29, 2014, https://www.linkedin.com/pulse/20140529131058-18098999-should-you-put-mba-behind-your-name-on-your-linkedin-profile (accessed July 17, 2015).

that best describe your function. "What do you want to be known for?"[81] Or found for? Avoid superlatives or flamboyant adjectives in your headline (e.g., The Industry's Best Sales Representative on the Planet).

The headline ultimately attracts viewers with the intention that they continue to read your profile and be impressed with your experience, skills, and accomplishments. When we discuss optimization, we will delve much deeper into the strategic use of your headline.

4. Location and Industry

The Location section appears below your Headline.

LinkedIn lists every significant metropolitan city in the country (more than 280 geographical location phrases at last count). Your location (or one very close) is likely listed.

It is important to list an accurate metropolitan city location on your profile. When employers and recruiters conduct searches, they often look for profiles of individuals who live in a particular city or region. Listing no location or a generic "United States" makes you almost invisible to employers and recruiters who may need a qualified candidate located in a certain metropolitan area or region.

When selecting a city, use a major metropolitan area instead of a suburb. This increases your odds that a HR recruiter will find you.

Be accurate when choosing an industry specialty. LinkedIn lists 145 industry phrases (at last count), so choose the one that best fits you. Your industry specialty is only viewable

---

81Whitcomb, *Job Search Magic*, p. 68.

to HR recruiters that use advanced platforms of LinkedIn. When employers and recruiters conduct searches, they may look for profiles from particular industries—ones from which they have made successful hires in the past.

Including an industry on your profile has the potential to get you fifteen times the amount of views than those who do not list an industry.[82]

To access your Location and Industry, click "Me" at the top of the LinkedIn page. From the drop down, select Settings and Privacy. Select "Account," then scroll down and select Name, Location, and Industry.

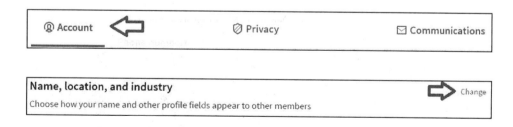

---

82 "10 Tips for the Perfect LinkedIn Profile," LinkHumans, SlideShare, published July 1, 2014, http://www.slideshare.net/linkedin/10-tips-for-the-perfect-linkedin-profile (accessed November 11, 2015).

5. Contact and Personal Information

LinkedIn allows you to provide contact information. Your Contact and Personal Information is located down the right side of your profile. It looks like this:

Click "Show more" and you're in. Click the pencil icon to make changes. This is a good place to put your personal email address and your cell phone number.

6. Summary Section

The Summary section is an area where you can write a narrative of your background, experience, and achievements. This is a biographical description of your career, so keep the content professionally relevant and use keywords. It appears directly below your name and location.

To edit or create a Summary, click on the pencil icon in the upper right hand corner of your profile.

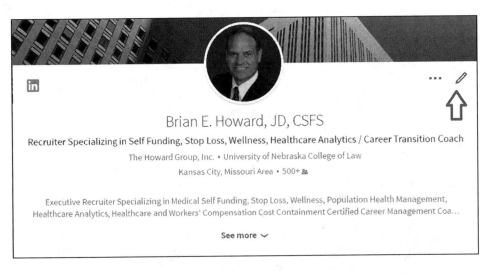

There is a difference of opinion regarding how the content of this section should be presented. Some advocate that it is an opportunity for you to write in the first person and show personality.[83] Others contend that it should be more in the third-person narrative. The choice is yours; however, make your decision based on how it will be best perceived by a potential hiring executive for your level of position.

Your Summary section has a significant impact on optimizing your LinkedIn profile and will be discussed at length in the pages that follow.

7. Experience

This is reasonably straightforward. Think resume. Use relevant keywords. Remember that your LinkedIn profile and your resume must match in general content. According to LinkedIn, "add[ing] your two most recent work positions . . . can increase your profile views by twelve times."[84] Strategic use of the Experience section will be discussed with optimization.

8. Education

Your education should align directly with your resume. Start with your highest degree and work backward in reverse chronological order. If you are a tenured job seeker, determine whether you want to include dates. Review the Education section of the Impactful Resumes portion of this book. LinkedIn users "who have an education on their profile receive an average of ten times more profile views than those who don't."[85]

Additional sections of your profile. LinkedIn has additional sections to further customize your profile. Depending on the HR recruiter or hiring executive, these areas may have an impact on their impression of you. To find these additional sections, look for a large blue box containing "Add new profile section" that appears along the right side of your profile.

---

83 Smith, Jacquelyn. "Here's What To Say In Your LinkedIn 'Summary' Statement," *Business Insider*, December 19, 2014, http://www.businessinsider.com/what-to-say-in-your-linkedin-summary-statement-2014-12 (accessed July 9, 2015).

84 Daniel Ayele, "Land Your Dream Job in 2015 with These Data-Proven LinkedIn Tips," *LinkedIn Blog*, January 29, 2015, http://blog.linkedin.com/2015/01/29/jobseeking-tips/ (accessed June 9, 2015).

85 LinkHumans, "10 Tips." *See also*, Smith, Craig, DMR, "200+ Amazing LinkedIn Stats" (Last Checked/ Updated October 2016) http://expandedramblings.com/index.php/by-the-numbers-a-few-important-linkedin-stats/. (downloaded November 28, 2016). This source indicates that 65% of job postings on LinkedIn require a bachelor's degree.

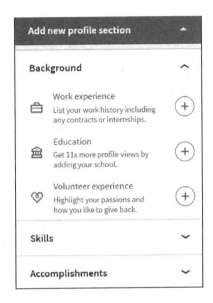

Click it and you will see an option regarding Background which will allow you to add information regarding your work experience, education, and volunteer experience. You will also see an option where you can add Skills. The last option is Accomplishments. This will give you a drop down list that includes publications, certifications, courses, projects, honors and awards, patents, test scores, languages, and organizations. We'll discuss some of these additional sections.

9. Volunteer Experience

Many employers look favorably upon profiles of those who volunteer or are involved in civic causes—it speaks to matching the culture of the company. "In fact, according to LinkedIn, 42 percent of hiring managers surveyed said they view volunteer experience equal to formal work experience."[86]

10. Skills and Endorsements

LinkedIn allows you to list fifty skills. Be reasonably specific and don't use all fifty. You don't want a HR recruiter or hiring executive to view you as a "jack of all trades and a master of none." You may appear desperate if you list too many skills. How many skills are too many? When you feel you are starting to stretch to include a skill, you have likely

---

86 Dougherty, Lisa. "16 Tips to Optimize Your LinkedIn Profile and Your Personal Brand," *LinkedIn Pulse*, July 8, 2014, https://www.linkedin.com/pulse/20140708162049-7239647-16-tips-to-optimize-your-linkedin-profile-and-enhance-your-personal-brand (accessed November 11, 2015).

reached the end. According to LinkedIn, listing five or more skills in your profile will get you up to seventeen times more profile views.[87]

Endorsements are a nice LinkedIn feature. They add credibility and a compelling nature to your profile as others agree with the skills you have listed (they can add others).

Endorse others. Remember, LinkedIn is a networking mechanism and a two-way street. The more you engage with others, the more they will engage with you.

11. Certifications

Listing certifications can enhance your value as a viable candidate for a position. Frequently a professional certification or designation is a significant differentiator from other job seekers.

12. Honors and Awards

List all notable honors and awards you have received, signaling to an employer that others have recognized you for your performance.

13. Organizations

Listing your memberships in professional associations can have an influence on employers because it reflects that you are in touch and following the industry. It can also be a source of networking and education.[88]

14. Recommendations

Remember that having others say good things about you is better than you promoting yourself.[89] "Recommendations are mini testimonials that people give you who have worked with you. You can request them via LinkedIn. It's another way to build credibility [for] you and your work. As appropriate, remember to return the favor when someone gives you a recommendation."[90]

Many recruiters review recommendations as part of their evaluation protocols. As a

87 Smith, Craig, DMR, "200+ Amazing LinkedIn Stats" (Last Checked/Updated October 2016) http://expandedramblings.com/index.php/by-the-numbers-a-few-important-linkedin-stats/. (downloaded November 28, 2016).

88 Yate, *Knock 'em Dead*, p. 86.

89 Matt, "Brag Book."

90 Frasco, "11 Tips."

minimum goal, get at least three recommendations posted on your profile from former bosses, colleagues, customers, or vendors you've interacted with.

15. Groups

LinkedIn groups are valuable, give you a platform to be an expert in an industry or topic, and help you gain insight and knowledge. "Your profile is five times more likely to be viewed if you join and are active in groups."[91]

HR recruiters and hiring executives search LinkedIn, and they also interact in LinkedIn groups.[92] With more than two million groups on LinkedIn,[93] there is no excuse not to join a group relevant to your industry or location. Eighty-one percent of users surveyed were in at least one LinkedIn group,[94] meaning hiring executives and recruiters—maybe even the one who will give you your dream job—are likely already members of, and might even be active in, a group. In a survey of LinkedIn users who found a job within three months of focused searching, 82 percent interacted with a group on LinkedIn.[95]

LinkedIn allows you to join one hundred groups, but only join those pertinent to your background, industry, and location. Determine a group's membership—larger ones offer more exposure. You will need to request membership to join a group.

To explore possible groups to join, click the Work icon at the top of your profile.

From the drop-down options, select Groups.

91 LinkHumans, "10 Tips."

92 Lindsey Pollak, "How to Attract Employers' Attention on LinkedIn," *LinkedIn Blog*, December 2, 2010, http://blog.linkedin.com/2010/12/02/find-jobs-on-linkedin/ (accessed June 4, 2015).

93 Arruda, William. "Is LinkedIn Poised To Be The Next Media Giant?" *Forbes*, March 8, 2015, http://www.forbes.com/sites/williamarruda/2015/03/08/is-linkedin-poised-to-be-the-next-media-giant/ (accessed June 5, 2015).

94 Pamela Vaughan, "81% of LinkedIn Users Belong to a LinkedIn Group [Data]," *Hubspot Blogs*, August 11, 2011, http://blog.hubspot.com/blog/tabid/6307/bid/22364/81-of-LinkedIn-Users-Belong-to-a-LinkedIn-Group-Data.aspx (accessed June 8, 2015).

95 Shreya Oswal, "7 Smart Habits of Successful Job Seekers [INFOGRAPHIC]," *LinkedIn Blog*, March 19, 2014, http://blog.linkedin.com/2014/03/19/7-smart-habits-of-successful-job-seekers-infographic/ (accessed June 9, 2015).

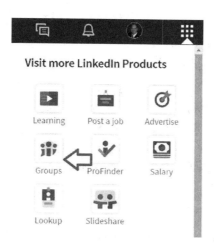

Then click the Discover option. LinkedIn may provide some possible groups of interest to you.

Once you join a group, it is much easier to relate to people. You have something in common. Common ground is a good thing when starting a networking communication.

16. Other Enhancements

You can also use a variety of media to showcase your skills (video presentations including SlideShare, pictures or screenshots, and text documents). These are optional and not required to get you found by a HR recruiter or hiring executive. However, they can add credibility to your experience on the job. Upload a video if you do public speaking. If you're skilled in graphic design, showcase your portfolio. If you write, add an article or a chapter of your book. Consider adding anything unique or impactful to prove and reinforce your skills, experience, or achievements.

Introducing LinkedIn Optimization

Optimization is taking full advantage of how the LinkedIn algorithms and programming work so you can be discovered for what you want to be professionally known for or found for. It means effectively using your keywords, putting those keywords in the correct areas of your profile, properly repeating those keywords, completing your profile, maintaining an adequate number of connections, and making your profile compelling. All of these elements, pulled together, optimize your LinkedIn profile for maximum effectiveness.

An optimized LinkedIn profile makes you more discoverable and more desirable when a HR recruiter uses LinkedIn to find a professional with your skills and background. Since 87 percent of HR recruiters use LinkedIn to identify and recruit candidates[96], having an optimized LinkedIn profile could lead you to your next career opportunity.

How Does It Work . . . How Does a HR Recruiter Use LinkedIn to Find Candidates?

There are numerous ways a HR recruiter can use LinkedIn to locate candidates. To illustrate one method, go to your LinkedIn home page or profile. Along the top next to the LinkedIn logo is a search box with a spyglass.

Put the following words in that space just as written: insurance AND sales. Click the spyglass. Your results will be millions of profiles appearing on the page (and potentially a couple of job openings). The example terms used are overly broad but it gives you a concept of how a recruiter uses LinkedIn by refining search terms (keywords) to identify candidates. The purpose of this section is to teach you how to optimize your LinkedIn profile so you are one of those top candidates.

The Goal of Optimization

Now that you have a general understanding of the functionality of the LinkedIn algorithms and programming, you need to know what you are striving for by optimizing your LinkedIn

---

96 Jobvite 2016 Recruiter National Survey www.jobvite.com (accessed February 4, 2017).

profile. Your goal, in descending order is: (1) to be listed (ranked) as the number one profile on the first page (the ultimate achievement), (2) to be on the first page, and (3) to be on the first three pages.

These goals can be achieved provided you have adequate career achievements and information and you follow the instructions for optimization. Depending upon your professional circumstances, you may need to evaluate your ranking by limiting it to your city or metropolitan area.

Keyword Location

Where your keywords appear on your profile does matter. The sections listed below are the primary areas where the algorithms and programming look to match keywords.

1. Headline
2. Summary
3. Job title
4. Experience/employment descriptions
5. Skills

There are advanced platforms that HR recruiters can purchase from LinkedIn that could expand this list, but these are the primary sections where the algorithms and programming match keywords.

Headline

You have 120 character spaces available to you in your headline, which is actually a lot of room. Since we know that this is a section where the algorithms and programming go to match keywords, make sure your keywords appear here.

The headline section provides an excellent opportunity for you to list a branding statement that describes yourself. What do you want to be known for or found for?[97] A convenient formula that works well for many job seekers is:

[Job function or title] + [A bridge phrase or action verb (e.g., "with experience in," "with expertise in," "specializing in," or "utilizing")] + [keywords: reference to products, services, skills, industry, and so on]

---

97 See, Whitcomb, Susan Britton. *Job Search Magic: Insider Secrets from America's Career and Life Coach.* (Indianapolis, IN: JIST Works, 2006), p. 68.

For example:

> Senior Sales Executive with Experience in Workers' Compensation, Pain Management, Leadership.

> Or:

> Product Development Professional Applying Behavioral Research to Health Care Technology.

Here are some real examples from LinkedIn profiles:

> Sr. Sales Executive Specializing in Executive Leadership, Referenced-based Pricing, Stop Loss

> Health Care Leader Skilled in Key Account Growth, Sales, Strategy, Analytics, Problem-solving and Partnership Optimization.

When choosing keywords for your headline, use those that are skills, knowledge, products, and services you have experience with. Most HR recruiters will use keywords that are skills- or knowledge-based to identify candidates on LinkedIn. Then, during the screening process, they explore and evaluate soft skills (e.g., work ethic, communications skills, etc.). We'll mention your soft skills in just a moment in the Summary section.

This raises an interesting concept that you need to be aware of. As you build your LinkedIn profile, you occasionally need to think like a HR recruiter. What keywords would a HR recruiter or hiring executive use to find a professional like you? More often than not, the keywords you use will align with those used by a HR recruiter. However, that is not always the case. For example, some companies use the title Business Development to mean sales. Other companies use that same title to mean marketing, branding, public relations, and so on. If you happen to have one of those titles that is not generally accepted or representative of your function, you will want to use terminology on your LinkedIn profile that is more accepted and used by a HR recruiter. The point is to double check your thinking along the way.

Summary

You have two thousand character spaces available to you for your summary[98], which is a ton of room. Do not get long-winded when writing your summary. Your summary is just

98 Foote, Andy, Maximum LinkedIn Character Counts for 2016, December 10, 2016 https://www.linkedin.com/pulse/maximum-linkedin-character-counts-2016-andy-foote. (accessed November 22, 2016).

that . . . a summary of your career, not an autobiography. Think of your summary as the executive summary of a white paper.[99]

An effective technique that takes advantage of the LinkedIn programming is to start your summary by restating your headline, word for word, and then expanding upon it to include other keywords that would not fit or were of secondary importance in your headline (perhaps your soft skills). Below are the "banner statements" contained in the Summary of the two Headline profile examples:

Senior Sales Executive Specializing in Executive Leadership, Referenced-based Pricing, Stop Loss, Self-Funding, Product Distribution

Effective Health Care leader skilled in strategy, key account growth, sales, analytics, partnership optimization, team mentorship and problem solving.

Remember, LinkedIn is looking to match keywords *and* tracking the number of times they appear when ranking you against other similar profiles. By restating your headline at the top of your Summary section, you create an introductory or banner statement running along the top of your summary. The HR recruiter does not think twice about it but you have taken advantage of the programming by stating keywords twice between your headline and your introductory banner statement in your summary.

After your introductory banner statement, write one to three (maybe four) paragraphs that summarize your career experience so far. This will include duties, responsibilities, and your keywords. As you write, be aware that this paragraph(s) must read smoothly. A good approach is to write the paragraphs and then insert keywords as appropriate. It's also a good technique to write your summary paragraph(s) – and other sections – in a Word document and then copy and paste it into the appropriate section. This way misspellings and grammar errors will be caught. This is important. A survey conducted by Jobvite indicated that 72 percent of HR recruiters view typos negatively on social media.[100]

The next component of your summary, following your career summary paragraphs, is your career accomplishments. These are your achievements you are most proud of. Start with, "Career Accomplishments Include:", then list your top three or four. If you are not

99 See, Kolowich, Lindsay, What is a White Paper, June 27, 2014 http://blog.hubspot.com/marketing/what-is-whitepaper-faqs#sm.0000lbm5cb9ke7e11nu1h1l4e63aj (accessed November 22, 2016).

100 Jobvite Recruiter Nation Report 2016, http://www.jobvite.com/wp-content/uploads/2016/09/RecruiterNation2016.pdf (accessed March 15, 2017).

sure whether to include a particular achievement, hedge toward not including it. You want these achievements to be your best ones.

This discussion on accomplishments fits directly into one of the tenets for optimizing your LinkedIn profile—Compelling. The concept of "compelling" will be woven throughout the rest of this discussion as we address other topics and strategies.

Once you have your accomplishments listed in your Summary section, either use the programming on your computer or go to the Internet and copy and paste an icon and place it in front of each of your accomplishments. When choosing an icon, choose something dark, like a bullet point ● or a black diamond ◆. These dark icons draw the eye of the HR recruiters and highlight your achievements in their minds. Whatever icon you select, use it consistently throughout your profile. Using different icons makes your profile look jumbled or gaudy. Here are a couple of examples:

Career Achievements include:

- Recipient of 20XX Female Executive of the Year

- Developed and executed business development, marketing and sales plan that yielded 30% year-over-year growth.

- Marketed and sold new business to large employers, generating 30% of the overall company revenue.

- One of six senior managers who re-engineered corporate-wide business practices resulting in savings of more than $13 million.

Career Achievements include:

- Implemented cost savings strategies throughout a variety of initiatives resulting in a cost savings over 1 million dollars.

Finally, at the end of your summary, provide your personal email address and cell phone number. This is a good strategy because people that are not connected to you cannot see your contact and personal information.[101] You want to make it as easy as possible for a HR recruiter to contact you and providing this information at the end of your summary makes it easy to do so.

---

101 Pearcemarch, Kyle, SEO for LinkedIn: How to Optimize Your LinkedIn Profile for Search (March 19, 2015) https://www.diygenius.com/how-to-optimize-your-linkedin-profile-for-search/ (accessed November 22, 2016).

Job Title

The job title area of your employment background is where LinkedIn looks for matching keywords. You have one hundred character spaces for your title.[102] If you have a title that is unique to your company, make sure to also include a more descriptive terminology so the HR recruiter can determine your actual function.

Experience

This is your employment history and it is a section where you should heavily use your keywords. For each employer, write one or two paragraphs describing your duties, responsibilities, product knowledge, distribution, territories, target markets, and so on. Beneath the paragraph(s), put: "Achievements" or "Accomplishments," then, like you did in your summary, list the important accomplishments you achieved in that position. This approach informs the HR recruiter of what your duties and responsibilities were and that you were successful in the role. For example:

INCREASED SALES:

- 141% in 20XX over prior year
- 197% in 20XX over prior year
- 179% in 20XX over prior year

Follow this formula for each employment going back fifteen to twenty years. In your Experience section, your career-level accomplishments listed in your summary will appear again under the employment from which they occurred. This is fine. It is recommended to put your dark icon in front of each accomplishment like you did in your summary.

Skills

List your keywords as skills, when appropriate. According to LinkedIn, the number of times you are endorsed for a skill has no weight on how many times the algorithms and programming recognize that particular keyword. In other words, having thirty people endorse you for a skill (keyword) does not mean the algorithms sees that keyword appearing thirty times on your profile. We will discuss an advanced technique using your Skills section in a moment.

---

102 Foote, Andy, Maximum LinkedIn Character Counts for 2016, December 10, 2016 https://www.linkedin.com/pulse/maximum-linkedin-character-counts-2016-andy-foote. (accessed November 22, 2016).

Keyword Stuffing

Keyword stuffing is *abusively* overusing your keywords throughout your profile to increase your ranking.[103] It's a strategy designed to game the system. Sadly, this is a strategy too often suggested by some LinkedIn profile writers and career coaches. According to discussions with LinkedIn customer service, the algorithms and programming are now (supposedly) designed to detect this strategy and can actually reduce your ranking.

The far better approach (and the one promoted in this book), is to construct a profile using accepted and common sense optimization strategies that present your professional background and experience in a genuine and sincere manner to make the most positive impression possible on the HR recruiter.

This finishes the discussion regarding the first tenet of optimizing your LinkedIn profile regarding keywords. We will now move to the next tenet of optimization—Completeness.

Completeness

The more complete your LinkedIn profile is, the higher it will rank compared to other profiles. According to LinkedIn, "Only 50.5 percent of people have a 100 percent completed LinkedIn profile."[104] Consequently, by having a complete profile you can outrank many other competing profiles.

Profile completeness is important. The LinkedIn algorithms and programming *display* search results (how you rank compared to other profiles) based on the following:

1. Profile completeness
2. The number of shared connections
3. Connections by degree (1st, 2nd, and so on)
4. Groups in common

Profile completeness is the "trump card" with the LinkedIn algorithms and program-ming.[105] The other factors of ranking do not matter if your profile is not complete. If you

---

103 See, Practices to Avoid When Optimizing Your Profile For LinkedIn Search. https://www.linkedin.com/help/linkedin/answer/51499/practices-to-avoid-when-optimizing-your-profile-for-linkedin-search?lang=en (accessed November 23, 2016).

104 Foote, Andy, Why You Should Complete Your LinkedIn Profile, (December 7, 2015). https://www.linkedinsights.com/why-you-should-complete-your-linkedin-profile/ (accessed November 22, 2016).

105 Ibid. ("Profile Completeness is a trump card in the search engine.")

need a refresher of what constitutes a complete profile, here are the components:
- Location and industry
- Current position (with a description)
- Two past positions (best practice)
- Education
- Skills (minimum of three)
- Profile photo
- At least fifty connections[106] (best practice)

You are already well down the road to completeness (and compelling) as you work on your profile using keywords. However, LinkedIn has additional sections that can be added to your profile beyond those that are most commonly used. They include:

Volunteering Experience

Publications

Certifications (Professional Designations)

Courses

Projects

Honors and Awards

Patents

Test Scores

Language

Contact and Personal Information

Organizations (Professional Associations and Affiliations)

Posts

Volunteering Experience, Organizations

There are a couple of considerations regarding these sections. First, volunteering experience is favorably viewed by employers, but it must be substantive. As previously stated, standing behind the card table selling brownies at the Cub Scouts meeting doesn't count. However, being a volunteer Red Cross first responder does. Second, avoid any reference to an organization or cause that could be viewed as controversial. This would

---

106 Ibid.

generally mean anything regarding politics, religion, race, and so on. Of course there are exceptions if your career is in politics, religion, and race relations.

Honors and Awards

It is perfectly acceptable to restate your accomplishments and achievements in the Honors and Awards section. This is especially true if the achievement resulted in an award. Repetition of your achievements affirms in the mind of the HR recruiter that you are a well-qualified job seeker.

Language

If you live in the United States and English is your native language, do not list it. It is assumed that you are fluent. This section is used for foreign languages.

Personal Details

Avoid providing any personal information that would be inappropriate for a HR recruiter to ask in an interview. Marital status and year of birth are two notable ones.

Connections

The more connections you have, the better the probability you will rank higher than other profiles.[107] Your ranking is, in part, influenced by how closely connected you are to a HR recruiter (or anyone else looking). The difficult part is you have no idea who could be looking on LinkedIn and how closely connected you are to them.

The best strategy to combat against or take advantage of this connection factor is to increase your connections and join industry-relevant groups. Try to get connected to as many professionally relevant people as possible. These are professionals that can hire you or help you. This would include colleagues and peers at other organizations including clients, vendors, competitors, and so on. If you want to work for a particular company, seek connections within that company. Strive to get a minimum of five hundred professionally relevant connections (possibly more depending upon your professional circumstances). The more professionally relevant connections you have, the higher the probability that you

---

107 Pearcemarch, Kyle, SEO for LinkedIn: How to Optimize Your LinkedIn Profile for Search (March 19, 2015) https://www.diygenius.com/how-to-optimize-your-linkedin-profile-for-search/ (accessed November 22, 2016).

will be more closely connected to the HR recruiter who is searching on LinkedIn. The closer the connection, the higher you will appear in the ranking of profiles.

You are allowed to join up to one hundred groups on LinkedIn.[108] Since your ranking is influenced by the number of common groups you have with a HR recruiter, it is very important to join relevant and well-populated groups, especially those groups that are in industries you belong to or are interested in.

Fully appreciate that your network has value and is an area of evaluation when a hiring executive or HR recruiter looks at your profile. An evaluation of the number of contacts in and the quality of your network creates a "Network Value Score." By analogy, it's like your credit score when applying for a mortgage. The higher your Network Value Score, the more valuable you may become as a quality candidate for the position.

If you are new to LinkedIn or have been inactive, work to get five hundred connections. The number of connections you have appears on your profile until you exceed five hundred. After that, it appears as "500+." You want HR recruiters and hiring executives viewing your profile to conclude that you have a network of professional colleagues. It can add to your professional value as a candidate. If you're staying within your field, it is not uncommon for hiring executives to see how many common connections you have with each other—the more the better. And it is not uncommon for hiring executives to reach out to these common connections and inquire about you as well. Hence this is another good reason to stay active with your network.

Compelling

A profile is compelling when it intellectually or emotionally moves the HR recruiter to contact you. There are several factors that can make a profile compelling. They include: your knowledge and skills, accomplishments, endorsements, recommendations, the overall appearance and completeness of your profile, and anything else that makes you unique in the eyes of the HR recruiter.

Your profile can be compelling based on your knowledge and skills. You know things or have done things in your career that a HR recruiter is looking for or is impressed by. You have experience and a skill set in need by the HR recruiter. This can range from knowing and having experience with a particular software program to having Profit and Loss (P&L)

---

108 General Limits for LinkedIn Groups, https://www.linkedin.com/help/linkedin/answer/190/general-limits-for-linkedin-groups?lang=en (accessed November 23, 2016).

experience with a large organization. There are thousands if not millions of things a HR recruiter could look for that are knowledge- or skill-based.

Documented accomplishments are clearly compelling. The most influential accomplishments are those that can be quantified with numbers, percentages, dollars signs, savings (in time and money), and the list goes on. Accomplishments can heavily influence a HR recruiter to contact you. Your accomplishments communicate that you are good at what you do.

The number of endorsements you have for a sought-after skill can influence the compelling nature of your profile. If a HR recruiter finds a profile with 99+ endorsements for a sought-after skill or experience, it is a clear indication that the professional could be a qualified candidate.

An advanced technique is to list one professional character trait you possess as a skill. Examples are work ethic, perseverance, honesty, and so on. Then, get as many connections to endorse you for that character trait as possible. Having a professional character trait listed as a skill and having an adequate number of endorsements is a differentiator from other profiles and will get noticed by a HR recruiter. Endorsements for a sought-after character trait open the door to what kind of person/professional you are seen as through the eyes of others. This enhances the compelling nature of your profile.

Recommendations can influence the compelling nature of your profile. Once your profile is identified as a "probable" qualified candidate by a HR recruiter, the number and content of the recommendations can influence the HR recruiter to contact you. As a general rule of thumb, try to get three positive recommendations for each employer going back to at least two to three employers.

And finally, the overall completeness and appearance of your profile can be a compelling factor. There are millions of well-qualified job seekers who fail to appreciate the career enhancing power of a LinkedIn profile. Potentially life-changing opportunities pass those people by through their failure to have a complete and professionally appearing LinkedIn profile. However, to your benefit, you will have such a profile that will open you to career opportunities that others will not have (or ever know about).

Put It to the Test

After you have revised your profile and optimized it, put it to the test. Get on LinkedIn and run a search for yourself. Put in one keyword or phrase that you are using in your profile along with your title in the Search field at the top of your profile.

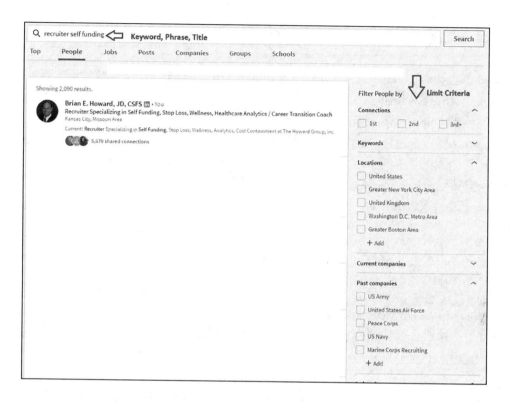

You may need to further limit the criteria by location. For example, "Regional Sales Director" AND Telemedicine AND Dallas. How do you rank? Did you appear on the first page? On the first two or three pages? Try another one of your keywords. How did that one work? If you are not coming up on the first three pages, double check to make sure you have all of the elements of a complete profile. Then, look at the profiles that appeared in front of you and see if you can make improvements based on what those candidates put on their profiles. Selective borrowing is permitted. Make revisions and test it again. Do what you can to improve your ranking to appear on the first page or the first three pages, if possible.

Understand that regardless of the revisions you make and the optimizing strategies you use, you may only be able to improve your ranking so much. Don't get frustrated. You can only do what you can with the algorithms based on the information in your profile. But, whatever you do, don't go overboard. Your profile must still appear professional and informative. Optimizing is a great strategy and it will improve your ranking, but creating an awkward-looking profile for ranking purposes defeats the ultimate objective . . . impressing a HR recruiter or hiring executive.

Strategies for Your LinkedIn Profile When You Are Unemployed

If you are unemployed, what do you put on your LinkedIn Profile? Do you announce your availability or would doing so reduce your attractiveness as a candidate? Fortunately, you have several strategic options.

As you consider the choices that follow, the primary consideration is this: how would a HR recruiter or hiring executive react to the approach you use for the level of position you are seeking? After we discuss the strategic options, we'll discuss factors that could influence your decision on which one to use.

Put an End Date on Your Last Employment. Your first option is to list an end date on your current employment. It's honest and your profile is up-to-date. HR recruiters will draw the conclusion that you are currently unemployed.

Announce Your Unemployment in Your Headline. As you know, the headline is the area immediately below your name. It is acceptable to use your headline as an advertisement of your availability: "Currently Seeking New Opportunities," or "In Transition," among others.

However, there is a more effective approach since the LinkedIn algorithms and programming searches the headline for keywords. Create your headline to include the keywords "Seeking Opportunities." For example, "Banking Professional Specializing in Commercial Lending, Seeking New Opportunities." This strategy capitalizes on your keywords and announces your availability.

Announce Your Availability as a Statement in Your Summary Section. Another option is to include a statement of your availability early in your Summary section. Your statement could be as simple as "Actively Seeking New Employment."

As you recall, your Summary section is also an area where the LinkedIn programming and algorithms look to match keywords. There is a strategic advantage of adding a sentence or two with keywords about position types, industries, and types of companies that would interest you. For example, "Actively seeking a new opportunity as an account manager in the employee benefits industry." This can help tighten your search, but be aware that it can also reduce potential opportunities. After you make this statement, continue with the rest of the summary in a traditional fashion.

List Your Availability as Your Current Employment. The consideration with this approach is the LinkedIn programming and algorithms look at position titles and position descriptions for matching keywords. So simply putting "Open to Opportunities" as your title does not take advantage of the programming. A better approach is stating an actual title or job function followed by "seeking opportunities." For example, "Sales Operations Professional Specializing in Health Care Seeking Opportunities." You have one hundred character spaces in the title area which should give you ample room to use this strategy. You could reword your headline and put it here as well.

For the company name, you can put "Unemployed." But, that sometimes can carry a negative stigma—though the weight of that stigma has faded in recent years. Instead, consider a more positive approach, such as putting "Exploring a Career Move," "Seeking New Position," or "In Transition" as your current employer.

Your position description provides some unique opportunities. If you resigned from your previous employment, the first sentence of your description could read something like this:

> Currently seeking a new position after voluntarily leaving [Past Employer] in good standing with recommendations.

Or,

> Actively looking for a new job in event planning after resigning my position at [Past Employer] with strong job performance evaluations.

If you were laid off, you could state the description something like this:

> Was subject to a company-wide layoff affecting [XX number employees, the entire marketing department, X number of departments]. Release was not performance-related.

If you were terminated for performance, it's probably best to leave that unspoken and use the position description space for other strategies.

For the rest of the position description space, create the messaging to put you in the best light. According to LinkedIn, there is now a two hundred character minimum and a two thousand character maximum in the position description area.[109]

The content of the position description could be a brief statement of your abilities and knowledge, using keywords. It could function as an abbreviated cover letter. You could also rework your elevator speech (if you use one as part of your overall job search) and put

---

109 Foote, Andy, Maximum LinkedIn Character Counts for 2016, December 10, 2016 https://www.linkedin.com/pulse/maximum-linkedin-character-counts-2016-andy-foote. (accessed November 22, 2016).

it here. The key consideration is to use the space wisely, not be lengthy, and consider how a HR recruiter would react to what you write. When pulled together, it could look something like this:

Title: Account Manager Seeking Opportunities in Employee Benefits

Company: Exploring A Career Move

Description: Was subject to a company-wide lay-off affecting over 100 employees at Insurance Company. Release was not performance-related.

Seeking an account management position to benefit an insurance organization with proven skills in client service, ACA compliance, implementation, renewals, and claim resolution. (Then customize the content based on your best judgment.)

Be a Consultant. You can list your current employment as consulting and your title as a consultant. Taking this approach is accepted "code" that you are unemployed but doing consulting projects to stay active and engaged.

The key to this strategy is the use of your keywords. Knowing that the LinkedIn programming and algorithms look at position titles, describe your title using keywords. For example:

Security Technology Consultant

Or,

Workers' Compensation Cost Containment Consultant

For company name, many use their last name or initials followed by "Consulting." You have a lot of latitude for the name of your consulting practice, just be professional in the naming.

Your professional description should contain your keywords, as previously discussed. This will help you when a HR recruiter or hiring executive searches for you.

Do Nothing At All. The final option is do nothing at all and if asked about your profile, go with "I forgot." This is not ideal, but the option is available to you.

Which Strategy Would Be Best for You?

The correct strategy(ies) depends on your unique professional circumstances. You may choose a select combination of approaches.

If you work in an industry where it is common to hire on a project basis, contractor-to-hire, or consulting basis, announcing your availability using these strategies makes sense.

The level of your position on the corporate organizational chart for the opportunities you are pursuing also has an influence on your strategy. Generally, these "announcement" strategies may be more acceptable to lower- to mid-range sales and management roles rather than true senior management or C-Level positions. The size of the organization you are targeting could be a consideration as well. Smaller more entrepreneurial organizations may be more receptive to announcement strategies. Exercise your professional judgement as to whether or which approach to use. Your choice hinges on how you believe a HR recruiter or hiring executive for your desired position could respond.

Job Alerts

LinkedIn will send you job alerts, through email or mobile communications, when an open position is advertised on LinkedIn that matches a job profile you create.

To create a job profile and to start receiving these alerts, begin by accessing your LinkedIn page and click the Jobs icon.

You will now see a page title, "Jobs you may be interested in."

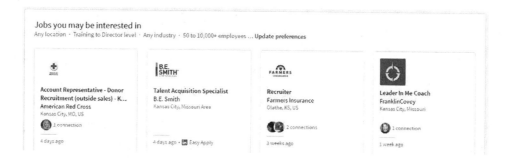

These are posted openings on LinkedIn that the programming believes you might be qualified for based on the information contained in your profile (this is yet another reason to have a complete and robust LinkedIn profile). Click on any of the job(s) of interest to you to read more or to apply.

To create job alerts, go to the top of the page where you see "Search jobs" and fill in the box with the criteria you are focused on.

Then, fill in your location in the "Search location" box. Once you have entered the information, click "Search."

You will now see a page with listed jobs.

On the right side of your screen, you will see an option to "Create search alert." Follow the prompts.

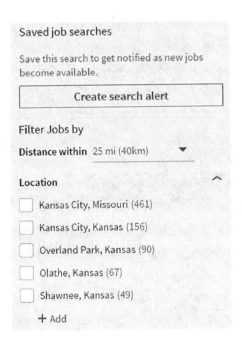

Company ∧

☐ OfficeTeam (3)

☐ The University of Kansas Health System (3)

☐ Ascend Learning (2)

☐ DH Pace Company, Inc. (1)

☐ BASYS Processing Inc. (1)

  + Add

Date Posted ∧

◯ Past 24 hours (1)

◯ Past Week (91)

◯ Past Month (1009)

◉ Any Time (1480)

Job Function ∧

☐ Health Care Provider (198)

☐ Sales (71)

☐ Human Resources (67)

☐ Business Development (60)

☐ General Business (13)

  + Add

Industry ∧

☐ Construction (341)

☐ Staffing and Recruiting (292)

☐ Hospital & Health Care (262)

☐ Financial Services (204)

☐ Information Technology and Services (187)

  + Add

Experience Level ∧

☐ Entry level (1094)

☐ Associate (164)

☐ Mid-Senior level (92)

☐ Not Applicable (86)

☐ Internship (30)

☐ Director (6)

☐ Executive (2)

When you click "Create search alert," you will be taken to a page where you can select the frequency and method of notification. Make your selections and click "Save."

You can repeat the process for other opportunities you are interested in. LinkedIn allows for several saved searches. Depending upon the programming, your saved searches could be shown under the search bar as "Saved jobs."

In addition, after you have started receiving job alerts, your results might also show under the search bar.

When you look into several jobs in one week, the LinkedIn programming concludes that you are a job seeker (although the exact number is guarded by LinkedIn as proprietary, seven is the number often referenced by career coaches). When that happens, you should automatically begin receiving emails from LinkedIn about jobs similar to the ones you researched.

The Open Candidates Feature on LinkedIn

LinkedIn has a feature where you can signal recruiters that you are open to new opportunities. This feature is called "Open Candidates."

To access this feature, click the "Jobs" option at the top of your LinkedIn profile.

From there you will see "Jobs you may be interested in." Scroll down and look for a link entitled "Update career interest." Click it.

Based on your Profile and Career interests
Any location · Any industry · 50 to 10,000+ employees ... **Update Career interests**

Scroll down and begin answering the questions about location, experience, industries (LinkedIn may offer suggestions), company size, and availability. When you activate the feature you are also given an Introductory section with three hundred character spaces.

Finally, let recruiters know you're open by activating the feature to "On" (top of the page).

Who can see your Open Candidate profile? Only recruiters who have paid for and use LinkedIn's premium "Recruiter's Platform" (prices begin at around $8,000 per license) can see that you have filled out the Open Candidate questionnaire.[110] HR recruiters, your current employer, and its affiliates should not be able to view your Open Candidate profile. However, LinkedIn provides this disclaimer: "We take steps to not show your current company that you're open, but can't guarantee that we can identify every recruiter affiliated with your company."

Naturally, if you are unemployed, there is no risk. Even if you are employed, the risk of discovery is reasonably small. Besides, it is not illegal, immoral, or unethical to be open to a new job that can enhance your career experience. Most employers know that the job market is a free agency market. Employees, especially today, look to maximize their career experience and that can mean pursuing new jobs when the time is right (this also includes your boss and other senior executives of your current and former employers).

Strategies for using the Open Candidate feature. For most job seekers, using the Open Candidate feature is a good idea. Recruiters can screen potential candidates not only based on qualifications, but those that are open to new opportunities. This shortens their work and can place you toward the top of their contact list. According to LinkedIn, "open

110 Uzialko, Adam, LinkedIn's Open Candidates: How to Search for a New Job, Quietly, October 6, 2016, http://www.businessnewsdaily.com/9468-linkedin-open-candidates.html (accessed November 25, 2016).

candidates" are more likely to be contacted by recruiters[111]. Use the Introductory section of the questionnaire to emphasize skills/background and accomplishments. Remember, you only have three hundred characters spaces so you have to be succinct. For example:

> Account management professional seeking a position with a health insurance organization, with proven skills in client service, ACA compliance, implementation, renewals, and claim resolution. Promoted three times, 95 percent client retention, recognized with client services award, have client recommendations.

If you are unemployed, there is virtually no reason for not using this feature. The only rare consideration (employed or unemployed) would be the perception based on the level of position you are seeking. Would a senior-level hiring executive, board of director, or possibly a retainer-only search firm pause to reach out to you because you are an Open Candidate on LinkedIn? Very unlikely (hopefully), but it is worth a moment of thought.

Measuring the Effectiveness of Your LinkedIn Profile

Having a complete profile, implementing optimization strategies, and making your profile compelling are necessary steps to maximizing the use of your LinkedIn profile in your job search. But the true effectiveness of your profile is the number of views it gets. If you are in a full-blown, active job search utilizing all the tools at your disposal, one measure of success is getting a minimum of twenty weekly search appearances. Twenty is not a scientific number but rather a minimum threshold number to use as a benchmark for the effectiveness of your LinkedIn profile.

You can track the number of weekly search appearances from your profile page—look for "Search appearances" that appears on your Profile page (under your summary introduction).

---

111 Bell, Karissa, LinkedIn will now help you secretly tell recruiters you want a new job , October 6, 2016, http://mashable.com/2016/10/06/linkedin-tell-recruiters-you-want-a-new-job.amp. (accessed November 7, 2016).

Brian Howard, JD, CSFS

Recruiter Specializing in Self Funding, Stop Loss, Wellness, Healthcare Analytics /
Career Transition Coach

The Howard Group, Inc. • University of Nebraska College of Law

Kansas City, Missouri Area • 500+

Executive Recruiter Specializing in Medical Self Funding, Stop Loss, Wellness, Population Health Management,
Healthcare Analytics, Healthcare and Workers' Compensation Cost Containment Certified Career Management Coa...

See more ∨

Your Dashboard
Private to you   ☆ All Star

419	1,839	158
Profile Views	Post Views	Search Appearances

Clicking on the "Search Appearances" will display the names of the companies from which people have searched and found your profile. Do those companies happen to be those you are reaching out to (or should be reaching out to)?

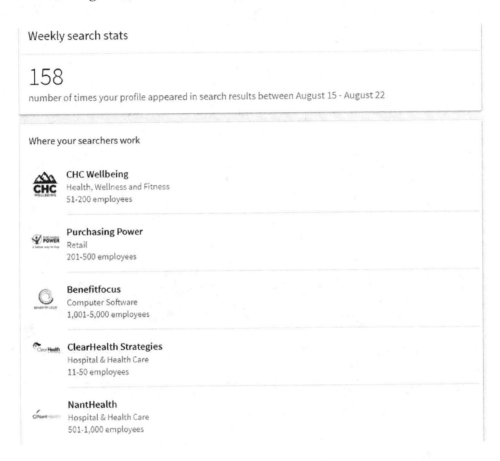

Below the list of companies are the titles of the people who have found your profile. Hopefully they are hiring executives, internal company HR, and external recruiters.

This LinkedIn feature can give you valuable insight on how well your LinkedIn profile is working for you (based on its content) and is also a measurement regarding the progress of your job search.

What Do You Do with Your LinkedIn Profile after You Get a New Job?

Once you land a new job, you have a couple of choices with your LinkedIn profile. First, you can create your Experience section in the same fashion as previously instructed.

There is another approach to consider. Understand the construction of your profile has been focused on you. It has been written to showcase you as a professional with the purpose of a job search. When you get a new job, you may want to shift that focus to your new employer. This is achieved by putting a paragraph in your new current employment that describes the company, its products, services, value proposition, etc. You can often get this information from the company website or company LinkedIn page.

After you insert the company description, follow the same advice as previously instructed with a paragraph about your duties and responsibilities, followed by accomplishments as they occur.

Keep Your Profile Current

Update your information and keep it current so it doesn't appear stale. According to LinkedIn, keeping your positions up to date on your profile makes you eighteen times more likely to be found in searches by recruiters and other members.[112]

LinkedIn is a dynamic site that changes frequently, adding some features and functionality and taking others away. Be aware of the programming changes and their possible implications for your profile use.

Sample of an Optimized LinkedIn Profile

Once you have implemented all of the optimization strategies, your LinkedIn profile should look similar to the sample profile that follows.

---

112 Smith, Craig, DMR, "200+ Amazing LinkedIn Stats" (Last Checked/Updated October 2016) http://expandedramblings.com/index.php/by-the-numbers-a-few-important-linkedin-stats/. (downloaded November 28, 2016).

Nancy Brock

Sales Executive Specializing in Healthcare Benefits Administration/SaaS, Wellness and Women's Health

Ovia Health • Washington University in St. Louis

Washington D.C. Metro Area • 500+ 🔗

Sales and Business Development Executive Specializing in Healthcare, Benefits Administration/SaaS Technology, Women's Health, Wellness, Consumerism, Work Ethic, Integrity.

Leadership Roles in Health Care Start-Ups, Early Stage Companies, and Insurance

Nancy has over 20 years of sales, business development, and client management leadership experience spanning employee benefits, wellness, population health, consumer-driven health, behavioral health and Employee Assistance Programs. Nancy has managed sales, account management, marketing, and product management teams and has worked with Fortune 500 employers, mid-size employers, payers and benefits brokers and consultants.

Nancy's expertise includes sales and marketing, strategic planning, distribution partner development & management, business plan development, account management, product management, project management, market research and intelligence, and P & L in wellness, population health, consumer-driven health and benefits administration.

Career Achievements include:

• Recipient of 2014 Top Female Executives
• Developed and executed business development, marketing and sales plan that yielded 30% year-over-year growth
• Marketed and sold new business to large employers, generating 30% of the overall company revenue
• One of six senior managers who re-engineered corporate-wide business practices resulting in overall savings of more than $13 million

nancy.brock@gmail.com
703-555-5555

246 Who's viewed your profile   224 Views of your share

Experience   +

 Regional Sales Manager

Ovia Health

Nov 2016 – Present • 5 mos • Potomac Falls, Virginia

Ovia Health is the leading digital health platform for women and families. Trusted and loved by millions, Ovia Health's mobile apps for fertility, pregnancy, and parenting have empowered over 5 million women to take control of their healthcare and start families with confidence. We are passionate about helping women and families understand their reproductive health and using technology to make it easier for them to do so.

Accountable for managing the full sales cycle of new enterprise opportunities in the Maryland South Atlantic region.

See less ∧

 Sales & Business Development Consulting

Independent Wellness Consulting

Sep 2016 – Oct 2016 • 2 mos • Potomac Falls, VA

Provide sales consulting services to wellness companies to help them demonstrate the value of solving their clients' problems, the cost of inaction, and the urgent need for change. Assist with the development of sales presentations and case studies.

See less ∧

 Vice President, Sales

bswift

2014 – 2016 • 2 yrs • Chicago, IL/Computer Software

Accountability for managing the full sales cycle of new business opportunities initially in the Mid-Atlantic region and then for the Eastern region. Sold benefits administration/exchange technology and services to employers with 1,000+ employees.

Achievements include:
• Top 5 in pipeline generation
• 2015 sold highest total contract value
• Hand picked by CEO to manage new vertical

See less ∧

 Vice President/Senior Consultant

Willis of Virginia, Inc.

2012 – 2014 • 2 yrs • Reston VA

Identify, secure and manage new business development opportunities. Partner with employers to solve human capital and benefit challenges. Develop comprehensive and tailored Total Rewards strategies and programs in collaboration with Willis Human Capital team. Conduct analysis, prepare strategic recommendations and coordinate review of documents to ensure compliance. Developed and coordinated conference on Innovative Next Practices for a Healthy and Productive Workforce.

See less ∧

Education   +

Washington University in St. Louis
MSW, Social Work

Graduated with an MSW from the George Warren Brown School of Social Work

See less ⌃

University of Michigan
BA, Psychology
Activities and Societies: Delta Gamma, William J. Branstrom Freshman Prize

Graduated from the University of Michigan School of Literature, Science, and the Arts, Ann Arbor

See less ⌃

Volunteering Experience & Causes   +

Participant
March of Dimes

March for Babies Annual Walk

See less ⌃

Fundraiser
Make-A-Wish Foundation of Greater Virginia
May 2013 • 1 mo
Children

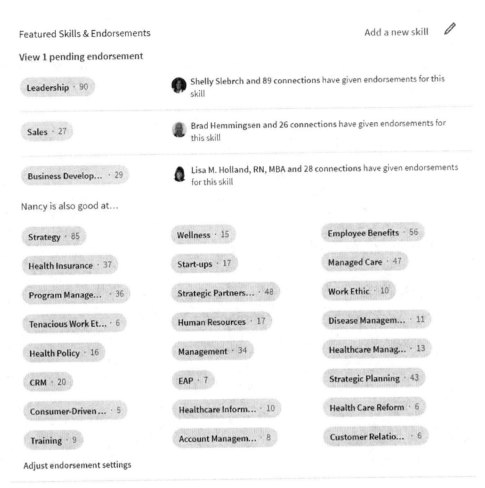

Featured Skills & Endorsements   Add a new skill ✎

View 1 pending endorsement

Leadership · 90   Shelly Slebrch and 89 connections have given endorsements for this skill

Sales · 27   Brad Hemmingsen and 26 connections have given endorsements for this skill

Business Develop... · 29   Lisa M. Holland, RN, MBA and 28 connections have given endorsements for this skill

Nancy is also good at...

Strategy · 85	Wellness · 15	Employee Benefits · 56
Health Insurance · 37	Start-ups · 17	Managed Care · 47
Program Manage... · 36	Strategic Partners... · 48	Work Ethic · 10
Tenacious Work Et... · 6	Human Resources · 17	Disease Managem... · 11
Health Policy · 16	Management · 34	Healthcare Manag... · 13
CRM · 20	EAP · 7	Strategic Planning · 43
Consumer-Driven ... · 5	Healthcare Inform... · 10	Health Care Reform · 6
Training · 9	Account Managem... · 8	Customer Relatio... · 6

Adjust endorsement settings

See less ∧

Recommendations

Ask to be recommended ✎

Received (33)   Given (27)

Tara Lathrop
Account Executive at
OneSource Virtual
November 3, 2016, Nancy worked
with Tara in the same group

Nancy and I were colleagues at bswift. She has a passion for health and benefits technology, is a strategic and creative problem solver, and is a collaborative team player. From her first week on the job, Nancy was eager to learn, and she took the initiative to successfully bring together a group of sales colleagues for a series of ongoing training and development activities, which added significant value and was universally well received.

One situation really stood out to me during our time together. Nancy won a very large new account for the company within just a few weeks on the job. She put together a very compelling and creative strategic business plan and presentation when the employer came to our office for a site visit. Later, this employer shared that this effort had differentiated Nancy and the company from the other vendors that they were considering. Nancy is a sales executive that I would highly recommend to any company.

Kelly Challenger
Senior Director, Marketing
June 20, 2016, Kelly worked with
Nancy in different groups

I worked alongside Nancy for a year executing lead generation campaigns in support of her region and the Public & Labor sector and she is by far one of the best sales executives I've ever had the pleasure of working with.

Nancy was always incredibly well organized, managed her accounts with the utmost professionalism while at the same time valued the relationships she had developed – both internally and externally – and handled them with the utmost care.

I was particularly impressed by Nancy's knowledge of the industry and her ability to get the job done. Whether it was executing a regional event in her area, or supporting an appointment setting campaign for her particular vertical, Nancy always gave 100% and was completely invested in its success. I've spent my entire career working with and supporting sales and Nancy is by far one of the best Account Executives I've ever had the pleasure of working with.

View 31 more recommendations ⌄

Accomplishments

+

6 **Honors & Awards** ✎
2014 Top Female Executives
Recognized for Outstanding Professionalism, Excellence, and Dedication

Feb 2014
Top Female Executives

Dedication, Leadership and Excellence

Recognized for demonstrating dedication, leadership and excellence

http://halloffame.cambridgewhoswho.com/HOF/2013/Q1/P4.html?I=14

Jan 2013
Cambridge Who's Who

Professional of the Year, Health Care Support Services

http://www.worldwidebranding.com/Members/VA/Nancy-Brock-1309800.html

2013
Worlwide Who's Who

Professional of the Year, Health Care Support Services

http://www.worldwidebranding.com/Members/VA/Nancy-Brock-1309800.html

2012
Worldwide Who's Who

Elite American Executives, Certificate of Recognition

http://eliteamericanexecutives.com/2014/01/10/nancy-brock/

Aug 2011
Elite American Executives

William J. Branstrom Freshman Prize

Awarded to first-term freshmen who rank in the upper five percent of their class within their school or college at The University of Michigan.

1981
University of Michigan

See fewer honors ︿

4 **Organizations**

Society of Human Resource Management

WTPF, The Business Forum for HR Professionals

March of Dimes Maryland-National Capitol Chapter, National Capitol Chapter

2011 – 2014

Northern Virginia Technology Council

Sep 2015 – Present

See fewer organizations ︿

2 **Publications**

Interview by Jean Chatzky, "Protect Your Health," December 2006   [See publication]
Interview on being a savvy healthcare consumer.

Harpo Productions, Inc.
Dec 4, 2006

Authors

The Road to Health Consumerism   [See publication]
Evolution of consumer-driven health plans and UnitedHealth Group's CDHP results.

VAHU News
Jun 2008

Authors

See fewer publications ^

Chapter 6

Cover Letters and Other Written Communications

Dost thou love life? Then do not squander time,
for that is the stuff life is made of.
— Benjamin Franklin[113]

Some employers focus on a cover letter, while others will bypass it and go straight to the resume. If the resume is strong, some employers will then go back and read the cover letter. Regardless of how an employer treats the letter, make sure that you invest an appropriate amount of time writing a persuasive and well-constructed cover letter. This immediately begins to differentiate you from other job seekers by highlighting strong points in your background and provides a sample of your writing ability. A well-written letter can serve as a customizable template for different job opportunities.

Types of Cover Letters

In general, cover letters fall into three categories:

---

113 Franklin, Benjamin [Richard Saunders, Poor Richard, pseud.]. *The Way to Wealth*. July 7, 1757, *American Literature Research and Analysis*, http://itech.fgcu.edu/faculty/wohlpart/alra/franklin.htm (accessed May 27, 2015).

A **letter of application** is used to match a specific employment position.

A **letter of inquiry** is written (frequently to HR) when you are exploring whether the employer may have a possible open position within the company.

A **marketing letter (or email)** is written to quickly grab the hiring executive's attention. The goal of this "attack" strategy is to showcase your qualifications and create enough interest so the hiring executive reads your resume and engages you in conversation. You are proactively marketing yourself directly to a potential hiring executive who could likely hire you for the position you seek (regardless of whether there is a known or posted opening).

The Cover Letter Success Formula

The kind of cover letter doesn't matter on this particular point: getting your cover letter read increases the odds of getting your resume reviewed and differentiating yourself. Be concise. With your cover letter (as well as all your written communications), proofreading is mandatory. Executives are reading not only for content, but for sentence structure and how you express your thoughts. Spelling or grammar errors broadcast that you either don't pay attention to detail or are careless. Have someone who's unfamiliar with your letter read it. You could also let your writing sit overnight. Some claim that reading it backward helps. And when it comes time to send your letters, don't send the same one to every executive. Having a template is fine, but customize each one. And don't mention salary, compensation, or benefits in a cover letter.

To maximize the persuasive nature of your cover letters, use the following approach, which has proven effective over the course of time:

- Create interest (first sentence)
- Match (next)
- Showcase an accomplishment/qualification (next paragraph)
- Provide additional information (paragraph three and perhaps four)
- Close

Here's an in-depth look at how to do this:

Create interest

You must quickly get the attention and interest of the employer. Personalizing the letter with their name (found by searching LinkedIn or the company website, or calling the company) will go a long way. Adding a "RE:" line (meaning "regarding") lets the executive know what your letter is about, and the position you're interested in. Generating interest increases the time the executive spends on your letter. All too often, people fail to generate interest by beginning their letters with the following types of opening sentences:

I am writing you today regarding any potential need you may have for a director of operations. I believe I have the qualifications you are looking for.

This type of writing is ineffective. Instead, begin your letters with something that will grab the attention of the hiring executive or be thought-provoking. Some examples are:

1. **Mention a personal or professional referral.** *Our mutual friend, Peter Huggins, suggested that I reach out to you.* Mentioning a common acquaintance is one of the most effect ways to capture a reader's attention (using the persuasion principle of social proof).

2. **Come out swinging with one of your top achievements.** *For the last four years I have been ranked as one of my company's top ten sales representatives for overall sales production.*

3. **Identify yourself by a unique or highly sought-after skill or knowledge base. This uses the persuasion principle of scarcity.** *I am a software engineer with a Microsoft Master's Certificate and five CCIEs from Cisco.*

4. **Refer to a statistic.** *According to the most recent polling, 43 percent of small businesses will explore concierge health care services for their company's health insurance needs, up from 21 percent just a year ago.*

5. **Offer to solve a business problem.** *If you need to decrease your company's operating expenses by 20 percent, without layoffs, I have a track record of doing just that.*

6. **Ask a relevant business question.** *Have you found it difficult to increase company revenues during this economic downturn? If so, that is my specialty.*

7. **Mention a recent company event or a news release that is significant.** *Congratulations on your acquisition of Plate Co., Inc. I understand this could increase your market share significantly.*

8. **Use a quotation**. *Jeremy Johnson of the American Marketing Association recently found that redefining target markets can increase effectiveness by almost double.*

9. **Cite a relevant industry trend**. *It is a well-known fact that national health care legislation is causing a silent exodus of experienced physicians from private practice. I have a track record of recruiting these doctors into on-site clinics.*

10. **Refer to a recommendation.** *There are very few executives that have the achievements and created as much increased value for companies as Rich. For example, 8 times revenue improvement over 5 years (resulting in the sale of the company), 30% growth in company revenues resulting in the sale of the company with a 10x multiple, among others. He has an undisputable track record of success.*

Match

After you have the hiring executive's attention, hold it by very briefly identifying your function, which matches one the company already has (best case), using their exact wording, if possible. This makes you relevant and encourages the hiring executive to read on. Here are a couple of examples:

> *As an industrial engineer with twenty years of manufacturing experience . . .*

> *I am a senior level account management professional with a specialty in wellness and care management . . .*

Depending on your writing style, this matching statement could be placed at the end of the "create interest" paragraph, added as the first sentence of the "showcase" paragraph, or be a short paragraph by itself.

Consider using the word cloud technique to match wording to possible needs of the employer.

Showcase an accomplishment/qualification

The accomplishment paragraph is even more important after you have created interest and matched a known company role. Focus the executive on key points, but do not repeat your resume. Make your accomplishments relevant by identifying the position's most important requirements, link your qualifications to them, and then show your accomplishments in each or most of the job functions. In other words, tell a prospective employer you can do the job and you have a track record of doing it well. These showcase techniques can also help to get your resume read.

If you want to pursue job opportunities as a director of operations (just as an illustration), start with your Master Job Description combined with research on similar open positions (or a job description from the employer). You may find a job description like this:

Director of Operations

Candidate must have at least ten years' experience managing multisite locations Individual will have experience with the following: process management systems, personnel management, performance improvement, and emergency response plans.

So, when writing your cover letter, use the exact wording to demonstrate your skills in the listed job requirements. This paragraph of your cover letter could look like this (important portions in bold for clarification):

*In the last fifteen years, I have worked as a **director of operations** for three manufacturers in the plastics industry. During my most recent position at See Through Plastics, LLC, I had success in the following areas:*

➢ ***Managed four manufacturing facilities in four separate regions of the country.*** *Exceeded production and profit goals for the last five consecutive years.*

➢ *Designed and implemented a **process management system** that resulted in **improved production efficiency** by 32 percent and increased product output by 20 percent.*

➢ *Created a workplace accountability matrix with floor supervisors that decreased absenteeism of workers by 15 percent while **improving productivity per worker** by 21 percent.*

➢ *Worked with company auditor to develop an auditing system that revealed resource and time inefficiencies. **Program saved 12 percent on resource orders** in the first year and reduced fulfillment time by over 20 percent.*

➢ *Worked with safety consulting firm to create and **implement a state-of-the-art emergency response plan for catastrophic events** and business interruption. Plan has been duplicated by other manufacturers.*

To keep the letter concise, only use bulleted items that address the position's most important requirements. In the above example, the job seeker may only use two or three of the five accomplishments.

In rare instances, there will be unique situations where accomplishments can be less important. This occurs when you may be one of relatively few in your field or area with a certain skill, certification, or knowledge that becomes an important element of your candidacy. Showcase your unique qualification in this paragraph.

Provide additional information

In the following paragraphs of the letter, elaborate on your experience, skills, background, and achievements. This is where you have a fair amount of latitude on what you want to showcase. Choose those topics you feel are the most relevant or impressive to the employer. Once again, inform the employer what you did, in addition to how this produced positive results.[114]

> *I am a motivated sales professional with a positive track record of opening new territories. At Ins. Company, I took over a three-state, virgin territory with no sales or business contacts. I researched and identified broker-dealers, set appointments, traveled, and made sales presentations. Within the first year, I generated over $1.2M in production and exceeded sales goals by over 300 percent.*

Another approach is to add a strong recommendation. This paragraph should be indented and single-spaced. To realize this technique's full impact, identify the person providing the recommendation by name and title. Here's an example:

> *My supervisor, Susan J. Smith, Director of Operations, Cyban, Inc. states:*
> *Jane has excellent communication skills. In addition, she is extremely organized, reliable, and computer literate. Jane can work independently and is able to follow through to ensure that the job gets done. She is flexible and willing to work on any project that is assigned to her. Jane was quick to volunteer to assist in other areas of company operations, as well.*

Remember, it is always more influential when others speak well of you rather than you promoting yourself.

Another technique you can use in this section is to reveal a professional insight about yourself to personalize the letter. It must be something relevant or important to the employer.

---

114 See also, Safani, "Tell a Story."

This paragraph can start with a phrase such as: "I am passionate about . . . ", "I am professionally rewarded when . . . ", "I have always been intrigued by . . . ", and so on. For example:

I am passionate about wellness. I get a great deal of satisfaction knowing that the wellness services I promote to clients will have a personal impact on the health and well-being of that employer's employees.

Use these paragraphs to inform the employer about any other piece of information relevant to your job search, such as relocation.

I will relocate to Portland in the next sixty days as a result of my wife's promotion.

Close

Conclude your letter by using a brief closing statement, followed by your intention to follow up:

Based on my track record of successful operational efficiency, I believe I have the qualifications and accomplishments to make a positive impact on ABC Inc. I look forward to discussing this opportunity with you and I will contact your office next week.

Don't restrict yourself to paper cover letters. Other effective methods include marketing emails (see Proactively Marketing Your Professional Credentials chapter and Appendix), as well as videos and YouTube (discussed later). Use multiple methods, as appropriate, in your self-motivated job search to gain greater visibility with employers and increase opportunities for interviews.

Cover Letters and Career Transition Job Seekers

For job seekers transitioning from one career focus to another or possibly changing industries, consider adding a paragraph informing the employer exactly how your skills translate or are directly transferable to the job opportunity. This explanation must be succinct. If it isn't, the employer may conclude that you are struggling to draw the analogy between your skills and the job. In that case, you lose. This information about your transferability of skills should be a part of the third or fourth paragraph. For example:

- "There is a strong correlation of my skills as a . . . and your open position for a . . . "

- "My skills and experience as an employee benefits account manager are directly transferable to your need of an internal benefits human resource specialist. (Now explain why) . . . "

★ Cover Letters and Recruiters

When contacted by a recruiter for a specific opportunity, you will be competing against other well-qualified candidates. The following technique can differentiate you from other job seekers.

Here's the scenario and how to gain a potential edge:

You are interested in and qualified for the opportunity, and the recruiter is willing to submit your credentials to the employer. Ask the recruiter if there is a job description or job posting. If so, get it and read it. In the same conversation or a follow-up call, tell the recruiter that you are going to send a brief cover letter (by email) regarding the position. Most, if not all, recruiters will accept the letter. Ask the recruiter, at his or her discretion, to include the cover letter as a part of your submission to the employer. Here's why: many recruited candidates don't bother with cover letters because they think a recruiter's involvement makes a cover letter unnecessary. Differentiate yourself from your competition and showcase your accomplishments and qualifications by writing a cover letter (remember the word cloud technique, which could help). Employers will note that you took the time and effort to write the letter, and draw the conclusion that you must be more interested than some of the other candidates who did not. And when the letter gets read, you have differentiated yourself even more.

Thank-You Letters

The primary purposes of a thank-you letter are to express your appreciation, reiterate your relevant background, qualifications, and successes, and differentiate you from other job seekers. Most hiring executives appreciate a thank-you correspondence after an interview.[115] And "some employers may expect a job interview thank-you card."[116] However, it has been

---

115 Accountemps, "Farewell to the Handwritten Thank-You Note? Survey Reveals Email, Phone Call Are Preferred Methods for Post-Interview Follow-Up," news release, June 14, 2012, http://accountemps.rhi.mediaroom.com/thank-you (accessed July 9, 2015).

116 "Do Employers Expect a Job Interview Thank-You Card?" CVTips, http://www.cvtips.com/interview/do-employers-expect-a-job-interview-thank-you-card.html (accessed July 10, 2015).

said that only 20 percent of all job seekers take the time to write a thank-you note.[117] If so, writing a thank-you note can differentiate you from many other job seekers. And not sending a thank-you note may reflect negatively on your candidacy.[118]

An important secondary purpose is to make sure the hiring executive remembers you. In a survey by *The Ladders*, a combined 76 percent said a thank-you note was "somewhat important" or "very important" to their hiring decision.[119] That's three out of every four! Therefore, capitalize on this opportunity to reinforce your skills and accomplishments.

Write a thank-you note after every interview. And keep it short. This is a thank-you letter, not a written interview summary.

To maximize the impact of your thank-you letter, use the following approach:

• Express your appreciation
• Match
• Emphasize past achievements
• Close

Let's look at each step in more detail.

Express your appreciation

Thank the hiring executive for their time. Then, move to rapport-building, depending upon the circumstances. Your first paragraph could look something like this:

> *Thank you for taking the time yesterday to meet with me regarding your implementation consultant position. I enjoyed learning how you derived the concept behind your state-of-the-art system.* (This is a compliment, using the persuasion principle of liking.) *As we*
>
> *discussed, my knowledge in this area could assist your department with the challenges it will face in the coming months.*

Or,

---

117 Helmrich, Brittney. "Thanks! 20 Job Interview Thank You Note Tips," *Business News Daily*, June 23, 2015, http://www.businessnewsdaily.com/7134-thank-you-note-tips.html (accessed July 9, 2015).

118 "Thank-You Note Etiquette," CareerBuilder, http://www.careerbuilder.com/JobPoster/Resources/page.aspx?pagever=ThankYouNoteEtiquette (accessed July 9, 2015).

119 "Give Thanks or Your Chance For That Job Could be Cooked," *TheLadders*, http://cdn.theladders.net/static/images/basicSite/PR/pdfs/TheLaddersGiveThanks.pdf (accessed June 5, 2015).

Thank you for meeting me on Tuesday regarding the regional sales position. I appreciate your time. And, by the way, good luck to your son during tryouts for the starting quarterback position.

Match

Because you were interviewed, you should know what the hiring executive is looking for in the position. Briefly restate and match your qualifications to the need.

During our plant tour last week, I was very impressed with your use of robotics in the manufacturing process. I can honestly say I have never seen such an impressive after-market manufacturing plant. My twenty years as an industrial engineer from near identical manufacturing environments makes me well-suited for the challenges of this position.

Emphasize past achievements

Express your interest in the position, and link two or three job requirements with your accomplishments. For maximum impact, try to make them relevant to company needs, a position's special qualifications, or topics mentioned in the interview. Your paragraph could look something like this:

I am interested in joining your company in an engineering operations capacity. As we discussed, my recent accomplishments include:

> *Implemented a manufacturing process improvement system resulting in an $800,000 saving.*

> *Designed and implemented an inventory auditing system that increased turnaround time by 30 percent and reduced spending by 12 percent.*

> *Developed and implemented a "Visions" business plan that forecast budgets for a variety of business operations including equipment and technology upgrades, new facility construction, and reduced operating expenses.*

Close

Here, express your continued interest and a plan to contact the hiring executive. The closing paragraph could look something like this:

What I achieved for Sinc Company, I can do for you. I will follow up with you in ten days, as you requested, to discuss additional steps.

Here is a real-life example:

> *Thank you for your time yesterday in consideration of my candidacy for your Payer Enterprise position.*
>
> *It was truly a pleasure to speak with you and learn more about your background and the culmination of experiences that led you to create <Company>.*
>
> *I was not only touched by your story, but impressed by the experience and knowledge you and your team contribute to <Company> and the patients your solution empowers.*
>
> *The desire to bring more value to health care by combining technology, science, and gamification, is cutting-edge and will change how we provide health care moving forward.*
>
> *I would certainly welcome the opportunity to be a valued member of your team and contribute to <Company's> Payer expansion.*
>
> *As we discussed, I thrive in environments where I can combine my clinical and sales acumen, and have been very successful in generating new insurance contracts for my employers.*
>
> *I have received numerous sales awards and accolades during my career and have attached an accompanying testimonial sheet that provides an overview of my potential to make a worthwhile contribution to your company. The document contains sentiments shared from coworkers throughout my sales career and provides color on what my peers share regarding my work.*
>
> *I am a strong team advocate that enjoys learning from my colleagues. I have excellent oral and written communications skills and can manage multiple projects easily.*
>
> *I look forward to hearing from you regarding next steps. In the meantime, please do not hesitate to contact me should you have questions or desire further information.*
>
> *Kindest Regards,*

Thank-You Letter When You Are Not Selected for the Job

This letter builds bridges for the future and is a very strong networking technique. It will differentiate you from others and create a favorable impression with the hiring executive. There are two good reasons for doing this. First, it can leave the door open for future opportunities with the company. It is not uncommon for employers to revisit previous candidates when new opportunities become available.

Additionally, since professionals within an industry often run in the same circles of influence, the letter distinguishes you and could lead to other business relationships with the hiring executive. Writing a professional correspondence after a decision not to hire you shows character and professionalism. You don't know where, when, and in what way your paths may cross again with the hiring executive. The letter sets up a positive engagement for the next time—be it business or personal.

Here is a sample letter:

Thank you so much for the opportunity to interview for the regional manager position. I understand that I was not chosen for the position. Although disappointed, I want to express my appreciation for your consideration throughout the interviewing process. ABC Company has a bright future and your leadership team is impressive.

I hope that we run into each other over the course of time at various industry events.

Laurie, it has been a true pleasure getting to know you and the other members of your team.

Please keep me in mind should your hiring needs change in the future.

Sincerely,

Thank-You Letter When You Withdraw from an Interviewing Process

It is equally important to send a thank-you letter when you choose to withdraw from pursuing a position. Doing so is professional and lets the hiring executive focus attention on others for the position.

Here is a sample letter:

I hope this email finds you well and having a good week.

I would like to withdraw my candidacy for the VP of Sales position at ABC Company. I have accepted an offer with a health care analytics company out of Chicago and wanted to make you aware of this change in status.

Thank you so much for your time, consideration, and speaking with me regarding the position.

I believe your company is positioned to do great things and will be championing your growth and success.

Best,

Email Follow-Up Letters

When following up through email, the same considerations and rules apply as previously mentioned. Things to remember: make your subject line relevant, omit a street address, and always include your telephone number.

Something to Think About

Some suggest that sending hard-copy cover letters, resumes, and thank-you letters is no longer as effective as it once was. People think, "It's all done by email these days." Perhaps that's true, but consider this: how many emails did you get in your last position? A lot, right? There are some hiring executives that receive two hundred or more emails a day (maybe you sent one of them). Obviously, not all of these emails are from job seekers, but the point is, these hiring executives are busy people who receive lots of emails.

In your last position, how often did you receive a personal letter (not junk mail)? Probably not often.

Here's the concept: due to the sheer volume of emails that a hiring executive receives, one possible technique to differentiate yourself (which is a primary goal in your job search), is to send a cover letter, resume, or thank-you note by US mail. *That which was old may be new again.* It's an idea you may wish to explore with some of your target companies and target contacts.

A variation of this approach is to send the cover letter by US mail and if there is no response, then follow up with an email message referring to the hard-copy letter you sent. Include a copy of the letter as an attachment or a summary of the letter's contents in the email's body.

Another Idea

If you decide to send a cover letter, resume, or thank-you letter by US mail, consider investing in customized envelopes. Since there is a lot of open space on an envelope to use, consider putting two or three of your top achievements in the lower left corner of the envelope. How often does a hiring executive see this? Probably rarely . . . and that might be just the differentiation you need for him/her to open the envelope.

Use your best discretion on how receptive a hiring executive for someone at your level would view these techniques.

Some Final Words about Written Communications

As you know, communication skills (written, verbal, and listening) are highly sought after.[120] Being able to write effectively and persuasively is an important element in your job search, and it will be evaluated (as well as whether you've proofread your materials). What you write about, how you communicate it, and the caliber of your sentence structure, word choice, grammar, and punctuation are measured against those of other job seekers. By following the Cover Letter Success Formula and proper thank-you letter writing techniques, you can feel confident that your written communications will differentiate you from other job seekers and grab the attention of the employer.

Have someone unfamiliar with the documents read them. Using an effective writing formula will be rendered useless if there are spelling, grammatical, and punctuation errors. The Appendix has sample letters for your review.

Shifting Gears

So far the topics we have been discussing have been preparing you to engage in job-search activities that lead to interviews by helping you establish the right mindset and setting up templates and to-do lists for success. At most, these preparatory activities should take between **one and two weeks** (as a *maximum*)—ideally much less. Anything beyond that could be busywork or a diversion for you to avoid the necessary work of engaging the job market and beginning your job search in earnest.

We are now going to shift gears into topics related to generating job leads and interviews.

---

120 Hanson and Hanson, "What Do Employers *Really* Want?"

Chapter 7

Professional Networking

Everything you want is just outside your comfort zone.
— Robert Allen[121]

Hidden Job Market

As you engage the marketplace in search of a new job, accept this statistic: it is widely believed that "at least 70 percent, if not 80 percent, of jobs are not published."[122] These jobs are referred to as the Hidden Job Market. Much has been written about the Hidden Job Market.[123] It is real. Landing your next position will combine online and offline strategies. This job-search book provides you the insight and strategies to achieve success through both avenues.

The Internet and social networking have dramatically changed how people search for a

---

121 "Quotes on Initiative," *Leadership Now*, http://www.leadershipnow.com/initiativequotes.html (accessed May 28, 2015).

122 Kaufman, "A Successful Job Search."

123 *Get Hired Fast!: Tap the Hidden Job Market in 15 Days* by Brian Graham, *Cracking the Hidden Job Market: How to Find Opportunity in Any Economy* by Donald Asher, and others.

job. As a result, networking techniques and strategies have taken on a whole new meaning.

Why don't employers advertise their open positions? For some it is a matter of company policy that they must post all job openings. However, many companies choose not to advertise for any of the following reasons:

- The sheer amount of respondents (with the vast majority wholly unqualified) makes for time-consuming work sifting through countless resumes.

- For truly specialized positions there are few or no qualified candidates.

- Employers want well-qualified, interested, and affordable candidates without the hours of effort it takes to locate them through advertising. This easing of the hiring process is part of the value recruiters bring to employers.

- Some employers choose to fill positions by word of mouth and networking.

How can you tap the Hidden Job Market effectively and efficiently? Follow the strategies and techniques in this book. Take a proactive approach to your search (don't just sit at home and apply for jobs online). Network both online and face-to-face.

There will be more about networking in the following pages. But, understand and appreciate this truth: networking works, but it can take time. "Those who give . . . get" is said to be the philosophical foundation to effective networking.[124] When you help others find what they want, they will remember you and return the favor (the persuasion principle of reciprocity).

124 Vlooten, Dick van. "The Seven Laws of Networking: Those Who Give, Get," *Career Magazine*, May 7, 2004, http://sciencecareers.sciencemag.org/career_magazine/previous_issues/articles/2004_05_07/nodoi. 1275810282259244595 (accessed June 16, 2015).

Networking

Networking is an essential part of building wealth.
— Armstrong Williams[125]

Networking for a job involves connecting with people you know and then the people they know to leading you to a job. It also includes professionally reaching out to those you don't know for the same purpose. It generally involves three types of contacts:

- Those people that can lead you to others that can assist you in your job search

- Those people that can introduce you to someone that can hire you

- Someone that has the authority to hire you

Job-search networking can take place in a wide variety of situations including face-to-face, online through professional networking sites (LinkedIn) and social networking sites (Facebook), professional associations, alumni events, and even the casual dinner gathering with friends.

It is estimated that between 60 and 80 percent of all jobs are found by networking.[126]

---

125 Williams, Armstrong. "A Few Simple Steps to Building Wealth," *Townhall*, June 13, 2005, http://townhall.com/columnists/armstrongwilliams/2005/06/13/a_few_simple_steps_to_building_wealth/page/full (accessed May 28, 2015).

126 LinkedIn, "Using LinkedIn to Find a Job"; Beatty, "The Math Behind the Networking Claim"; Rothberg, "80% of Job Openings."

Statistically speaking, your next job will come as a result of your networking efforts.

This next concept is important and goes straight to the heart of professionally networking for a job: it's not how many people you know, but rather how many people know you. Ponder that for a moment to understand it. How many people know you well enough that they would refer you to someone else or possibly go out of their way to help you, even if it's in a small measure? It's this kind of relationship networking that drives a job search.

Fear of Networking

Unfortunately, many job seekers hesitate to take full advantage of networking because they're intimidated or are afraid of being viewed as pushy, annoying, or self-serving. Put those feelings aside. Networking is not about arrogant self-promotion. Instead it's about building relationships. When you think about networking as building relationships—or creating professional friendships—many of your fears will disappear.

Accept this next statement as gospel truth: whether your networking is formal or informal, online or offline, there are people out there that want to help. It's your job to get out there and let them!

Do the thing you fear, and the death of fear is certain.
— Emerson[127]

Why Networking Is So Effective

There are several reasons why networking is an effective way to find your next opportunity:

- **It taps into the Hidden Job Market.** Networking gives you access to the 70 to 80 percent of all jobs that are not advertised.

- **It decreases the time it takes to land a new position.** Networking is a proactive job search tactic. People you know or have been referred to are more likely to speak or meet with you personally. The more communications you have, the closer you get to a job offer.

---

127 "Ralph Waldo Emerson Quotable Quote," Goodreads, www.goodreads.com/quotes/60285-do-the-thing-you-fear-and-the-death-of-fear (accessed May 28, 2015).

- **It reduces competition.** Job postings tend to draw a pile of resumes. Networking makes you the preferred candidate of a much smaller candidate pool.

- **It introduces you through a common connection and expands your current network.** People do business primarily with people they know and like. As your network expands, so will your opportunities as you are introduced to more and more people.

- **It helps you practice for interviews and builds self-confidence**. Networking creates phone conversations, lunch dates, and informational interviews. These are opportunities to practice your interviewing skills. This will boost your self-confidence, awareness that your job search is moving forward, and feelings of success as you improve overall. Having confidence translates into better communications which creates more interviews eventually leading to more job opportunities.[128]

Types of Networks

Conceptually there are two job-search networks: personal and professional. Your personal network includes family, friends, neighbors, and doctors, as well as your dentist, financial advisor, accountant, and members of church, civic, or philanthropic groups you attend. Everyone else you interact with in your personal life is also included here. Websites in your personal network include Facebook and Twitter, among others.

Your professional network is developed from your career and consists of people that are work colleagues, connections at other companies, former bosses, senior management, association contacts, and so on. The leading online site for professional networks is LinkedIn.

Both personal and professional networks can be extremely powerful in directing you and connecting you to potential job opportunities. Which network will yield the most leads will depend upon your circumstances; your networks could perform equally well.

Each one of your contacts connects you to their network. And any member of that network could know about an available opportunity. Let's say you have solid relationships with twenty people in either your personal or professional network. Now let's say they each know twenty people. That's four hundred people you can get to know reasonably quickly without much effort.

For some people, twenty connections is a very low number. It's possible that your network, especially on the professional side, could be in the hundred-plus range. You do

---

128 Moynihan et al., "A Longitudinal Study," quoted in Kurtzberg and Naquin, *Essentials*, p. 30–32.

the math on how large your extended network can be—chances are, you'll be pleasantly surprised.

Evaluating the Strength and Quality of Your Professional Network

Prior to actively networking, take some time and evaluate your current professional network. Are there enough quality, relevant contacts to drive your job-search efforts? Give yourself one point for each of the following questions that you answer yes:

- Is your professional network comprised predominantly of people within your industry or position type?
- Does it contain connections that can lead you to other connections that have influence, perhaps even to potential hiring executives?
- Do you feel your professional network is large enough?
- Are you a member of enough industry-specific LinkedIn groups, associations, or relevant local groups?
- Do you feel your network can help you?

How did you do?

5 points. Great job on your network!

4 points. Your network is excellent, but could stand some improvement.

3 points. You need to spend time building your network.

2 points. Your network needs serious attention.

0 or 1 point. Get your network a lifeline, stat!

If you need to improve your network, put extra time and effort to get introduced and connected to others that can enhance the strength and quality of your contact base. The more time and effort you devote to your network, the quicker it will grow, and the quicker you'll connect with your next opportunity. Start with your strong connections (in your inner circle of trusted contacts) and ask for their assistance. They will probably be willing to help, but contacting them and asking to be introduced to their network contacts will take time. Many will help, some may not. Either way, thank them for their time and move ahead.

Who to Connect and Network With

The point of networking for a job is connecting and communicating with people who can help you or hire you. So, who would that be? Below is a list of targets, along with "help" or "hire" designations to get you thinking:

1. Hiring executives from competing companies or from your current or past employers (hire you and help you)

2. Peers and colleagues, selectively chosen, from your current company or past employers (help you)

3. Hiring executives from vendors, customers, suppliers, or business partners from your current or past employers (hire you and help you)

4. Peers and colleagues from these vendors or business partners (help you)

5. People who are "centers of influence"—these could be contacts from a wide variety of sources including personal, philanthropic, civic, and nonprofit organizations (help you)

Many other connections exist—just make sure these possible connections can move your search forward. No matter the type, most of these people can be identified and contacted through a search of LinkedIn.

Create Your Professional "Cabinet"

The President of the United States has a Cabinet. It is a select group of trusted advisors composed of the vice president and other prominent government officials of the executive branch, totaling sixteen (not including others who are a part at the president's discretion).[129] You also need to create a Cabinet of trusted advisors. Here is a definition to guide your thinking, selection, and development process:

A professional (networking) Cabinet is a select group of people in your professional life who you can trust and call upon, knowing that they will undoubtedly help you in any way reasonably possible. This would include providing you with advice,

129 "Constitutional Topic: The Cabinet," U.S. Constitution Online, http://www.usconstitution.net/consttop_cabi.html (accessed November 10, 2015).

introductions, mentorship/tough love, referrals, insight, and recommendations, among other things. It is a reciprocal relationship; they know they can count on you to do the same for them.

Let's examine a few components of this definition.

A select group—Your Cabinet will likely be small, comprised of five to ten people, perhaps a few more if you can create and maintain close relationships. It's likely that your Cabinet will be people with whom you have developed (or are currently developing) a close relationship.

Professional life—Your Cabinet is a group of people in your professional life. These people may be your friends, but the foundation of the relationship started in your professional life.

Trust—These people must be trustworthy. They are, in large part, confidants to whom you can be vulnerable regarding professional matters.

Undoubtedly help—These are people you can count on and who have your best interests at heart. These people are your go-to inner circle.

In any way reasonably possible—You must understand and appreciate that there are limits. Like the president's Cabinet, each member has an area of expertise. This is also true with your Cabinet. Your Cabinet will likely consist of professionals who have unique abilities, insight, connections, and so on. In fact, over time you want to have a reasonably diverse Cabinet.

A reciprocal relationship—As with any network, the relationship must be a two-way street to be productive. You must be willing to give when your Cabinet member needs you.

A Cabinet is a very important networking group to create and have. It is the group you can rely upon in a pinch. They are your network's foundation. How many people do you know who you can contact almost immediately and ask for help with full confidence that you will receive it? If that number is not at least five to ten, you need to grow your Cabinet.

Create Your Sales Company

The next layer of your network is your "Sales Company." The words used to describe these network contacts were chosen by design.

Sales. As you know, salespeople promote the products and services of the employer. They sell the benefits of those products and services. They assist buyers. They are ambassadors for their employers in the market. They also provide feedback to their employer. By analogy, you want to create a layer of connections who will assist you, promote you, and be your ambassadors in the job market when given an opportunity.

These are the people you have good professional and collegial relationships with. You have interacted with them professionally, and perhaps socially, on some level. These are people you are reasonably sure (though not completely, like your Cabinet) will help or lend a hand if the opportunity presents itself. Put into percentages, your Cabinet is 100 percent sure to help. Your Sales Company is 60 percent and above. It's more likely than not. There are no scientific percentages, but connections in your Sales Company are those people you can call on who are likely to help. This help can take many forms, including:

"I'll keep my eyes open."

"You might want to read this article on XYZ Company."

"You may want to network with Kipp Sawyer."

"Call Ruth Moore, my boss. We're looking."

Always be a professional networker. Thank everyone who responds and offer to help them if they need anything.

Company. The word "company" was chosen for its military definition. A military company is one hundred to two hundred soldiers.[130] Therefore, picking the midpoint, your Sales Company should number around 150 contacts. The 150 number also has some scientific basis—it happens to be the Dunbar Number, created by British anthropologist Robin Dunbar. Based on his studies, he theorized that there is a numerical limit to the number of

---

130 "Operational Unit Diagrams," United States Army, http://www.army.mil/info/organization/unitsandcommands/oud/ (accessed November 10, 2015).

individuals with whom a stable interpersonal relationship can be maintained. That number is 150.[131]

The point is this: you want to have around 150 connections in your Sales Company.

Let's think through the power of what this could mean for your job search. Let's assume that you have a healthy network—ten Cabinet members and 150 in your Sales Company. Now, let's assume that only 40 percent of your Sales Company actually provides assistance to you in some form (remember the 60 percent number—so we are being pessimistic about the level of help for this example). Let's do the math: 40 percent of 150 is sixty, plus ten (Cabinet members are 100 percent reliable) gets you to seventy. You have seventy sales reps, advisors, promoters, and ambassadors out there helping you and promoting you in some measure. Think about that for a moment . . . that's a lot. Are you beginning to grasp the importance and power of a healthy network?

The Peripheral and Pruning

Outside your Cabinet and your Sales Company are the rest of your connections. The people you know, are acquainted with, or simply connected to on LinkedIn. They are peripheral, but still important.

All human relationships ebb and flow. People enter your life and stay or fade away over time for any one of a thousand reasons. This will be true with your network. The people in your network will migrate between or out of your network circles. Cabinet members move to the Sales Company and vice versa. Some retire or pass away. New connections appear on the scene. Maintain and cultivate relationships and be aware of what you have with your Cabinet and Sales Company.

Then there are times when you need to prune your network. This is when the relationship with the connection has diminished in value to a point where there is no mutual (professional) benefit for the relationship. It would be like a director of robotics being connected to a person who has become a pastry chef. The connection is just not there, at least not on a professional level. From a job-search perspective, these would be connections who can't hire you, help you, or be a center of influence for you.

On LinkedIn, these are the connections you may choose to "remove." When you do this, the connection is not alerted that you have severed the connection. And, more often than

---

131 Konnikova, Maria. "The Limits of Friendship," *The New Yorker*, October 7, 2014, http://www.newyorker.com/science/maria-konnikova/social-media-affect-math-dunbar-number-friendships (accessed November 10, 2015).

not, your circle of professional acquaintances is or has become divergent enough that it will go completely unnoticed. There'll be no hard feelings.

LinkedIn

LinkedIn has dramatically influenced networking during a job search. There are some cautionary strategies and notes to keep in mind.

1. **Use good judgment when connecting or extending invitations.** Determine whether a potential connection could be helpful or a center of influence for you. Connect with those who are in your industry or field of interest.

   Extend invitations to peers in your industry and those one to two levels above your title or function. Going above one or two levels may stretch the logical relevance of connecting.

   If you extend an invitation that is not accepted, it's okay. Do not to take it personally.

2. **Join Groups.** As previously mentioned, there are over two million LinkedIn groups.[132] Statistically, there are groups that will apply to you—join them.

   Once you are in a group, it is easier to connect and get introduced to people of interest to you. Always customize your invitation for a better response and success rate.

3. **Follow target companies.** Look up the company page for any company you are interested in. Click the "Follow" tab. All activity from that company's page (potentially job openings), will appear on your LinkedIn home page. This is a great feature to track the company's activities and potential hiring needs.

LinkedIn conducted a six-month study of senior-level professionals (vice president titles and above) and their use of LinkedIn during their job search. The results clearly indicated that these senior-level professionals knew "the value of building and nurturing professional relationships in order to be successful in their job search"[133] (networking). The study found

---

132 Arruda, "Is LinkedIn Poised."

133 Ayele, "Land Your Dream Job."

that "80 percent were sending connection requests, 50 percent were participating in groups, and 40 percent were engaging on LinkedIn via shares, likes, and comments."[134]

Spreading the Word—Asking for Help

Having access to a network will not help you find a job until you get the word out about your situation. Start by making contact with your strong connections (your short list and Cabinet). Initial contact can be either by email or by telephone. A personal call is always best even if it is a follow-up to an email (or LinkedIn InMail).

Focus your networking on connecting and exchanging information. This enhances or builds a relationship that, over time, becomes mutually beneficial. Maintaining professional friendships is a give-and-take process. Take time to catch up on family, mutual friends, industry trends, and so on, if a connection is strong. After that, segue to the topic of your job search. Do not ask for a job (especially if your connection is in a position to hire). Trust in the fact that if your connection can hire you or refer you to someone that can, they will. Instead, enlist your contact as an information source, ally, or a lookout for your job search. Ask for information, insight, and advice.

Never bash your former employer in an interview. That same rule extends to networking contacts as well. Most don't want to hear negative comments. There will be some that will want "the dirt," either because they are competitors or they are simply prone to gossip. Don't fall for it. Keep your comments professional and use your exit statement (or a variation).

Be as specific as possible about the type of position, company, or industry you are interested in (more on this in a moment). Aimless or generic networking requests are often vague and your networking contact will struggle to remember what you need. Providing specific information is easier for your them to remember—and to recall that it was you.

When reaching out to a new connection, inform him/her how you are connected. Use a referral name or common association, membership, or LinkedIn group whenever possible. Then, with humble sincerity, professionally inform the connection of your situation. Like a strong connection, enlist this new connection as an information source or lookout for your job search. Don't forget to provide this person with your contact information.

If you are unemployed, consider sending your resume to your connection if given permission to do so. In your email cover letter, restate or inform the connection of the types of opportunities you would be interested in. Do not include any salary information.

---

134 Ibid.

Grant permission for the connection to pass along your resume to others if it would be appropriate, in their opinion, to do so.

For every connection you make, be sensitive to their time. Make the connection, have the conversation, but do not overextend your conversation. You will know when it is time to wrap it up. Boring or overloading a connection with information does not help your job search.

When you speak with a networking connection, be present in the moment. Give your full attention to the conversation. Focus. Listen. Avoid distractions. Strive to form a relationship that goes below the surface. This could take some time and a few engagements, but it's worth it. Having a few deep networking relationships is far more beneficial than a lot of superficial ones.

Networking in a Local Market for a Local Position

For local, general (non-industry-specific) job searches, network with those with occupations that are dependent upon networking for their livelihood. These people include real estate agents, financial planners, stockbrokers, mortgage lenders, bankers, and insurance agents, among others. They interact with the public every day and are frequently privy to information from these interactions that could lead to a job opportunity.

Another group to network with is those involved in civic organizations, and philan-thropic and fund-raising activities. These people often interact with local business lead-ers and hear about certain openings.

Get Busy! (and Keep Momentum in Networking)

Some job seekers struggle to get out of the gate when it comes to networking. This could be because their network is not developed, their network has grown cold from lack of contact, or they fear coming off wrong when making contact. But remember, networking is how most jobs are found.[135] The thing to realize is most everyone is willing to help if you give them a chance.

Networking is an ongoing process. Here's the goal—especially if you are just starting your search: fill your calendar with a minimum of twenty appointments in the next two to three weeks. Network every day in some form. Talk to someone, preferably someone

---

135 LinkedIn, "Using LinkedIn to Find a Job"; Beatty, "The Math Behind the Networking Claim"; Rothberg, "80% of Job Openings."

new (this is a great help so you don't slow down after an initial flurry of quick contacts). These appointments can be scheduled telephone calls or face-to-face meetings for coffee, breakfast, lunch, or something else. Get busy making contact. When you book twenty appointments, reach for the brass ring and book twenty more. When you achieve that goal then move on to the next. Get the idea? And . . . don't stop. As your search progresses, time commitments will erode the amount of time you can network. That's okay. There are only so many hours in a day. And it could be a good indication that your search is progressing (if you're getting interviews). But, overall, don't stop reaching out completely.

Maintaining Your Network

To network successfully, remember that you are building mutually beneficial relationships. That means giving freely to others, as well as receiving. Try to give, without the expectation of receiving, whenever appropriate. Nurture these relationships. Avoid being a hit-and-run networker, disappearing after you get what you want. With an appropriate level of communication, you will create a network that will benefit you and your network for years to come, and perhaps a lifetime.

Professional Associations

Professional associations are one of the most powerful networking tools you have. One of the best things you can do to shorten your job search is to join and be (reasonably) active in a professional association. Associations exist to promote the interests of the industry it serves *and* the careers of its members—through networking.

Some of the most connected and networked professionals you'll ever meet will belong to professional associations. These people get a charge out of being connected in your industry. So, as you discover them, connect with them, network with them, and (professionally and diplomatically) leverage them as a resource for your job search.

Professional associations are mostly volunteer organizations. With the exception of a select few positions in large national associations, professional associations depend on members to volunteer in order to get things done. This is achieved through various committees tasked with certain functions. With your job search in mind, which committees could bear the most fruit from networking? Two committees in particular can be most helpful.

Membership Committee—This committee gets you involved and interacting with potential new members as well as current members. It's a terrific committee to be involved with for easy introductions and networking.

Program/Speaker Committee—This committee identifies and approaches industry leaders to speak at association events. Being involved with this committee is a great way to get connected to thought leaders in your industry. It also improves your influence in the industry by being known by these movers-and-shakers, not to mention your ability to name drop because of knowing them (the persuasion principle of social proof).

Finally, being a member of a professional association gives you access to the membership directory. This directory can be easily used to identify professionals in your industry for networking (as well as to identify companies for any marketing purposes). Properly handled, your membership in an association will frequently, though not always, gain you a brief networking conversation with another member.

The more deeply connected you are (or can become) in professional associations, the greater your chances of tapping into the Hidden Job Market and shortening your job search.

Association/Industry Conferences

Association and industry conferences are great events for job-search networking. They present an opportunity to meet face-to-face with industry colleagues and hiring executives. You can learn which companies are potentially hiring. Occasionally you can get insider information on companies of interest to you. If you are a seasoned professional that has attended professional conferences, you know there is as much covert recruiting and informal interviewing taking place as there is actual business interaction with potential clients and customers.

Conferences can be expensive once you factor in the registration fee, travel, and lodging. However, attending and investing in one major industry conference is a good job-search strategy.

Discover whether the sponsoring organization has local chapters. Some do and may frequently hold monthly or quarterly meetings. Local chapter meetings tend to be breakfast or after-hours meetings. The cost for these local meetings is usually little or nothing, if you are a member of the organization. Attend as many as possible and build your network.

Use the following strategies to get the most out of attending a professional conference and further your job search:

1. Do research using the attendee and exhibitor lists. Every industry conference requires you to register. Registrants often get an advanced copy of the attendee and exhibitor lists (potential employers). Look at both lists for any hiring executives who will attend. This is invaluable information for you. Make it a goal to meet and speak with them. Research the executives on LinkedIn, and see if you have anyone in common who can introduce you via email or LinkedIn before the conference.

Research the companies who will be at the conference as well. Check out each company online, as well as their jobs page, if one exists. See if they are looking to hire someone with your skills and background. Also, find out from the conference materials when the exhibit hall is open. You'll probably do most of your job-search networking while other potential job seekers are aimlessly wandering the booths just checking it out. Too many job seekers come to conferences unprepared. Your research will edge out your competition.

2. Come prepared with your elevator speech, resume, and business cards. Be ready to use your elevator speech. Bring plenty of resumes, but only offer one if asked. Put each resume in an envelope with your name on it so it can be transported easily (and discreetly) in a suit or portfolio. Business cards are a must, especially for circumstances that don't allow for an extended discussion about employment. Make the contact, have a good conversation, and exchange business cards. You can communicate more fully later and supply a resume (if appropriate). Make sure you put a short note on the back of each business card you receive, so that you can remember something about the person or your conversation with them. This is a lifesaver when following up later.

3. Keep your attire conservative and employ a solid conference game plan. First impressions are critical, so conservative business attire is a requirement. Overdressed is better than underdressed. Dressing in conservative attire portrays professionalism and taps into the persuasion principle of authority. Survey the layout of the conference before you arrive (using the conference materials). Map out the companies that interest you, and put them in order of your personal preference, high interest to low interest. Keep in mind, your order may have to change if a lower-priority company has a booth very close to a higher-priority one. When you arrive at the conference, see if any new companies registered at the last minute and were not included in the attendee list. They may need to be added to your "company hit list." If you see someone you know at a conference, saying hello is fine, but clinging to them is not.[136] You're here to expand your network and connect to your next job, not waste precious time socializing.

4. Remember: every conversation is an interview. Use your elevator speech and remember the three keys to kick off a good interview or conversation: make eye contact, offer a firm handshake, and show enthusiasm. Be prepared with a few questions for the person you are speaking with. If in doubt, "What do you think of the conference so far?"[137] works well. (See the topic that follows for other icebreaker questions.) You are most likely being interviewed from the moment you speak with a company representative or hiring executive, but don't bring up the topic of open positions right away. That may make things awkward. Read the situation before asking. Most people will understand your ultimate goal and will offer help, either at the conference or during post-conference communication.

5. Following up is crucial to your success. You'll likely use email to do this, and contacting every relevant connection you made at the conference may take a lot of time. But you never know which connection will lead to your next job. Use all of the business cards you collected and create a brief follow-up email (or LinkedIn InMail) to each (which is where the notes you recorded on the back of each card pay dividends).

The idea of walking into a conference filled with strangers can be intimidating. This is completely understandable and you are not alone in that feeling. However, networking is very important to your job search. Follow the steps in this section. Research. Plan your strategy. Bring your business cards and practice your elevator speech. And then meet people. After the first few, initiating conversations will get easier and you won't be able to wait to talk to the next person.

Icebreaker Questions for Conferences and Events

Often the most intimidating part about networking at a conference or event is starting a conversation. It's uncomfortable after an introduction to deal with that awkward moment of silence. The trick to overcoming the awkwardness is to be prepared with a handful of conversation starters—icebreaker questions.

When engaging in a conversation, be present and focus. Use open-ended questions whenever possible starting with "what" and "how." Start all networking conversations

---

136 Weiss, Tara. "Find Your Job by Going to a Conference," *Forbes*, March 24, 2009, http://www.forbes.com/2009/03/24/conference-job-seeking-leadership-careers-networking.html (accessed July 10, 2015).

137 Ibid.

with the idea of creating a "conversation surplus" for the other person. Let them fill the conversation bucket about them. Be a good, interested listener. Only speak of yourself when they ask. Otherwise, keep the focus on them.

More often than not, a networking conversation balances out and ends up being equal in terms of the sharing of information and time spent in conversation.

If the conversation ends with a significant surplus in your fellow attendee's favor, that's fine. Praise yourself for being a good listener. You don't know how that seemingly lopsided conversation might benefit you in the future.

Here are some good icebreaker questions to spur conversation:

- What do you do? (Follow up with a request for their opinion [their "take"] on an industry issue, trend, event, or something else.)

- What motivated you to come to this conference/event?

- What do you think of the lineup of speakers?

- What did you think of the last speaker?

- What are you finding most interesting [or valuable] about this conference?

- Attendance looks good. Do you come every year?

- What's keeping you [or your company] busy these days?

Once the conversation begins and the initial discomfort dissipates, an engaging conversation can start to develop. As a good networker, always offer to help a contact whenever you can with the understanding that they will do what they can to help you. Remember, in networking, those who give . . . get.

Goals of the Networking Conversation

Your primary goal in a networking conversation is to display and utilize professional networking techniques. Yes, you are networking with the purpose of advancing your job search, but you will gain more traction and advance your search further by being patient and strategic.

This is done by actively listening, asking questions, offering insight, and so on. Avoid a making a statement about your situation until the contact asks a question about you. By being present, professional, and engaging in conversation, you have built rapport. Then when you state your situation, there is more likelihood the contact will help you.

Listen carefully and learn—what you discover may help advance your job search (you never know). You could also pass on to others what you discover and possibly help them in a myriad of ways.

As a part of your networking communications, you are looking for three kinds of information (from each networking encounter, if possible):

Advice. This is any kind of insight you can receive about anything related to your job search. The topics here can be wide and varied. As a general theme, most people respond positively to a request for advice. It's a compliment that you are interested in their thoughts and expertise.

Information. This is anything related to the market, including jobs as a whole, trends, companies that are hiring, receiving funding, introducing new products, downsizing, and so on.

Referrals. This is enlisting every contact into your Sales Company, if they would be willing to help, as much as they're able. You want to have your networking contact communicate with you about job opportunities or refer or introduce you to other contacts.

Realize that these networking goals or requests are not asking for a job. They are really requesting help in the form of information that can advance your search.[138]

Face-to-Face Networking as an Introvert

Networking can be more challenging if you are introverted. Meeting new people face-to-face just does not come as easy to you as it does to others. Fortunately, there are some practical strategies you can use to defuse much of the anxiety of networking. They are:

- **Remind yourself of the value networking brings to your job search.** Sixty to eighty percent of all jobs are a result of some form of networking.[139] Psyche yourself up the best you can.

- **Go to smaller events.** Avoid conferences or association events that are attended by

---

138 See also, Phillips, *Guide to Professional Networking*, p. 50–51; Pete Leibman, "9 Keys on How to Email a New Networking Contact During a Job Search (written by Career Expert, Pete Leibman)," *CareerMuscles* (blog), January 6, 2011, https://careermuscles.wordpress.com/2011/01/06/9-keys-on-how-to-email-a-new-networking-contact-during-a-job-search-written-by-career-expert-pete-leibman/ (accessed November 10, 2015).

139 LinkedIn, "Using LinkedIn to Find a Job"; Beatty, "The Math Behind the Networking Claim"; Rothberg, "80% of Job Openings."

the thousands; look for opportunities where the attendees are more in the hundreds instead.[140]

- **Focus on groups where you have a common interest or common purpose.** For example, if you're a nurse in workers' compensation, look for a group that comprises nurse case managers. Conversation will be easier because you have knowledge of and interest in the topics of conversation. These types of functions often have educational sessions, which give you a reason for being there if you feel the need to state one.

- **Before attending a function, create a list of three or four icebreaker questions.** Use the previous section on icebreaker questions as a guide. Preparation is key. At an event with unfamiliar people, you may become distracted by your surroundings and forget a few things—having your list of questions will make conversations with other attendees easier.

- **Know how to close a conversation.** When the conversation has run its course and the silence begins to feel awkward, have a closing line that will politely allow you to move on. For example, "It has been a pleasure speaking with you. I'm sure you have others to meet as do I. Do you have a card?"

When properly done, networking will open doors to opportunities. To be a successful networker, give far more than you ever expect to receive. Over time, you will discover that you have received more than you gave.

For a more in-depth discussion on networking during a job search, check out *The Motivated Networker* which has been endorsed by Dr. Ivan Misner, Founder of BNI (Business Network International) - the world's largest business networking organization. Dr. Misner has been dubbed "The Father of Modern Networking" and is one of the world's leading experts in business networking:

"The Motivated Networker is the most comprehensive networking book on the market on how to use networking to find a job. Well-written, thoroughly researched, and practical, The Motivated Networker covers important networking topics and introduces the "ICE" Method for job-search networking. It is a must-read for all job seekers!"

---

140 Townsend, Maya. "The Introvert's Survival Guide to Networking," *Inc.com*, http://www.inc.com/maya-townsend/introvert-networking-guide.html (accessed November 4, 2015).

Chapter 8

Social Media: Twitter and Facebook

There is in this world no such force as the force of a man determined to rise.
— W. E. B. DuBois[141]

Please Note: Twitter and Facebook change their format, features, appearance, and functionality regularly. These changes can enhance the experience but may also restrict the usefulness. This topic on Twitter and Facebook is current at the time of writing.

Social media has quickly become part of the arsenal of tools used by job seekers when conducting a job search. It has been reported that 14.4 million job seekers have used social media to search for a job.[142] The percentage of job seekers using social media continues to increase year after year.[143] This is likely due to its increasing effectiveness and its use by younger generations who have grown up with the technology.

---

141 Pine, Joslyn. Ed., *Book of African-American Quotations*. (New York: Dover Publications, 2011), p. 51.

142 The Muse, "Job Seekers: Social Media is Even More Important Than You Thought" by Brooke Torres https://www.themuse.com/advice/job-seekers-social-media-is-even-more-important-than-you-thought

143 PRC, "Searching for Work in the Digital Era" http://www.pewinternet.org/files/2015/11/PI_2015-11-19-Internet-and-Job-Seeking_FINAL.pdf

We have already discussed LinkedIn. It is the most prevalent online professional networking site. We will now explore using Twitter and Facebook.

Twitter

Recruiters use Twitter for talent acquisition.[144] Getting dialed into Twitter can be another tool you can use in your job search and to be found by recruiters.

One unique feature about Twitter that enhances its job-search value is that you can follow just about anyone you wish, including companies, target contacts, thought leaders, HR personnel, and corporate recruiters, without requesting permission (unlike LinkedIn and Facebook). This openness can be a profound resource for information, identifying job leads, job opportunities, and communicating with those that can help you and hire you.

If you are new to Twitter, here are some pointers to get you started:

Create Your Twitter Account. Go to www.twitter.com and click on sign up. You will enter your name, email address, and a password; then go on to click sign up. You will be taken step-by-step to set up your account.

Create Your Twitter Username (Handle). This is nothing more than a name that appears as you tweet (a term for a posting made on the Twitter website). You're permitted fifteen characters for a username or handle.[145] You can use your own name, nickname, or any other descriptive name—so long as it is professional.

Set up Your Twitter Profile.[146] Your profile bio is limited to 160 characters including spaces, so you must be succinct with your description. Review your elevator speech, branding message, and network/resume business cards. Then, formulate your bio. Explore other Twitter profiles for ideas if needed.

Add a photo, likely the same one that appears on your LinkedIn profile. Since your Twitter profile is short, add a link to other sites, most notably LinkedIn.

Here are a couple of partial example profiles to get you thinking:

144 2016 Recruiter Nation Report fka Social Recruiting Survey http://www.jobvite.com/wp-content/uploads/2016/09/RecruiterNation2016.pdf

145 "Character Limit and Changing your username" https://support.twitter.com/articles/14609 Twitter Help Center, (accessed March 14, 2017).

146 "Setting up and Customizing Your Profile" https://support.twitter.com/articles/127871 Twitter Help Center, (accessed March 14, 2017).

Award-winning care management sales professional . . .

Seasoned operational management executive . . .

Once you have an account, establish a handle, and write a profile, you are ready to go. Now that you're set up, here are some steps to use Twitter in your job search:

Create a second account if necessary, then follow target companies and people. For job seekers with established personal Twitter accounts, it's recommended to create a second one solely for your job search. Identify and begin following target companies of interest to you. This can give you an edge over other job seekers, and serve as a great source of information to further your search, since most major or established organizations have a corporate Twitter account. A growing trend among employers is using Twitter to announce open positions.[147] Following industry thought leaders, hiring executives, human resource professionals, recruiters, and so on can help as well.

Use hashtags well. Twitter uses hashtags (the # symbol) as an index or filing system of sorts. It's a way to search Twitter for topics or specific information. You can use this indexing system to look for job leads. Below is a short list of hashtags that can lead you to possible job openings:

#jobs

#jobsearch

#employment

#resume

#careers

#nowhiring

Think creatively with the use of hashtags and you may discover hidden openings.

You can use the hashtag indexing system to narrow your search by location or function. For example:

"#Dallas" + "#jobs"—jobs in Dallas

"#jobs" + "#sales"—jobs in sales

"#jobs" + "#accounting" + "#omaha"—accounting jobs in Omaha

---

147 Undercover Recruiter, "List of 140 Employers Posting Jobs on Twitter" by Jorgen Sundberg, http://theundercoverrecruiter.com/list-employers-posting-jobs-twitter/ (accessed March 16, 2017).

Create content. When you write a tweet, Twitter limits you to 140 characters, including spaces and a link. You must be brief and to the point with your messages.

You can tweet and retweet (forwarding someone else's posted message) as much as you like, just don't overdo it. The key is to create interesting and relevant content. This can be tricky, so abbreviating words in your tweets is acceptable and necessary. Share news, links, and professional insight. Respond to other people's tweets and answer questions. The most important thing is to think before you post. As a professional job seeker, your tweets reflect directly on you. Others form an opinion and an impression of you based on what you post and how you express it. Using Twitter can be a helpful tool in your job search by providing you a platform to demonstrate industry knowledge. Just be cautious not to be too self-promoting.

Overall, Twitter's use and acceptance can be industry specific. In other words, some industries may use it more than others. Regardless, Twitter is gaining wider acceptance by employers every year. Twitter is a job-search tool that should be seriously considered and used as part of your strategy. Its impact will rely on your use and your industry's acceptance and use of it.

Facebook

When it comes to Facebook, the lines between social and professional networking have blurred. Facebook has historically been viewed as a purely social networking venue for kids. That has changed. As younger professionals enter the job market and advance their careers, many have repurposed Facebook into a professional networking tool, with a personal touch. In fact, many job seekers view Facebook as a job-search tool that showcases the whole person, not just the professional.

Companies have caught on. Most larger, established, and forward-thinking companies now have a corporate Facebook presence. They use Facebook to attract job seekers and to check the character of job applicants.[148]

As a job-search tool, Facebook is similar to LinkedIn. You will discover similarities as we discuss Facebook. Some of these points will be shorter, because concepts have already been more thoroughly covered in the LinkedIn section. Similarities include:

---

148 CareerBuilder, "Number of Employers Using Social Media to Screen Candidates Has Increased 500 Percent over the Last Decade," news release, April 28, 2016, http://www.careerbuilder.com/share/aboutus/pressreleasesdetail.aspx?ed=12%2F31%2F2016&id=pr945&sd=4%2F28%2F2016 (accessed March 16, 2017).

Profile. Like LinkedIn and Twitter, you need to create a professional Facebook page.[149] From the top navigation bar click the expansion arrow next to the question mark icon. You can then click "Create Page." Choose from the list of categories that Facebook provides. From those categories, there are subcategories to choose from. Be sure to align all of your profiles, Facebook, Twitter, and LinkedIn.

If you prefer to utilize your personal Facebook account and you have been using it socially with your friends, it's time to get out the mop and bucket and clean it up. Remove all unprofessional posts and photos. From this point forward, all posts and photos must be acceptable to the professional viewing audience (hiring executives, corporate HR professionals, executive recruiters, and so on).

Similar to LinkedIn, use keywords and industry terms-of-art to enhance your "findability." Consider linking to or mentioning your LinkedIn profile. Make sure it is consistent with employment, dates, and so on.

Classify your friends. From your Home page, go to the left side of the page to "Explore" and click on "Friend Lists." From there you can create a "New List." Create a list of your professional friends/contacts. The benefit of this is that you can post information directed only to your professional contacts. As you add professional friends, classify them to this list. Depending upon the number of friends you have, it could take you a while to do this, but it is worth it. Be sure that any professional contacts you add are relevant to you.

"Like" and follow target company pages and search firms. By doing this, you will receive information about job openings, announcements, and news releases on your home page and your notifications list.

Searching on Facebook. You can use the search function within Facebook on a wide variety of topics (likes, interests, groups, and so on). Type your search term into the search bar at the top of your Facebook page and click enter. More than one search term can be entered into the search bar.

> *Omaha Nebraska Medical Executive*
>
> *St. Luke's Hospital President*

Once your search results load, you can then refine your search by People, Groups, Pages, and more.

---

149 Facebook "Pages" https://www.facebook.com/help/282489752085908/?helpref=hc_fnav.

Post relevant content. Publish useful information and pass along good content as it should come your way. Remember to think and be smart with what you post.

Privacy Options.[150] Facebook has many privacy options such as managing who can view your full profile, pages, friends lists, photos, etc. It is recommended to review and set your privacy options appropriately for a job search.

Some final words on Facebook. Traditionally viewed as a purely social site, Facebook is now clearly a significant resource tool for a job search. Will Facebook ever surpass LinkedIn as a professional networking site? Who's to say? It's certain Facebook is another tool that today's job seeker can use to advance and shorten a job search.

A Caution about Online Networking

Online networking is a powerful job-search strategy and tool. Properly used, it can and will advance your job search. It can also be a tremendous time-waster. It is easy to get caught up clicking away and connecting with others that have only a remote chance of advancing your job search, but "you never know." Or, you can end up having delightful online communications that make you feel good—which are okay—but really do not serve any job-search purpose, but "you never know," right? Wrong.

Be careful. Before you know it, two hours of your precious time can be gone and your search hasn't budged one inch. The advice here is simple: be aware of the purpose of what you are doing and the amount of time you are spending on online professional and social media sites. If you catch yourself asking whether your activities on online networking sites are advancing your job search, you've likely crossed the line into busywork disguised as a job search.

What Employers Discover and Look for on Social Media

As discussed, it is undeniable that social media will play a role in your job search. The significance of that role depends largely on how much you use social media. But employers also use it.

To help you better understand the role of social media in your job search, CareerBuilder. com conducts a yearly survey that asks hiring managers and human resource professionals if, how, and why they incorporate social media into their hiring process.

150 "Basic Privacy Settings & Tools" https://www.facebook.com/help/325807937506242/?ref=contextual Facebook Help Center (accessed March 17, 2017).

The results from the 2016 survey found that out of the 2,186 hiring managers and human resource professionals, 60 percent of employers use social networks to screen potential job candidates (this trend continues to grow).[151] That means more and more companies browse your social media profiles to evaluate your character and personality. What they find about you will influence their hiring decision.

In the CareerBuilder survey, employers that chose not to pursue a job applicant after researching social media sites indicated the following reasons:

- Job seeker posted inappropriate pictures, videos, or information—46 percent

- Found evidence of job seeker's use of alcohol or drugs—43 percent

- Job seeker made negative remarks about previous employer or fellow employee—31 percent

- Discriminatory comments made about race, gender, religion, etc.—33 percent.[152]

- Poor communication skills—29 percent

However, over 32 percent of hiring executives discovered information that improved a job seeker's candidacy, including:

- Job seeker's background matched qualifications of position—44 percent

- Got a good feel for candidate's personality—43 percent

- Professionalism—44 percent

- Creativity—40 percent

- Communication—36 percent[153]

According to CareerBuilder, the research clearly indicates that employers utilize social media to gain additional insight into job seekers' behavior and personality outside the interview. They use all tools available to help ensure a good hire. Which means you should make certain your social media profiles are as effective in your job search as they can be.

---

151 McDonnell, Amy "60% of employers are peeking into candidates' social media profiles" April 28, 2016 http://www.careerbuilder.com/advice/60-of-employers-are-peeking-into-candidates-social-media-profiles

152 Ibid 8.

153 Ibid.

Chapter 9

Working with Search Firms

*Just begin and the mind grows heated; continue, and the task
will be completed!*
— Goethe[154]

According to surveys conducted by the American Staffing Association, over 90 percent of employers have or would use an executive recruiter to fill open positions.[155] This section will cover how to find recruiters that fit your industry or position and how to work with them effectively to enhance your job search.

What Recruiters Can and Cannot Do for You

Recruiters can be a terrific resource during a job search. They should not be your leading

154 "Johann Wolfgang von Goethe Quotable Quote," Goodreads, http://www.goodreads.com/quotes /316359-just-begin-and-the-mind-grows-heated-continue-and-the (accessed June 11, 2015).

155 DISYS, "Top 5 Reasons to Use Staffing Firms as Your Primary Hiring Strategy," http://www.disys.com/ top-5-reasons-to-use-staffing-firms-as-your-primary-hiring-strategy/ (accessed June 19, 2015); "Get Help With Hiring . . . And More: Working With Staffing Firms: What's in It for Me?" CareerBuilder, http://www. careerbuildercommunications.com/staffing-firms/ (accessed June 19, 2015).

source for landing your next job, simply because they are hired and paid by employers to find well-qualified candidates, not find jobs for job seekers.[156] That being said, the search and placement business is a billion dollar industry,[157] and job seekers get identified and placed by recruiters every day. The trick is to be found, and have the right qualifications, at the right time. Here is a non-exhaustive list of the benefits of aligning yourself with a recruiter:

1. They can introduce you to job opportunities with their clients.

2. They often have insight on opportunities with their clients before they are made public.

3. They can help you determine your market value.

4. They can frequently provide you with much more information about the position, company, and culture than what you can discover on your own.

5. They can prepare you for interviews and inform you about hot buttons to hit upon and landmines to avoid.

6. They can give advice on how to manage the interviewing process, often because they are a consultant on position types and timing of communications with the employer.

7. They can provide insight and advice during offer negotiations.

8. They can counsel you through the resignation process (should that apply to you).

There are also things that a recruiter cannot or will not do for you:

1. Hold your hand and become your nursemaid during your job search.

2. Get you a job. Remember, recruiters are hired to find qualified candidates for their clients (employers), not find you a job.

3. Unless you become a viable candidate in an active search with the recruiter, they will not spend an inordinate amount of time with you discussing your resume, the job market, interviewing strategies, and other free advice.

---

156 "Don't Do That!—Mistakes To Avoid When Working With Recruiters," *True Source* (blog), November 2012, http://www.true-source.com/2012/11/dont-do-that-mistakes-to-avoid-when-working-with-recruiters/ (accessed June 9, 2015).

157 "Employment and Recruiting Agencies in the US: Market Research Report," IBISWorld, March 2015, http://www.ibisworld.com/industry/default.aspx?indid=1463 (accessed June 11, 2015).

The key to working with recruiters is knowing what to expect and controlling your own expectations. Recruiters can be a valued resource but the responsibility of your search lies in your own efforts.

Retainer and Contingency Search Firms

Before we discuss how to target and contact recruiters, it's beneficial to have a basic understanding of the two types of search firms you're likely to encounter as a professional-level job seeker: retainer and contingency. We'll briefly describe the differences and then move on to how to engage and work with them.

If a firm works on a retainer basis, they are generally paid an up-front fee to begin search activities. Then, at certain predetermined times along the search time line, the firm is paid another installment. Final payment is usually made upon completion of the search assignment. Fully retained searches are generally used for senior executive and C-level positions with larger organizations.

A contingency firm is paid differently. As the name implies, their fee is contingent and earned only when a referred candidate is hired by a client. It is strictly pay-for-performance.

It used to be said that contingency firms are paid for performance while retainer firms are paid for process, regardless of whether the position gets filled. In large measure, it is this "paying for performance rather than process" that has led to the continued growth of the recruiting industry's contingency side. In fact, many retainer firms now conduct contingency searches to compete for the revenue flow of clients that prefer a contingency arrangement. Contingency firms also conduct retainer searches, and function in similar ways with the same resources, blurring the distinction between the two types.

What this means for you, as a job seeker, is that it doesn't matter how the firm is paid. What does matter is whether the firm can match you to an open position with one of its clients.

How to Find Recruiters

Identifying and contacting recruiters is not as difficult as you might think. Below are three effective methods. It's recommend that you use all three.

1. Calling hiring executives in your industry

2. Calling colleagues in your industry

3. Researching recruiters online (notably LinkedIn)

Let's discuss these approaches in detail.

★ Call Hiring Executives

One of the best methods for identifying recruiters is to reach out to hiring executives and ask for referrals. Think about it: who better at identifying and referring you to potential recruiters than the executives that hire them, right?

This method has three major advantages. First, it is an easy call to make. You are asking for help, and most people will help you if they can. Asking hiring executives for referrals is a safe and reasonable topic for your call.

Second, this method will lead you to the industry's top recruiters. Connecting with them will expand your reach for potential opportunities.

Finally, and most importantly, you will be speaking with hiring executives that could have an opportunity, such as described in the Hidden Job Market, or know of one in the industry. Hint: it's extremely helpful here to be ready with your elevator speech.

How do you go about calling these hiring executives? Here are the steps:

• Identify companies that interest you.

• Research and determine who the likely hiring executive is for the position you would be interested in.

• Pick up the phone and make a call. Engage the hiring executive in a conversation, explain your situation, and as part of the conversation, ask whether he/she could identify and pass along to you the names of a few recruiters. (A script for this call is to follow.)

This technique is effective because you *call* the hiring executive. The ultimate goal is to speak to the executive and have a voice-to-voice conversation. Avoid using email for this approach. It dilutes the effectiveness.

Because this technique is such a powerful way to network with hiring executives, here is a script you can modify:

Introduction:
"(First name of the hiring executive or Mr./Ms.), this is (state your name). I'm a clinical nurse manager with thirteen years' experience in the population health management industry. I am looking to make a career move and I would like your advice and assistance regarding my search."

Confirm you have the right contact:

"If I have it right, you are the hiring executive (or use the executive's title) for case and nurse managers. Here's what I'm looking for . . . I would like the names of recruiters that specialize in (title of your position) that I can contact. I am hoping you could refer me to a few recruiters that you like."

Assume the hiring executive will help:

"Do you know of any recruiters that you feel good about? Maybe some good ones you've used in the past?"

Show appreciation and (maybe) ask one question:

"Thank you. Let me ask you since I have you on the phone: What do you think the effects will be of the new health care legislation on the population health management industry?"

If you're unemployed, close and offer to send your resume:

"Again, thank you. I appreciate your help. If it's okay, I'm going to email my resume to you just so you have it. Feel free to forward it to others as you deem appropriate."

For anyone that helps you, send a thank-you email (and as appropriate, include your resume). Depending upon the conversation, it could be appropriate to send a LinkedIn invitation.

There are a couple of reasons why calling hiring executives for referrals to recruiters is a powerful technique. First and foremost, it gets you talking with hiring executives that could lead to a job opening with that company. Second, hiring executives are the people who typically approve the payment of recruiting fees. Therefore, when you call a recruiter later saying you were referred by one of their paying clients, that will help get their attention, and they should take or quickly return your call. The recruiter will not want say that they did not speak with you if the hiring executive asks later.

When properly executed, this approach will get you several names of recruiters that likely specialize in your industry or position type. When you start to hear the same names of those held in high regard, you've likely discovered your industry's best recruiters—and, in the process, possibly some to avoid.

Most importantly, you have connected with hiring executives in the industry. Those contacts can pay big dividends in your career in the short- or long-term.

Call Your Colleagues in the Industry

The advantages of contacting your own industry colleagues are many. You can have open and frank discussions regarding recruiters. You will be able to create a list of several recruiters that call your colleagues. You might learn about a few recruiters that you may elect not to contact. And, networking with colleagues may result in job leads.

These calls are easy to make. The hazard is you can easily get tied up in long conversations that eat up your time and distract you from your real goal of getting a new job.

Researching LinkedIn and the Internet

Search LinkedIn for recruiters. By using the keyword feature you may limit your search to recruiters with a specialty that matches your background, experience, or interests.

Another fast way to obtain names of your industry's recruiters is to search the Internet. There are online services that maintain nationwide databases of recruiters. One website where you can describe a recruiter by industry and location, and find one to match your profile, is www.mrinetwork.com.

For local searches, the local business journals frequently include names of search firms in their Book of Lists. The firms are frequently listed by the number of recruiters and list the specialties of each firm.

Contacting a Recruiter

If your first contact with a recruiter is by email, keep it short and informative. Identify your role or function (title) and highlight a couple of accomplishments. Do not send a lengthy email. Recruiters are time sensitive and the mere appearance of a long email will discourage them from reading it. Attach a copy of your resume. Ask for a call, but follow up with the recruiter in a couple of days if you have not heard back.

If your first contact with a recruiter is a proactive call, start your conversation by getting their attention. Begin with an attention-getting statement. The most persuasive approach is to name the person that referred you, if you have one. Another way would be to mention an accomplishment: "Bob, my name is Linda, and I am an award-winning marketing professional with seventeen years of experience in the plastics industry. I am exploring a career move and I would like discuss how we might be able to work together."

Stay in routine contact with the recruiters you feel can help you. This can be done with a call or email. Most all recruiters will permit this kind of routine communication. The key here is to keep your name in front of the recruiter without becoming a pest. Turning off a recruiter is closing a door to a potential opportunity. It's a fine line that really depends on the level of position you are seeking. Contacting a recruiter once every three or four weeks is adequate.

Finding a Recruiter That Can Help You

When talking with recruiters, ask questions. Here are some questions to help determine whether the recruiter is a good match for you, now or in the future:

- In what industry do you do most of your work?
- What types of positions do you fill?
- Based on my background, am I a viable candidate for you?
- Can I send you a LinkedIn invitation? (If you fit within the recruiter's specialty)

When there is not a match with the recruiter's specialty

If the recruiter tells you they can't be of assistance, ask for the names of any other recruiters they may know who can help you. If they don't know of anyone, do not be disappointed. They may not have contacts that specialize in your area of interest. You could also ask the recruiter for general assistance, but be sensitive to the recruiter's time. Here are a couple of questions you could ask:

- What is your opinion of the job market?
- If you were in my shoes, what would you be doing to advance your job search?

When there's a match between your background and the recruiter's specialty

If there is a match between your background and the recruiter's specialty, provide and volunteer any information requested by the recruiter, especially a resume if you have not already provided one. Get connected to the recruiter on LinkedIn.

Even if there is a match, understand that most of the time, they will not be able to help you immediately. This is simply a function of timing. They may not have an active assignment that fits your background, geographic location, or other factors. Just because they cannot place you today does not mean that they cannot place you in the future.

Recruiters can be a rich resource for your job search and the industry you work in. To foster a good relationship with recruiters, it is good etiquette to offer your network of connections that may help them in any way. Developing this kind of relationship with a recruiter is priceless. Recruiters have long memories. Helping a recruiter can benefit your career greatly in both the short and long term.

Some Final Advice Regarding Recruiters

Remember that recruiters work for the employer, not you. They will call you if and when they have a potential opportunity that fits your qualifications.

- Connect with recruiters who specialize in your industry or position type—preferably both.

- Stay in touch with recruiters, but don't become a pest.

- Always return a recruiter's call promptly. Evaluation begins with your responsiveness—and recruiters almost always have a reason for calling.

- Always give referrals. Ask if you can help the recruiter. Even if you're not interested in a particular opportunity, try to help the recruiter find someone who might be qualified.

- Never decline an InMail message from a recruiter on LinkedIn. Some recruiters have a professional policy of never again contacting job seekers if they decline a message. It's better to respond and say you're not interested than to decline.

- If you are contacted by a recruiter, never ask the recruiter to identify the client by name or prematurely ask about compensation unless that information is volunteered by the recruiter.

- Never lie about anything in your professional background, go around a recruiter to contact an employer about an opportunity without permission, or use a recruiter to elicit a counteroffer from your current employer.

Targeting the right recruiters and connecting with them can be an effective channel to job opportunities and job-search advice. Simply be professional and responsive at all times.

Chapter 10

★ Proactively Marketing Your Professional Credentials

Far better it is to dare mighty things, to win glorious triumphs, even though checkered by failure, than to take rank with those poor spirits who neither enjoy nor suffer much, because they live in the gray twilight that knows neither victory nor defeat.

— Theodore Roosevelt[158]

Networking will generate job-search activity. However, there is another technique that you should also use to maximize your exposure to the job market—Proactively marketing your professional credentials. When networking and proactive marketing are used together, you will be utilizing the two most effective job-search techniques available. Earnest and properly executed use of both approaches will significantly shorten your job search.

Proactively marketing your professional credentials will differentiate you from the majority of other job seekers, but it requires initiative and perseverance.

We are about to discuss two techniques for proactively marketing your professional credentials. These techniques will create activity in your job search in the form of

---

158 Theodore Roosevelt, "The Strenuous Life," (speech, The Hamilton Club, Chicago, IL, April 10, 1899), http://www.bartleby.com/58/1.html (accessed May 28, 2015).

conversations, networking, referrals, leads, and interviews by diving straight into the heart of the Hidden Job Market.

The first is a cold call. It involves calling a prospective hiring executive and presenting yourself as a well-qualified job seeker. You will then, as needed, make follow-up communications through additional calls or email correspondence. This approach requires courage, perseverance, and the emotional strength to accept some verbal rejection. However, it is arguably one of the quickest ways to get interviews in the Hidden Job Market. Why? Because you are presenting yourself as a solution to a hiring need before an opening is advertised.

For some, the idea of making cold calls as a part of a job search feels uncomfortable, too pushy, or too aggressive. The technique is not for everyone. There is an alternative.

The second technique can be equally effective and initially easier to execute. It requires that you create and send an impactful email to a hiring executive, followed by telephone calls and additional emails. The follow-up calls are more of a warm call since you have reached out to the hiring executive after email correspondence. It can take some of the edge off of making a call to someone you do not know.

Regardless of which approach you take, it is absolutely necessary that you pick up the phone and call executives who could potentially be hiring. At the outset, make sure your voice mail message at home is appropriate and your cell phone greeting is professional.

To take full advantage of these techniques and tap into the Hidden Job Market requires that you identify employers of interest, identify the hiring executive, and communicate a compelling message about your abilities and how you can benefit the employer's organization.

Here are the steps to creating and executing an effective proactive marketing plan:

• Identify your target companies.

• Determine the hiring executive's identity.

• Research the hiring executive's telephone number and email address.

• Write a compelling call script and email cover letter about your credentials.

• Execute. This is either starting with a call or email.

The Work

Proactive marketing takes effort, but it is one of the most effective ways to uncover opportunities that may not even exist *except* in the mind of the hiring executive or in confidential conversations among senior managers or even board members.

Your proactive efforts could represent the most labor-intensive commitment of time you invest in your search. It may take three to five days of solid research time for you to identify target companies, the right (or probable) hiring executive, and his or her current email address and phone number. It is recommended that you make the commitment of time to do this work early in your job search (and do it early in your day).

The proactive method requires a shift in your thinking. You are now looking for a company you want to work for, instead of a job . . . so to speak.[159] As you discover and learn about interesting companies, put additional marketing effort toward these companies, perhaps via a drip email and call strategy (discussed later).

As you identify those high-interest companies, follow them on social media (LinkedIn, Twitter, and so on) as well as more traditional news sources (press releases, Google alerts, and more). Connect with relevant employees and executives on LinkedIn. Consider asking for a research interview(s), which is another technique mentioned later. The more you can learn, the more you network, and the more you make them aware of your professional credentials, the greater your chances of getting an interview. Review Getting Off to a Successful Start in Chapter 1 to ensure you're organizing your research properly.

Get (and Stay) Organized

Keep the information collected as a result of your research organized on an Excel spreadsheet using this or a similar format:

Company Name / Industry / Contact Name / Title / Email address / Phone Number / Notes
The notes column will help you keep track of dates of contact, what you have sent, and more.

You can also visit JibberJobber (www.jibberjobber.com) and Career*Shift* (www.careershift.com). These are services designed to help keep job seekers organized during their job search.

Determine Your Target Employers

There are a variety of methods and sources to identify target employers. They include:

1. Competitors of your current employer

---

159 Whitcomb, *Job Search Magic*, p. 273–274.

2. Companies where your LinkedIn contacts work

3. Companies you can identify by reviewing profiles on a LinkedIn group

4. Association membership lists

5. Industry conference attendee, exhibitor, and vendor lists

6. Clients, suppliers, and distributors of your current or past employers

7. Books of Lists with major employers by industry type (most metropolitan areas have them)

8. Purchased lists (services that sell databases of companies and contacts) including:
   - infousa.com
   - hoovers.com
   - standardandpoors.com
   - jigsaw.com
   - listgiant.com
   - goleads.com
   - vault.com

Start with your short list of targeted companies. Then, collect information on one hundred more companies. It may sound like a lot, but it might be the only one hundred companies (plus your short list) you'll need to research to get an offer (or two). If you exhaust the original group of companies, research more.

Identify the Hiring Executive

This is a process of research. You are looking for the executive that has the authority to hire you—not HR. This executive can be identified in several ways:
   - Company website
   - LinkedIn
   - Phone call to the company

If you are in doubt, contacting two or three executives in the company is fine. Always contact the most senior executives—those that are one to two levels above your current position.

Research the Hiring Executive's Email Address

This can be tricky, but the best way is to review the company website. Go to the contact page and look for an email address. If there is not one, go to the news and events page. Normally a press release for the company will have the marketing employee's email address. That can give you the formula that companies use for their email addresses. If you cannot find an email anywhere on the website, just use the website address and put an @ symbol before it.

Another way is to look up employees of the company on LinkedIn. Sometimes employees provide their company email address, which will give you the email formula you need.

As an alternative, use different forms of the hiring executive's name and then the company web address or the email address you have found on the website in the Google search. For instance, most companies use the formula firstinitiallastname@xyz.com. Google that and see if you have any results. If not, try different formulas: firstname.lastname@xyz.com. You can usually find email addresses this way because people sometimes use work emails for personal use.

Below are some different formulas you can use to search for email addresses:

jsmith@xyz.com

john.smith@xyz.com

smithj@xyz.coms

john@xyz.com

johns@xyz.com

johnsmith@xyz.com

There is a useful website (service) that can be helpful in finding email addresses. Check into www.hunter.io.

Using the Telephone

Some professionals and executives hesitate to proactively market themselves and their credentials using the telephone. In today's job market, it is imperative to utilize every resource and technique available to shorten your job search. The telephone must be part of your job-search arsenal.

To help ease the physical use of the telephone, consider investing in a hands-free headset or use a Bluetooth device on your cell phone. This will free up your hands so you can write and you won't have to hold the phone to your ear with your shoulder. Being hands-free will have a positive effect on your tone of voice and keep you more relaxed when making calls.

The Positive Impact of Using the Phone

There are several good reasons why you need to make calls to hiring executives as a part of your job search. Almost every point under "The Advantages of a Self-Motivated Job Search" can be achieved by using the phone during your search. Using the phone also helps you:

1. **Differentiate yourself.** Calling a hiring executive to discuss your background and possible opportunities sets you apart from other job seekers. Employers value initiative.

2. **Create a positive mental impression.** When you are on the phone, the only variables that count are: your background, qualifications, enthusiasm, and positive phone voice.

3. **More quickly establish a relationship.** Your call personalizes the engagement and communication. It is said that 60 percent of most hires are made based on personal chemistry, according to a study by the University of Michigan on hiring managers.[160] A conversation helps build that chemistry (using the persuasion principle of liking), which can lead to an interview.

4. **Create urgency.** By calling an employer, you create the perception that you will not be on the market long. The hiring executive will see that you are proactive in your job search and are researching future opportunities thoroughly. All of this helps you create value (using the persuasion principle of scarcity).

5. **Gather information to be more prepared for possible interviews.** An initial phone conversation with the hiring executive may help you learn what issues are important to that company or executive. You can then prepare answers to possible interview questions based on that information.

---

160 DiResta, interview by Canters, "How to Blitz."

Excuses for Not Using the Phone in a Job Search

(If you have no inhibition in using the telephone to call hiring executives as a part of your job search, you can bypass this topic.)

Over the course of time, every excuse imaginable has been raised as to why individuals will not use the phone. These excuses basically encompass the following:

1. "It's beneath me."

Check your ego at the door and think of these calls as nothing more than networking calls with a purpose (and a script). Accept the fact that virtually everyone (including those you will call) has faced unemployment or a career transition at some point. It was as uncomfortable for them as it is for you now. They understand what you are doing and going through. Most will help if they can. Using the telephone to connect and network is not beneath you, but rather shows what you're made of.

2. "I have better uses for my time than leaving a bunch of voice messages."

Actually, you don't. Leaving voice messages and playing a little phone tag is all part of the process. You must show persistence. You may have to call someone several times before speaking to them. A hiring executive takes note of persistence—as long as you don't cross the line and become an annoyance. As a general guideline, make three attempts. If you do not get a response, it's safe to move on.

If you keep missing an employer that has called back, ask to schedule an appointment that is convenient for both of you. Ask if the hiring executive's administrative assistant can contact you to set up the appointment.

3. "I have sent so many emails and resumes, and networked extensively. They'll be calling me!"

Conducting a job search is about using every avenue available to you to advance your search. This means taking the initiative to reach out to hiring executives. Failing to do so simply prolongs your job search.

4. "My resume, background, and qualifications are strong. Once the word really gets out, they'll call me!"

Maybe, maybe not. Even when a hiring executive takes the time to read your cover letter or email and looks at your resume, it is easy to get sidetracked or distracted. The executive has business priorities to attend to. You need to do something to bring your value back to the forefront. One simple phone call will make a remarkable difference.

5. "They could hang up on me!"

This excuse is ridiculous and so what if they do? Regardless, it is so rare that it is almost not worth mentioning. When was the last time you hung up on an industry colleague asking for help? You would not do that and neither will they. You are asking people for their assistance. They will not hang up on you.

6. "I don't want to be rejected."

This excuse, for some, can significantly slow a job search because at the root of the excuse is fear. Fear, whether real or perceived, is a formidable emotion. If this is an obstacle for you, call upon your courage to overcome it. Read the virtues to practice during a job search at the beginning of this book.

No one wants to be rejected. Although you will encounter the word "no" or a statement such as "I don't think I can help you" or any number of responses that will not advance your job search, don't get discouraged. Rejection is an inescapable part of the process. But bear in mind: rejection is not personal, it's business. They are not rejecting you as a person. And every no gets you one step closer to a yes.

Here is the reality: you will either use the phone in your job search or you won't. But if you do, you will reap significant rewards that will positively affect your search and your career.

If you choose not to use the phone, the following things will likely happen (and you probably already know what they are):

1. Your job search will take longer.

2. You risk settling for any job (just to be employed).

3. You risk slipping into a passive job search relying on posted job openings. (And by now you know, that is not an effective strategy.)

Phone Zone

Find a quiet place free of distractions where you can focus and concentrate on the task at hand. It can be your home office or den where the risk of interruptions and background noise (including kids and pets) is minimized. Prior to making calls, remove all unnecessary paperwork and nonessential items from your work surface or desktop. The only things you need are:

- Your call list
- Your script for leaving a voice message
- Your presentation of what you will say when you speak to the hiring executive
- A script for answering common responses or objections
- A copy of your resume
- Success stories
- Pen, paper, maybe something to drink
- Your enthusiasm

Phone *Phear:* The Pre-Game Jitters

It is perfectly normal to have some anxiety about calling hiring executives. For some of us, it happens. Your entire job search won't collapse because you have a case of the nerves. In fact, a healthy dose of nerves is an indication of an outstanding performance to come. Below are some tips to turn nervousness into focused effort:

1. Script and practice the delivery of your message. Know what you are going to say (more on that in a moment).

2. Concentrate on delivering your message/script with confidence. You are on the phone. They cannot see you.

3. Remember that you know everything about the subject at hand: you. In other words, there won't be a question you can't answer.[161]

4. Adopt the attitude that every hiring executive you will call has a possible opening. Never assume that it is a bother that you called or that the answer will be no.

Here is a suggestion that helps most job seekers: when it comes time to start making calls, generate five calls in succession, without breaks, as efficiently and effectively as you can. Remarkably, once you break the ice and create a rhythm, the reluctance fades. Progress is being made. As you get the feel for it, you will be surprised how many quality calls you can make.

---

161 See also, Claycomb and Dinse, *Career Pathways*, Part 5, "Phone-phobia."

The Marketing Call Script

The following is a sample script to use when speaking to a hiring executive.

Introduction:

The introduction identifies who you are. If you can, reference a mutual business colleague or business association. That common ground often helps break the ice.

> *"Mr. Tyrrell, my name is Gene Watson. I was referred to you by Bob Johnson."*

> *"Mr. Tyrrell, my name is Gene Watson and I am a care management sales professional. I don't believe we've spoken before, however, we both belong to the (care management association)."*

If you do not have a common reference point:

> *"Mr. Tyrrell, my name is Gene Watson and I am a care management sales professional and I am currently (or formerly) with (Company Name)."*

Ask permission to continue the call:

Hiring executives are busy, and they will appreciate the thoughtfulness.

> *"I realize that I've called you out of the blue. Did I catch you at a good time?"*
> *"I hope that I can get a few minutes of your time?"*

Get their attention:

Similar to your elevator speech and cover letter, make a clear statement about one of your showcase accomplishments. Grab the hiring executive's attention.

> *"I am a care management sales professional and for the last four years I exceeded sales quotas by 27 percent. My sales have been achieved by selling through fee-for-service consultants, payers, and directly to larger companies."*

> *"I am an underwriting management professional and with my previous employer I rewrote the underwriting guidelines which resulted in the growth in our block of business from $25M to $80M over four years."*

Purpose for the call:

Now that you have introduced yourself and gotten the hiring executive's attention, state the reason for the call . . . to set up an interview.

"I'm looking to make a career move and I would like to meet (or speak) with you to discuss how I can contribute to the success of (Company Name)."

Relate to the employer (optional):

If possible, try to make a statement (if you can) that relates to the employer. This can be a statement specific to the company, a trend, or an issue facing the industry.

"By the way, I understand that you have just rolled out a new cost containment service line."

"As we both know, the new health care regulations that take effect next year are going to change business."

If you do not have enough information about the company or industry, you can omit the "relate" portion of the script.

Close:

Close the call with a request for an interview (the ultimate purpose of the call).

"I am available (to meet with you or speak with you in more detail) in the afternoons next week if you would be interested in meeting (or speaking further)."

"I can make myself available Tuesday morning or after three p.m. on Thursday. Which time frame might work best for you?"

The purpose here is to get an interview. And the key to success is to ask for one.

After you finish the script:

Once you finish speaking, you will likely encounter a moment of silence. The hiring executive is processing what you have said. This is not the kind of call they receive every day. Remain quiet.

The hiring executive will respond with one of two things: a question that indicates interest (a "buying sign") or an objection/deflection. If the response is a question, this is good. Provide a short, responsive answer. There could be a follow-up question, which is great. Provide a response. However, at some point you need to again request an interview, either one over the phone or in person.

> *"Mr. Tyrrell, it sounds like we might have some things to discuss. Let's schedule an appointment to (talk in more detail/meet in person)."*

> *"Mr. Tyrrell, it appears that there may be an opportunity where I can bring some value to your company. When could we schedule a time to speak in more detail?"*

There will be calls when your script will not go exactly as written. The hiring executive might interrupt with a question. Anticipate this happening. Simply respond accordingly.

Objections

If you get an objection (or deflection), it will likely be one of the following:

1. "I don't have any openings."

More often than not, this response is truthful. The first priority of any smart hiring executive is to achieve company goals through people, and be on the lookout for talented professionals. Offer to send your resume. If it gets read, another opportunity within the company could be a possible fit. And, most importantly, ask a question—get the hiring executive talking if you can. It is this part of the engagement where you build rapport. Something as simple as:

> *"I understand. May I forward my resume to you in the event something changes? One question: what do you see as the industry's most important trend right now?"*

> *"That's all right. Can you think of someone else you could refer me to that might have a need? Your referral will be appreciated by both of us."*

2. "Can you send me your resume?"

The response here is to agree but ask a question to hopefully get an interview or further the dialogue and continue to build a professional relationship. Responses could include one of the following:

> *"I will. However, my resume is just a paper representation of the value I can bring to (Company Name). When could we sit down and discuss my background so you further understand what I can bring to the table? I can make myself available to your schedule."*

"I will. What job title or opportunity should I refer to when I send it?"

"I will. What specific skills or experience are you looking for?"

3. "I really don't have time to talk right now."

> *"I understand. Is it possible to schedule a brief ten-minute call later?"*

4. "You'll need to talk to Human Resources."

This may or may not be a brush-off, but at least you will have a name for someone in HR and when you make contact, you can use the name of the hiring executive that referred you. Respond with something simple, like:

> *"Great. When I speak to HR, whom should I ask for? And what position should I tell them you asked me to contact them about?"*

Ask One Question after the Objections

If you can, ask one question after you respond to the hiring executive's objection. A good method to initiate this question is: "Let me ask you a question." There are myriad questions you could ask, but choose one that is germane to the conversation.

Rejection

An important point to remember when you make these calls: you will be rejected eventually (in one form or another). You need to keep telling yourself that people are not rejecting you as a person. Most of the time, it is the situation with the company—they aren't hiring, they don't employ people with your background, or something else. So each time you are rejected, renew your positive attitude with the next call. With each rejection you get, you are closer to an affirmative response (an interview). It's a process of elimination.

> *I can summarize the lessons of my life in seven words—*
> *never give in; never, never give in.*
> — Winston Churchill[162]

---

162 Cornerstone Coaching LLC, "What Winston Churchill Can Teach Us About Inevitable Success," (blog), February 26, 2014, http://www.cornerstoneadvisoryservices.com/blog/what-winston-churchill-can-teach-us-about-inevitable-success (accessed May 28, 2015).

Screening

As you make calls, you will undoubtedly encounter a gatekeeper—a person whose function is in part to protect the hiring executive's schedule. Be ever so kind and polite to these people. Befriend them if possible. As a general rule, they will have one question for you:

"What is this regarding?"

When speaking with the gatekeeper, be straightforward and honest and refer to the hiring executive by first name. Something like:

> *"I am an executive sales professional in the care management industry. I am exploring a career move and it has been suggested to me to reach out to Bob. Is he available?"*

Voice Mail

Most of the time, you will get the hiring executive's voice mail; you can use this as an opportunity to leave a brief message. The voice mail could go something like this:

> *"Bob, this is Kevin Johnson and I am an operations professional who successfully saved my most recent employer over $5M in operating costs by streamlining our customer relations call center. I would like to connect with you at your convenience to further discuss my background and how I can contribute to the success of (Company Name). I can be reached at 123-456-7890."*

How many voice messages should you leave? There is a fine line between being persistent and becoming a pest. Only you can make that determination. However, three to four over the course of a week or two would likely be the maximum. Remember that you can reach out to the hiring executive by email as well and blend your contact methodology.

Email Marketing Your Professional Credentials

An alternative approach when proactively marketing your professional credentials is to initially reach out to hiring executives by email (on LinkedIn InMail). Refer to the Cover Letter Success Formula in Chapter 6 to write a compelling email cover letter.

Marketing emails essentially follow the identical formula for content as any other letter with some distinct differences that should be observed to increase effectiveness. These differences include:

Subject Line. Good use of the subject line is vital. It must be short and impactful. A poor subject line would read: *"Accountant looking for work."* A good subject line would read: *"#1 Provider Technology Sales Representative."*

A good approach is using the headline from your LinkedIn profile, and modifying it as needed.

Street Address. This is a communication sent by email, not by the US Postal Service. Do not put a street address in the email. A date is unnecessary as well since it is automatically generated when you send the email.

Attaching a Resume. Here you have to make some decisions. Some companies have servers with robust firewalls that screen out all unfamiliar emails with an attachment. You can either send an attached resume or not. If your email that had a resume attached is returned with an undeliverable kickback, try again without the resume attached. Another consideration is your current employment status. If you are unemployed, it is recommended that you attach a copy of your resume. If you are currently employed, think through whether you want to provide a copy of your resume. When it comes to attaching a resume, customize the name of the document. It should at least be your full name with a space between your names *e.g.* John Smith.docx. A better approach would be your name plus a branding statement (e.g., John Smith Lean Six Sigma.docx). Or, add a position type or function (e.g., John Smith Senior Engineer.docx).

Close. Your email close should be different from other letters due to the reply function with emails. It is recommended that you ask the recipient to act in response to the email. An example of a good close would be:

> *"If you have an interest or a need for a proven account manager with a documented track record of success, please reply or call me."*

Telephone Number. Always put your telephone number in your marketing emails. The hiring executive may want to bypass the reply button and speak to you directly. Give them a way to do so.

The Appendix has examples of marketing emails for your review, including a suggestion about using videos (which will be discussed below).

Sending Your Marketing Email

Once you have identified your target companies, identified the (probable) hiring executive, obtained an email address, and written a compelling marketing email, it is time to send them.

Send each email individually. *Do not* send a mass email and waste your time and effort.

Instead, copy and paste your template email, and then customize each email as needed. Spell check. Give it one last look for appearance and send.

When you get an undeliverable message to an email you've sent, don't get discouraged or distracted. When you've completed sending the other emails in your original batch, deal with the kickbacks. Double-check the spelling and the email formula. Call the company to confirm the email address, informing the person on the phone of the email address you used and that you received a kickback. This approach frequently works.

Email Marketing through LinkedIn

Sending marketing emails as LinkedIn InMail is acceptable. Depending on the level of LinkedIn account you have, the number of InMails you have is limited. Therefore, try reaching hiring executives first through their company email. Use LinkedIn InMail as a secondary strategy if reaching the executive through company email proves futile.

Follow-Up Calls

After you send your marketing emails, wait a day or two and see if you get responses. Obviously, you want to immediately follow up on any emails you receive indicating interest. After a day or so, you will need to start generating calls to the hiring executives you sent emails to. You will use virtually the same scripts previously provided but with a reference to the email you sent to the hiring executive. Your voice message should also reflect that you sent an email a few days prior.

These calls should seem more like a warm call, and easier to generate, since you have already reached out to the hiring executive. You are now simply following up. Remember, the ultimate purpose of the call is to get an interview.

★ Drip Email Marketing

An effective strategy when marketing your professional credentials is "drip" marketing, which is when you send messages to a hiring executive over a period of time. The drip concept is to send a marketing email and then systematically contact the same hiring executive with additional emails containing different information. The goal is to generate interest from the hiring executive to secure an interview.[163]

There are several important points to be aware of when using this technique. Be organized, record who you have contacted, with what information, and when. Space your drip emails at least two or three days apart. Do not send a resume on the first contact.[164] Wait until you get interest or some positive response from the hiring executive before submitting a resume (or better yet, get an interview scheduled and then send your resume).

There is a variety of information you can select for your drip messages. Start with a description of your professional credentials and then follow up with emails containing:

1. A recommendation or endorsement

2. A list of references—especially if there is a chance that the hiring executive might know one of them

3. A short success story

4. A short list of accomplishments, especially if they may resonate with the hiring executive[165]

5. Positive comments from job performance reviews

6. An abridged summary from a personality assessment

7. A list of marquee clients or distribution-channel partners (or contacts) if you're in sales or account management

If you are asked for a resume, this could be a good sign. Just remember, the purpose of drip marketing is to generate interest and secure an interview.

Most job seekers that use the drip marketing approach find it easy to execute and less stressful than follow-up phone contact (however, you still need to call the hiring executive).

---

163 Hill, Paul. *The Panic Free Job Search: Unleash the Power of the Web and Social Networking to Get Hired.* (Pompton Plains, NJ: Career Press, 2012), p. 203.

164 Ibid., p. 205.

165 Ibid., p. 205–206.

Overall effectiveness depends on the hiring executive. Some may respond more favorably to a follow-up call because they recognize and appreciate the initiative. For others, it makes no difference.

Blend the email marketing and phone contact approaches. Follow your business instincts on the number and methods of contact. Show persistence, but again, don't become a pest. If you are not getting a response after several overtures, move on.

★ The Research Interview

This job-search technique can yield promising leads. A research interview is a very brief conversation, either by telephone or face-to-face, with an employee who currently works for a target company. The point of the conversation is to ask open-ended questions that elicit responses regarding their experiences working for that company.

The reason why the research interview works so well is twofold. First, people like to talk about themselves and share their experiences with others. Just assure your contact that the conversation is confidential.

Second, as a general rule, people like to help others. Once you establish confidentiality and show your genuine interest in their responses, people tend to speak openly. When people realize that their experiences and opinions are the focal point of the call, without a hidden agenda, the information will flow.

Here is a step-by-step guide to setting up a research interview:

1. Identify an appropriate number of targeted companies in which you have a sincere interest.

2. Identify an appropriate contact within that target company. Use LinkedIn to get referred to that person if possible.

3. Call, email, or use LinkedIn InMail and request an appointment by clearly stating the purpose for the conversation (to learn about the company). If appropriate, mention a contact the two of you have in common, or the person who recommended you reach out to them. Establish an appointment time for a fifteen- to twenty-minute conversation.

4. Prepare, in advance, four or five open-ended questions on topics of interest to you. The key is to get them talking about themselves, the company, their position, and so on. As a rule, stay away from the topic of salaries and compensation.

5. Since you set up the appointment, be the one to generate the call. Be punctual and ask your contact whether it is still a good time.

6. Conduct the research interview by asking your questions. Keep things to fifteen to twenty minutes to be mindful and respectful of their time. If you start to run over, acknowledge it; frequently the contact will say it is okay to continue.

   It is not uncommon for people to ask about your job search as a part of this conversation. This is where the magic of this approach often happens. They will volunteer information about internal openings (can you say Hidden Job Market?), lead you to network with others inside or outside the company, mention job leads with other companies, and so on.

7. Always write a thank-you note or email. Send it promptly after the conversation.

If there happens to be an open position within the company, ask whether your contact could refer you to the appropriate person. Also (and this is important), ask whether the company offers referral bonuses to employees for referring qualified job seekers. If so, this creates an obvious incentive for your contact to refer you. According to recent surveys, nearly two-thirds of companies encourage employee participation in recruiting by offering referral bonuses.[166] These bonuses often exceed $1,000.[167]

A research interview is a great strategy. It is an easy and comfortable call to make (similar to calling hiring executives about recruiters) and the topic is safe and reasonable for the company employee.

Using Videos or YouTube in Your Job Search

Embedding a short video (or YouTube link) into email messages to hiring executives is unique, effective, and can differentiate you from others, *if done correctly*.

First and foremost, your video must be professional. If it is not, you can significantly harm your job-search efforts. If you decide to pursue video, consult the section on Webcam

166 Jobvite Recruiter Nation Report 2016, http://www.jobvite.com/wp-content/uploads/2016/09/RecruiterNation2016.pdf (64% of recruiters report awarding monetary bonuses to incentivize referrals into their organizations.) (accessed March 15, 2017).

167 "Bonus Programs and Practices," *WorldatWork*, June 2014, http://www.worldatwork.org/adim Link?id=75444 (accessed June 1, 2015).

or Skype Interviews in the next chapter. Many of the same considerations listed there will apply to your video (your attire, look into the camera, and so on).

The purpose of the video is to introduce yourself as a professional, create interest with the hiring executive, and differentiate yourself from other job seekers. Used in this way, it is not a lengthy video resume. Therefore, keep your video short; the recommended length is a minute to a minute-and-a-half.

The video personalizes you. The hiring executive can see you, pick up on your personality, and learn about your background. The video operates as a first impression, which is very important (see First Impressions in the next chapter). Remember to smile.

What do you talk about? After introducing yourself, discuss your qualifications, accomplishments, and professional traits. A logical starting point is your elevator speech. Start out strong with an attention-getting statement. This could be your biggest accomplishment or qualification, or you could reference an industry trend. Refer to the attention-getting recommendations listed previously. Many of those will work here. (As you may have figured out already, many of the concepts and techniques of a job search weave together, interrelate, and complement each other.)

It is imperative that you script, memorize, and practice what you are going to say. Then make sure you can deliver the speech in a conversational tone and manner (just like your elevator speech). This video will be viewed by hiring executives and recruiters. It must be perfect.

Where you shoot the video can have an impact on its effectiveness and the hiring executive. For example, if you are targeting positions that will require air travel, consider shooting the video at a quiet area of an airport (the key here is the setting must clearly *be* an airport). If you are in manufacturing, consider shooting the video on the floor of a manufacturing facility.

Putting high-level graphics into the video can make it distinctive. You can include a voice-over while the graphics are on the screen. Frequently, companies that design and create websites could help you produce a video with graphics.

When All Else Fails . . .

There comes a point when it becomes apparent that a hiring executive is simply not going to respond to your messages (emails or calls). If this happens, there's one last thing you can do before you "close the briefcase" and move on. Send one last short email describing your background and ask that should the hiring executive become aware of any openings that would be a match to please pass along your information. This technique enlists the hiring executive as a resource that could be helpful to your search.

Here is an example to get you thinking when composing your email:

> *Anita,*
>
> *I've reached out to you a few times over the past week or so. I'm sorry we have not connected. By the way, congratulations on your recent acquisition.*
>
> *I am an operations professional in the plastics industry. I managed four manufacturing facilities in four separate regions and exceeded production and profit goals for the last five consecutive years.*
>
> *I am in a job search looking for a senior operations position in the plastics or rubber industries based in the South (Texas would be ideal).*
>
> *Should you become aware of any positions that could be a match, feel free to pass along my information. My resume is attached.*
>
> *Best Wishes,*

Let's take a closer look at the email:

- It is short and to the point. This is important. Resist the temptation to provide too much information about your background and circumstances. You've already done that with previous communications.

- It mentions a compliment, which could help get the rest of the email read. If you do mention a compliment, make sure it is sincere and substantive. If not, leave this part out.

- It identifies your function and an accomplishment you have achieved. It clearly states that you are in a job search, what kind of position you're looking for, and where.

- It grants permission to the hiring authority to pass along your information, allowing them to help you, should they become aware of an opening. The hiring authority does not need to reply to you that your information has been passed along.

As you use this technique, every once in a while you will get a reply email acknowledging your message or a job lead. As with all job leads, it can lead to further networking and possibly your next job.

Where to Spend Your Time and Effort

Now that you know the various avenues to locate open career opportunities, where do you distribute your time and effort? There is no definitive answer to this question. However, for most career-minded professionals, the following breakdown is representative:

- 70 to 80 percent or more on networking and proactively marketing your credentials

- 10 to 15 percent with recruiting firms (initial and follow-up contact)

- 10 percent (or less) on job boards or direct applications

How to Honestly Measure Your Progress

As previously mentioned, one way to measure the success of your job search is the number of views of your LinkedIn profile. You want to keep that number above twenty at all times, if possible. Profile views, though a measure of your job-search progress, are not interviews.

The most important thing to measure regarding the progress of your job search is:

First-Time Interviews!

These interviews are your first conversation with a company representative (the actual hiring executive, HR, or someone else), and the purest reflection of your efforts toward getting a new job. Your goal is to get as many first-time interviews as you possibly can. When you get a first-time interview, make it your goal to get another as quickly as you can with another company. Get on a roll.

There is a plethora of other activities you can track and you should selectively do so (namely, the number of calls you make to hiring executives). But when the day is done, first-time interviews are the honest measurement of moving your search toward getting a new job.

If you are dissatisfied with your results regarding first-time interviews, frequently it is a result of your effort, or lack thereof. Are you making enough proactive outreaches—email, LinkedIn, calls? Are you continuing to network? Are you focused and putting concentrated effort into your search? Be honest with yourself.

The second most important thing to measure regarding the success of your job search is:

Second-Time Interviews!

These are interviews beyond the initial screening. You are in the company's evaluation phase and "in-play."

If you are not advancing out of first-time interviews, communicate with those employers that passed on you and get as much honest feedback as they'll give you. Remedy what you can and make changes.

Counting true, actual, and substantive interviews is the purest measure of your job search. The only way to get a job is to get an interview. And, the more interviews you have, the better your odds of landing a fulfilling position in the shortest time possible.

The Ultimate Truths

To move your job search forward you must get interviews. To get interviews, you must talk to a lot of people. The preceding information gives you techniques and tactics to engage people in conversations, and written communications to get interviews.

However, to actually land a job (as a result of your interviews) requires that you differentiate yourself from other job seekers by providing real-life examples of your skills and resulting accomplishments. More on how to achieve that in the pages that follow.

Chapter 11

Interviewing

To get something you never had, you have to do something you never did.
— Jose N. Harris[168]

How Much Are Interviews Worth?

Did you know that during an average round of golf, the actual amount of time the golf ball is in contact with the club face is a fraction of a second per swing?[169] Playing eighteen holes of golf results in a very small amount of ball contact overall. Remarkable. The same ratio of contact to length of an athletic contest likely holds true with other sports where there is an instrument striking an object (hockey, baseball, and tennis immediately come to mind). Now think of all the time these professional athletes spent over the course of their lives practicing, staying fit, being coached for hours, and so on to perfect, as much as possible, the technique and muscle memory to execute a swing that results in such a sliver of contact

---

168 "Jose N. Harris Quotable Quote," Goodreads, http://www.goodreads.com/quotes/415120-to-get-something-you-never-had-you-have-to-do (accessed June 22, 2015).

169 "Ball at Impact," Golfswing.com, http://www.golfswing.com.au/139 (accessed February 15, 2016).

time. This analogy represents the small amount of time you spend interviewing relative to the total amount of work hours over the course of your career.

Let's do some math: assume you work forty hours a week for fifty weeks a year (two weeks a year for vacation and personal time off). This totals two thousand hours of work time a year. Assume that you will work for fifty years—as a society we are choosing to work longer into our lives.[170] Therefore, your total number of career working hours is one hundred thousand hours. A little staggering when you think about it.

Statistically speaking, the average professional could have as many as ten jobs over the course of their career[171] (for some it could be more or less, but ten is representative in today's free-agent market, and it makes the math easier). Assume that it takes twenty-five hours of total interview time to secure a new position. This includes the interview process for the job you're hired for, as well as all of the positions you interviewed for that did not work out. And, we know that interview processes have been lengthened for a variety of reasons.[172] So, ten jobs that took twenty-five hours of interviewing per job equals 250 hours of interview time over the course of your career. The ratio of 250 interview hours for one hundred thousand hours of career work time gets you .25 percent. When viewed this way, those interview hours take on more importance. (And we're not done.)

Consider the financial impact an outstanding interview can have on your career and personal life. Assume that you were, *on average*, able to improve your compensation by $10,000 every time you changed jobs. (It is recognized that there is a plethora of circumstances that affect this generalization. There could be times when it is more or less, but on average, assume an improvement of $10,000 per job change. Play along here; it's to prove a point). So, ten jobs over the course of your career, with an increase of $10,000 per position, equals

170 Woods, Jennifer. "Working Longer—Whether You Want to or Not," CNBC.com, December 23, 2014, http://cached.newslookup.com/cached.php?ref_id=105&siteid=2098&id=10359558&t=1419339600 (accessed June 9, 2015).

171 Bureau of Labor Statistics, "Number of Jobs Held, Labor Market Activity, and Earnings Growth Among the Youngest Baby Boomers: Results from a Longitudinal Survey," news release, March 31, 2015, http://www.bls.gov/news.release/pdf/nlsoy.pdf (accessed May 29, 2015).

172 Susan P. Joyce, "After the Interview, What is Taking Them SO Long?" *Work Coach Café* (blog), September 17, 2012, http://www.workcoachcafe.com/2012/09/17/after-the-interview-what-is-taking-them-so-long/ (accessed February 15, 2016); "2015 Candidate Behavior Study," CareerBuilder, http://careerbuildercommunications.com/candidatebehavior/ (accessed February 15, 2016); Jena McGregor, "Interviewing for a Job is Taking Longer Than Ever," *On Leadership* (blog), *Washington Post*, June 18, 2015, http://www.washingtonpost.com/blogs/on-leadership/wp/2015/06/18/interviewing-for-a-job-is-taking-longer-than-ever/ (accessed February 15, 2016).

$100,000. Multiply that over a career of fifty years and that gets you $5,000,000. The value could be more when you consider the investment value of some of that money.

Okay, if you find yourself thinking about these numbers, the analogy, and the ways you could shoot more holes in it than a block of swiss cheese, you've missed the point. The numbers and the analogy are not perfect. But, again, that's not the point. The point of the illustration is to impress upon you that interviews are critically important to your career enjoyment and financial well-being. Approaching interviews with a cavalier attitude or flying by the seat of your pants is professionally foolish. There's simply too much at stake. When it comes to interviewing for a job, take it seriously. Prepare. It's worth a lot of money, and it means a lot to your career, you, and your family.

Let's review for a moment. Remember from Understanding the Employer's Mindset in Chapter 3, an employer hires with two main goals in mind: to make money or save money.[173] An interview is the platform that addresses those ultimate goals, through information exchange.

How an Employer Views an Interview

Employers want to answer five major questions as a result of the interviewing process:

1. Can you do the job? (skills and experience needed to perform the job)

2. Will you do the job? (motivated to actually perform the job functions)

3. Will your performance have a positive impact on company goals? (subjective prediction of future performance . . . will you be any good at it?)

4. Do you fit in? (cultural fit)

And, if those four questions are answered yes, then . . .

5. Are you affordable? (compensation)

When all five of these questions are answered affirmatively, you have a shot at the position. Other job seekers may meet the criteria too. Failing to pass any one of these hurdles will result in the employer pursuing other job seekers for the opportunity. Let's look at how you can give yourself the best chance to win.

---

173 Whitcomb, *Job Search Magic*, p. 274.

Can You Do the Job?

Questions in this portion of the interview will be about your technical skills, ability, and knowledge, as well as your transferable skills. It is an evaluation of your qualifications for the job and a determination of whether you can actually perform the functions of the position. Emphasize your skills and abilities and match the basic elements needed to perform the job functions.

Will You Do the Job?

Motivation is pivotal to success in any job position (or job search), and is a professional quality all hiring executives want to see in a job seeker. The hiring executive needs to know whether the job seeker will be motivated to actually perform the job functions.

As a job seeker, you must convince the hiring executive that you have the required abilities and are motivated to use them. This is achieved by educating the hiring executive about your passion for the job, work ethic, internal drive, and examples of taking the initiative and going the extra mile. Revealing that you have researched the company, position, and perhaps the hiring executive's background can also be a reflection of your motivation.

If the hiring decision comes down to two equally qualified candidates, the one that has demonstrated motivation and enthusiasm wins.

Will Your Performance Have a Positive Impact on Company Goals?

Here, the hiring executive will attempt to predict your future performance on the job, and compare you to other job seekers. You may have the necessary skills and be willing to use them, but will your performance significantly and positively impact and advance company goals, be an improvement from the previous person in the position, improve team performance, and so on? This is where competition for the position takes place in the mind of the hiring executive. It's about proving results and convincing the hiring executive that you can make things better. They want to hire the best.

It is imperative during the interview to stress accomplishments, your history of success, and work ethic. Ask about how you will be measured in the position, position goals, and projects. Then reference your accomplishments to match and exceed expectations.

Generally, in today's business environment, many employers are very sensitive about short-term goal achievement. They have a problem, and they need it solved yesterday. The lead time to get quantifiable results in a position is getting shorter. Therefore, in interviews, focus your responses the best you can on providing value and results to the employer in a short period of time. (Just be careful not to overpromise and under deliver.) Portray yourself as an expert who knows how to do a task and shorten the start-up time, leading to quicker ROI from hiring you. In other words, you can hit the ground running.

Do You Fit In?

Cultural fit with the organization and personal chemistry with those you will work with is a big deal. Statistically, 60 percent of most hires are based on personal chemistry.[174] Employers tend to hire who they like even though more qualified candidates may be available.

Cultural and personal chemistry questions explore likability, connection, communication, values, interests outside of work, and dress/appearance. When the hiring executive shifts gears into more personal topics, they are assessing your cultural fit and personal chemistry.[175]

Are You Affordable?

To land an offer, your compensation must generally fit within the hiring range for the position. The more qualified you are, and the more they like you, the more justification exists to move you to the higher end of that salary range. Sometimes, if your qualifications and cultural fit are strong enough, employers will go beyond the original compensation range to capture extraordinary talent. It does happen, but don't pursue positions in the hope that the employer will do so. All employers are conscious of budgets and parity issues. There are limits to what they can or are willing to do.

Strategy for a Successful Interview

A successful interview involves four basic elements:

1. **Uncovering the employer's need.** You achieve this through research, reading job descriptions, listening, and asking probing questions.

---

174 DiResta, interview by Canters, "How to Blitz."

175 Jobvite Recruiter Nation Report 2016, http://www.jobvite.com/wp-content/uploads/2016/09/RecruiterNation2016.pdf (accessed March 15, 2017).

2. Communicating to the employer that you can satisfy that need. You achieve this by matching and relating your skills and experience to the needs of the employer.

3. Persuading the employer to hire you. You achieve this by emphasizing your past accomplishments and relating them to the employer's need. Differentiate yourself.

4. Showing enthusiasm for the position. It has been repeatedly shown that top qualified candidates that show enthusiasm for the position are more successful in receiving job offers.[176] Simply put, everyone wants to be wanted and the more you convince an employer you want the job, the more likely you are to get it.

As you read through this chapter, keep these four strategies in mind. Their themes are woven into all of the substantive interviewing topics and techniques that follow. The concept is similar to "Solution Selling," a sales methodology where the salesperson focuses on the customer's pain(s) and addresses those pains by introducing his or her product and services.[177] As it applies to your job search, you must position yourself as the solution to the hiring need.

Strategy for Opening the Interview

This is an interviewing strategy that can be very effective if the interview opens in a way that gives you the opportunity to use it. If it doesn't, don't push it.

After pleasantries are exchanged, take the lead by asking the hiring executive to verbally describe what he or she is looking for. Listen carefully. You are about to hear the answers to the test.

This proactive approach can give you a strategic advantage. Whatever information the hiring executive provides as to what he or she is looking for (plus the information you gathered from your research) are the target qualifications, professional character traits, needs, and issues the executive wants for the open position. Explain how you can fulfill these targeted needs or wants by referencing your background, accomplishments, professional character traits, and past experiences (whatever might be the emphasis of the

---

176 U.S. Department of Labor, "Soft Skill #2: Enthusiasm and Attitude," Skills to Pay the Bills, http://www.dol.gov/odep/topics/youth/softskills/Enthusiasm.pdf (accessed June 19, 2015); Adams, Susan. "How to Ace Your Job Interview," *Forbes*, March 1, 2013, http://www.forbes.com/sites/susanadams/2013/03/01/how-to-ace-your-job-interview-2/ (accessed June 15, 2015).

177 "What is Solution Selling?" Sales Performance International, http://solutionselling.learn.com/learncenter.asp?id=178455 (accessed June 8, 2015).

hiring executive's description). Successfully doing so can remove questions he or she may have about your qualifications for the position. The tone of the interview may relax and take on an exchange of information rather than an examination and evaluation of qualifications.

First Impressions

Research has repeatedly shown that hiring executives heavily base their evaluations on their initial impressions of a job seeker.[178] Therefore, the first thirty to sixty seconds of an interview are crucial to your success. The hiring executive creates first impressions of you, positive or negative, in that quick snippet of time.[179]

If the hiring executive draws a negative first impression, there is a tendency to ask tougher questions to validate the initial negative impression. Or, the hiring executive could elect to minimize the engagement and make the interview short.

On the other hand, if the hiring executive has a positive first impression, there is a tendency to ask easier questions and even overlook deficiencies in qualifications.

Create an initial positive impression by dressing conservatively (over 50 percent of a person's impression of you is determined by physical appearance),[180] smiling, having a firm handshake, and making opening remarks that demonstrate your sincere interest in meeting the hiring executive.

Be aware of your countenance (your facial expressions) during the interview. Try to keep it positive even when you hear less favorable information about the opportunity. Gather information and be slow to judge. The hiring executive will be watching, and your unintended facial impressions could portray your negative thoughts (even though you may not yet have full information). This could have a bearing on the lasting impression the hiring executive has of you.

Creating an initial positive impression means you won't be playing catch up during your interview.

---

178 Zolfagharifard, Ellie. "First Impressions Really DO Count: Employers Make Decisions About Job Applicants in Under Seven Minutes," *Daily Mail*, June 18, 2014, http://www.dailymail.co.uk/sciencetech/article-2661474/First-impressions-really-DO-count-Employers-make-decisions-job-applicants-seven-minutes.html (accessed June 5, 2015).

179 Regis University Career Services, "Interviewing Strategies for CPS Students and Alumni," Regis University, http://www.regis.edu/About-Regis-University/University-Offices-and-Services/Career-Services/Student-and-Alumni/Interviewing-Strategies.aspx (accessed June 19, 2015).

180 Jamal, Nina, and Judith Lindenberger. "How to Make a Great First Impression," *Business Know-How*, http://www.businessknowhow.com/growth/dress-impression.htm (accessed June 2, 2015).

If you believe that the hiring executive's first impression is not positive, you have some heavy lifting to do, but it can be done.[181] There are a couple of things you can do. First, ask questions about the job and answer using your success stories. By showcasing your past performance you might be able to move the needle back in your direction. Second, name-drop if you can (capitalizing on the persuasion principle of social proof). If you know that the hiring executive and you have someone in common, mention the name. That might be enough to redirect the dialogue into positive territory. Even if your performance is superior, you may not overcome an initial negative impression or rough interview start. Do the best you can to get off to a good start.

Interview Progression

Most interviewing processes have three distinct phases: screening, evaluation, and consensus (final decision).

Screening. Frequently, screening interviews are conducted by phone with the primary focus of determining whether you have the requisite background, qualifications, and experience to do the job. Your goal for this interview is to make the cut and move forward in the interviewing process.

Evaluation. In this phase, the hiring executive(s) will dig deep into your background by asking specific and pointed questions about your technical knowledge and how you have performed in previous positions. You'll get into the nitty-gritty. Beyond your skills and capabilities, cultural fit and personal chemistry are also being evaluated. Occasionally, a psychological profile or interview with an industrial psychologist may be a part of the process. Most organizations use the results as part of the hiring decision, not a litmus test of whether to hire or not.

The last form of interview that can be a part of an evaluation process is an approval interview. It is with senior management (president, CEO, or someone else) and can either be traditional in length or brief. This is an opportunity for the individual to meet you and give approval. With a certain degree of frequency, you may encounter one favorite interview question from this person, because many interviewers have one that they ask everybody.

---

181 "Cognitive scientists say it can take up to two hundred times the amount of information to undo a first impression as it takes to make one," Zack, Devora. "10 Tips for People Who Hate Networking," Careerealism, May 4, 2015, http://www.careerealism.com/hate-networking-tips/ (accessed July 17, 2015).

This is usually when the interview is going to be brief and the executive has limited time. Be on your A game here—it matters.

Consensus (final decision). This is when the decision about who to hire is made. This meeting may not happen for a few days or even a week after all the interviews are complete. It is a total assessment of your candidacy for the position, including overall qualifications and fit, and how you compare with other candidates.

Interview Preparation

The interviewing process starts before you engage the employer in conversation. Here is a list of things you should do when preparing for an interview, regardless of format:

Research the company. Learn as much as you can. Get on the company's website and LinkedIn page. At a minimum you must know:

1. The products and services offered by the company

2. Who the buyers/consumers of these products and services are

3. How these products and services are valued or needed by the buyer/consumer (the company's "value proposition")

4. Who a few of the company's market competitors are

5. News, recent events, and any announcements regarding the company (often the website will have a "News" tab)

Check out the websites Glassdoor (www.glassdoor.com) and Vault (www.vault.com). These are websites where employees of companies can post comments about the company, both positive and negative. Be discerning about what is written.

If time permits, reach out to colleagues and ask what they know about the company. If you are interviewing with a publicly traded company, read the annual report, the CEO's letter to shareholders, and ask a financial planner or stockbroker for their assessment. Most job seekers won't do any of this. Referencing the most recent annual report will differentiate you from other job seekers, and your knowledge and insight will impress the employer.

Research the position. Read the job description, if there is one. Call colleagues that may have useful information, especially if a colleague works for the employer you are interviewing with.

Research the hiring executive(s). Get on LinkedIn and research the background of the hiring executive(s). Understand their career history and look for any common ground. Having something in common, either professionally or personally, creates personal chemistry—a principle of persuasion and an integral part of hiring. It's been shown that employers hire those they "most like being around," so establishing personal chemistry can significantly increase your odds of advancing in the interviewing process and getting hired.[182]

Research the industry. This is particularly important if you are changing industries. Research trends—these are the hot topics that are shaping and impacting the industry. What is the future outlook for the industry? Familiarize yourself with the companies in the industry. Determine the best you can, who the industry leaders are and who are up-and-comers. Get educated.

Script answers. Take the time to script the answers to known or reasonably anticipated questions you will receive. Put yourself in the hiring executive's chair and think of the likely questions you would ask and script your answers. Then, if those questions are asked, you will be prepared and will be able to succinctly provide a response.

Prepare questions. Prepare questions to ask based on your research about the company, the position, the hiring executive, and the executive's area of responsibility. Refer to your list of questions from your Target Opportunity Profile.

The interview is a two-way street. The hiring executive is evaluating you for the position, but you are evaluating the company, position, reporting structure, and culture. It is an opportunity for you to figure out if this job at this company matches you.

Here are some powerful questions job seekers have asked that sparked engaging conversation:

- Why is this position available?

- What do you see as the most important task or challenge facing this position over the next six months?

- Looking back on this job and how it's been done in the past, what would you change?

- Who would you point to as a top performer in this job? What traits made him/her so good? What actions made him/her successful?

---

182 Sutton, Robert I., PhD. *The No Asshole Rule: Building a Civilized Workplace and Surviving One That Isn't*. (New York: Warner Business Books, 2007), quoted in Kurtzberg and Naquin, *Essentials*, p. 18.

- What obstacles do you foresee the selected candidate encountering that would hamper success in this position?

- What performance standards will define success in this position?

- What does success look like in the first ninety days?

- What stands between where the project/situation/company is today and where you want it to be?

- Why do you work for this company?

Take some time to do this research and prepare (you might only need to do it once). It will help you in your evaluation of opportunities. An interview is an exploration of many things, but ultimately you (and the employer) are both looking for the best possible fit.

Interview Formats

The following types of interviews occur during the screening and evaluation stages of the interviewing process. If you are an experienced professional, you have probably been through one or more of these. They are:

- **Telephone** - conducted either by the executive or human resources

- **One-on-One** - just the hiring executive and you

- **Skype/Webcam** - can be used at any stage, and allows the executive to see you

- **Succession** - usually used as a second or home-office interview, this type is multiple one-on-one interviews, typically with people from different departments—tailor your questions to the executive, such as asking an operations executive about efficiency and cost savings, and do your best to prepare questions for different departments

- **Group** - either of your potential peers, or of managers from different departments; direct your response to the person asking the question; bring up topics if you're in a peer group, but let superiors lead the conversation if in a manager group

- **Psychological** - either in person, or over the phone; a psychologist is likely evaluating you to see if your personality lines up with the position you're pursuing—be yourself, don't overthink, and don't give answers you think the interviewer wants to hear

- **Stress** - extremely rare, and designed to see how you react; you will not encounter this one, but if executives act angry, rude, or condescending to you or one another, it's likely an artificial scene—stay positive with your responses

- **Meal** - can be over breakfast, lunch, or dinner

- **Behavioral and Performance-Based** - questions here will focus on specific examples of your past behavior as indications of your future performance

Practice Interviews

One of the best things you can do to prepare for interviews is to conduct practice or mock interviews. This is especially true if you have not interviewed for a job in several years. Interviews can be stressful, and practicing reduces anxiety, boosts confidence, and leads to better performance. Prepare for all interviews thoroughly, so you won't treat the first real interview as your practice interview. It's entirely possible you could get into that interview, realize the position is more intriguing than you thought, be unprepared, and regret your performance.

To conduct a practice interview, ask a trusted colleague for assistance. Explain the purpose of the role-play. It is not an exercise to trip you up, but rather to prepare you. Use your resume to give your colleague a general outline to follow. Provide seven or eight likely questions you believe you may be asked, given your background and career history. To be truly effective, ask your colleague to research five or six interviewing questions from the Internet beyond those you provide.[183]

When conducting the mock interview, try to stay in character as much as possible. You can come out of character as you need to discuss responses, but remember the more realistic you make it, the better prepared you will be.

Evaluate your performance and responses with your colleague. Be open-minded to

---

183 Smith, Jacquelyn. "How to Ace the 50 Most Common Interview Questions," *Forbes*, January 11, 2013, http://www.forbes.com/sites/jacquelynsmith/2013/01/11/how-to-ace-the-50-most-common-interview-questions/ (accessed June 9, 2015); Thad Peterson, "100 Potential Interview Questions," Monster, http://career-advice.monster.com/job-interview/interview-questions/100-potential-interview-questions/article.aspx (accessed June 11, 2015).

their critique and suggestions. Make necessary adjustments. Having more than one practice interview (instituting any changes in approach and responses) is encouraged.

Answering Traditional Interview Questions: The UPAC Method™

As you can well imagine, you will be asked many questions in the interviewing process. The UPAC Method is an intuitive approach to answer these questions. Its effectiveness comes from the accomplishment component. When possible, mention an accomplishment that supports your answer.

U   **Understand** the question (ask for clarification if necessary).

P   **Provide** the employer with your (concise) answer.

A   Add an **Accomplishment** that supports your answer.

C   **Confirm** that you answered the hiring executive's question satisfactorily, redirecting the question if needed.

Here is an example of this technique:

Question: "We are looking for a product-training professional who can design and implement a training program for newly hired sales and account management professionals. What has been your experience in that area?"

U   You understand the question and what the employer is asking. Proceed with a response.

P   *Over the last five years with Barlowe ASP, I designed and implemented two training programs for current and new employees, many of whom were sales and account managers.*

A   *The most recent was a custom-designed program that I worked on with a well-known technology-education consulting firm. We designed the content of the program incorporating both the technology elements of the products and sales approaches. We created a comprehensive manual and high-touch presentations using the most interactive touch screen technology available. I then scheduled five half-day, in-house seminars. Each seminar was led by one of the firm's consultants that was knowledgeable in that particular subject area. The seminars were a smashing success.*

The vice president told me that I had exceeded all expectations.

C *Did I answer your question?*

Telephone Interview

Frequently, screening interviews are conducted over the phone. In this format, you must rely on verbal communication only. Slow your rate of speech and enunciate.

The advantage of a phone interview is the hiring executive can focus on the substance of your answers without distractions. Job seekers can have information in front of them to refer to as needed. Taking notes is useful during the interview and for follow-up communications. Here are some tips to improve your odds of a superior performance during a telephone interview:

Prior to the Call

1. **Prepare.** Research the company and position with the same due diligence as you would for a face-to-face interview. This preparation will shine through to the hiring executive, especially if you're asked, "What do you know about our company?"

2. **Phone Zone.** Create the identical quiet place that you did when you made your proactive marketing calls. Remove unnecessary paperwork and items from your work space and keep your resume, company information, job description (if you have one), success stories, questions to ask based on your research, water, pen, paper, and so on, nearby.

As a matter of human practicality, go to the bathroom before the call. Some telephone interviews are reasonably short (twenty to thirty minutes) while others can last over an hour.

If possible, use a landline. Cell phone connections are less reliable and you risk dropping the call. If you do not have a landline, make sure your cell phone is fully charged and you take the call in a place where you know you have good reception.

During the Call

You have done your homework for the call and created your phone zone. Here are some strategic suggestions that will prove helpful during the call:

After exchanging pleasantries, ask the hiring executive what he or she is looking for. Listen carefully. You are about to hear the answers to the test. Then, by reference to your background, experiences, and successes, fulfill those needs and wants, and sell your accomplishments.

Smile and stand up. Doing both of these things will have a positive impact on your tone of voice and portray a positive attitude. Standing will improve energy during a longer call.

Dress the part. Consider dressing for the telephone interview as you would a face-to-face interview. This will put you in an interviewing frame of mind.

Remember your questions. Use the ones you created during your interview preparation. Questions from you are a sign of interest.

Be careful not to over-answer. Most telephone interviews are screening calls. The hiring executive is frequently seeking information about qualifications. Answer questions completely, but don't get mired in minutia unless asked for more information.

Listen. Don't formulate what to say next while you should be listening to the hiring executive. Be active and engaged. Take notes but do not worry about complete thoughts. Fill in the details after the call is complete.

Ask for concerns. Have the hiring executive identify any obstacles and known challenges he/she can foresee that could hamper or prevent you from being successful. Ask: "Do you have any reservations about me succeeding in this role?" Refer to your background to defeat any perceived obstacles or issues presented by the interviewer.

Ask about the next steps. Do this at the end of the call. Indicate interest in proceeding to the next step. Consider asking whether you will be advancing in the interviewing process, which appeals to the persuasion principle of consistency and commitment (provided you've had a successful interview thus far).

Follow up. You must send a follow-up thank-you communication. The most time-efficient way is through email. Refer to the Cover Letters and Other Written Communications chapter of this book for examples.

The Unannounced Telephone Interview

There are occasions when a call will come unannounced. Although seldom the case, this could be by design by the employer. But often the unannounced call is a result of a scheduling mix-up, perhaps due to time zone differences. If this happens, simply tell the hiring executive that you are in the middle of something. You can reschedule the call or simply delay it by fifteen minutes. Give yourself time to gather your thoughts to make the call productive.

Webcam or Skype Interviews

Many employers use these to help speed up the interview process. In fact, it has been referenced that as many as six out of ten companies use webcam or video interviews in their hiring process.[184] For some job seekers, this format for an interview is new and can be unnerving.

If you are unfamiliar with the use of Skype, relax. It's not as intimidating as it sounds. The first thing to do is get an account. Go to their website (www.skype.com) and sign up. It's free. Write down your "address"—it's your Skype phone number. Put it somewhere so you don't forget it. Get a camera from the computer store if your computer is not equipped with one. Cameras are reasonably inexpensive. Hook it up.

After you are set up, here are key strategies to help you succeed during a Skype interview:

1. **Get comfortable with the technology.** Be sure it's set up on your computer, and familiarize yourself with the basics. Adjust the webcam to pick up your face, shoulders, and maybe down to the middle of your torso. Practice with the webcam and chat with friends or family prior to your interview. This will reduce anxiety. When the time comes to answer interview questions, look into the webcam's lens to give the impression of eye contact. Good posture is also important here. Do your best to remain still (on camera, movement can be delayed and therefore distracting). Be natural, and relax.[185] Technical issues may still come up. Take them in stride.

---

184 OfficeTeam, "Survey: Six in 10 Companies Conduct Video Job Interviews," news release, August 30, 2012, http://officeteam.rhi.mediaroom.com/videointerviews (accessed June 5, 2015).

185 Eric Bricker, "How to Ace Your Video Interview," *On Careers Blog, U.S. News & World Report,* July 11, 2013, http://money.usnews.com/money/careers/articles/2013/07/11/how-to-ace-your-video-interview (accessed December 1, 2015).

2. Control the scene. Similar in concept to the phone zone, set up a clean, professional background for the interview. Be aware of what is behind you.[186] Make sure any pets are out of earshot.

3. Wear professional attire. Dress like this is a face-to-face interview. There are a few special considerations. Don't wear clothes with busy patterns, as they tend to distract others. And dress completely, not just from the waist up.[187]

4. Have the hiring executive's telephone number. If the technology fails, you'll want to schedule a telephone interview as a fallback.

Screening Interview Conducted by a Human Resources Representative

This type of interview can be hazardous because this individual likely has little or no influence on the ultimate decision to hire you (unless you are pursuing a position in HR), but has the power to eliminate you as a candidate for the job. Your goal for this interview is to survive it and move forward in the process.

Understand that HR professionals who conduct screening interviews are frequently evaluated based on the number and quality of candidates they pass along to the hiring executive. The last thing they want to hear from the hiring executive is, "This candidate is weak." Or, worse yet, "What in heaven's name were you thinking? This candidate is not remotely qualified." So, study the job description and match your qualifications to it. Work to put the HR representative at ease that you are qualified and will make them look good.

Most times, interviews with human resources can be a bit scripted. The HR representative has a set number of questions or topics to cover with each candidate. The key, and the tricky part, is to provide the correct or acceptable answer. Too often, the HR representative looks for elimination factors rather than the totality of your qualifications.

With some limited exceptions, the questions you will likely encounter will be the general kinds of interviewing questions or statements, such as:

• Tell me about yourself.

• What are your strengths?

• What are your professional weaknesses?

• Why are you interested in this position?

186 Ibid.

187 Ibid.

- What do you know about our company?

- Why are you interested in our company?

- Why did you leave your last job (and others)?

- Why are you looking?

You will also encounter questions about your resume, why you made particular career moves, and reasons for leaving or staying at particular positions. Do not show any resistance to the questions regardless of your feelings about this type of interview.

Toward the end of the interview, you will undoubtedly hear, "Do you have any questions?" Realize that this person will probably not know much about the actual functions of the job you are pursuing, other than to repeat what might be on the job description. Do not put this person on the spot by asking in-depth position questions. Instead, stay in the safe zone and ask a few general questions this person should be able to answer, such as:

- What do you like about the company?

- What has made the company successful?

- What are the company's future goals and vision?

Remember to be respectful, polite, and friendly. Endear yourself. The reality is that the HR representative holds the future of your candidacy in their hands.

Meal Interview

This interview could be the most difficult type—it can happen at any step in the interviewing process, with any meal (breakfast, lunch, or dinner), and can trip up even the most confident of job seekers. Making this type of interview successful involves navigating a host of variables.

There are several reasons why employers conduct meal interviews:

1. **Convenience.** The hiring executive can multitask by conducting an interview during a meal.

2. **Confidentiality.** Other office personnel do not know that interviews are taking place for a particular position.

3. Information gathering. This includes your background and qualifications, just in a social setting.

4. Evaluation of personal factors. These would include social skills (useful for gauging how you would conduct yourself with clients, vendors, suppliers, key business partners, and so on), and your table manners. If you are the leading candidate, an added bonus of a meal interview could be to impress you.

The reasons for a meal interview don't really matter. What does is that hiring executives believe they can tell a lot about job seekers by the way they eat and interact in a social setting. Frequently, these interviews can go longer than traditional in-office interviews. Part of the key to success during a meal interview is not to be lulled into a sense of casualness. Make no mistake—this is an interview, not friends getting together just to catch up.

A meal interview is typically more conversational than a traditional face-to-face interview. It is fine if the conversation veers into personal topics. Remember, personal chemistry plays a significant role (up to 60 percent) in who the employer hires.[188] Follow the employer's lead. However, listen closely for when the conversation turns into questions or dialogue regarding your qualifications.

Here are some helpful things to remember about meal interviews:

1. Research the restaurant. Get the GPS out and know how to get there. Review the menu. Get some ideas on what to order.

2. Do not order messy foods like barbecue, pasta with lots of sauce, or any food that you would need to eat with your hands.

3. Order food that can be easily eaten with a fork and that can be cut into smaller pieces (that will help if you need to answer a question after taking a bite).

4. Do not order expensive entrees. Stay within the restaurant's mid-price range (you could make price part of your restaurant research).

5. Turn off your cell phone. Give the hiring executive your complete, undivided attention.

6. Be polite. Use "please" and "thank you." Be courteous to the servers.

7. Do not order alcohol, even if the hiring executive does. Being under the influence of alcohol during an interview shows poor judgment, impacts your answers, and takes you off your game.

188 DiResta, interview by Canters, "How to Blitz."

8.   Brush up on your etiquette and table manners. Know how, which, and when to use the utensils. Good table manners will give you an edge over other job seekers.

9.   Allow the hiring executive to lead the conversation. The interview questions may not occur until the meal is finished.

10. After the meal, show your appreciation to the hiring executive. Remember, the restaurant was likely chosen because he/she likes it. Compliment the choice of restaurants.

After the meal, do not worry about the check. The hiring executive will pay the tab. Make sure to ask about next steps. Write a thank-you note and send it within twenty-four hours of the meal interview. (Note: You should write a thank-you for every interview and especially meal interviews. The hiring executive did pay the tab.)

If you handle it professionally, a meal interview can give you a distinct advantage over other job seekers. It is an opportunity to build personal chemistry, display your social skills and table manners, and convey your abilities and accomplishments in a social setting.

Behavioral Interview

Behavioral interviewing is an effective and common interviewing technique. You must be prepared to answer these kinds of interviewing questions. If you have not interviewed in a while the format could be unfamiliar to you. A behavioral interviewing question requires you to describe situations or past experiences where you have demonstrated certain skills or behaviors. It is based on the premise that past behavior is the best indication of future performance. These questions are designed so you have to describe a situation, what you did, and the results of your actions. How did you use your skills and professional qualities to achieve success in your past?

Most behavioral interviewing questions begin with "Tell me about a time when . . . " or "Describe a situation where . . . " Theoretically, behavior-based questions help hiring executives avoid making hiring decisions based on emotions or gut feelings. Instead, the hiring executive is able to gather objective information that assesses your job skills, abilities, experience, successes, and so on.

These questions can be unnerving. They require you to quickly think of specific situations in your past where you used specific skills. We generally don't remember things in this way . . . we just do the job using our skills. It is due to the unpredictable nature of these questions along with the nervousness associated with an interview that can stump any job seeker.

Although there is a myriad of topics or competencies an employer can inquire about, some of the most common are:

• Technical ability

• Analytical thinking

• Communication skills

• Time management, prioritizing

• Leadership

• Problem solving, innovation

• Collaboration

• Ability to learn, adapt

Notice that many of these competencies are the sought-after skills, transferable skills, and professional qualities previously listed in this book. There could be several behavior-based questions for the same competency.

Preparing for and Answering Behavioral Interview Questions

The first thing to do in preparation for these questions is to review (or write) your success stories. You should have five or six examples describing your use of different skills and competencies. Reviewing or writing these success stories gets your mind thinking in terms of telling stories. It tends to awaken your memory about situations when you have used your various skills. As you remember situations, write a success story.

The next thing you can do to prepare for these questions is to "sit on the other side of the desk." Put yourself in the shoes of the hiring executive and think about behavior-based questions you might ask if you were hiring for the position you are pursuing. One technique that occasionally helps is to actually think or speak the beginning of a behavior-based question. That is, "Tell me about a time when . . . [then you finish the question]." This will occasionally make you think of questions that you had not previously thought of and you can now prepare for.

Read the job description. There are sometimes clues in a job description about the important skills or experience being sought. Those are often the areas that behavior-based questions will be directed toward.

Answering behavioral interview questions successfully involves being able to describe an experience directly related to the question (competency) being asked about. Use your success stories whenever possible. Here's how to answer effectively:

1. **Understand the question.** Listen carefully and be sure you understand what is being asked. If you do not, ask the hiring executive for clarification. It is permissible for you to reframe the question and repeat it back to the employer.

2. **Determine the professional competency being asked about.** Then think of a situation in your professional experience that illustrates the competency being addressed. Thinking in terms of identifying the competency makes it easier to recall a situation when you used that competency. Take a moment. Don't panic if something doesn't come to mind right away. Ask the executive for more time if you need it.

3. **Tell a brief success story that describes a situation illustrating your skill or competency.** Highlight how your skill influenced the end result.

4. **Confirm that your response answers the question.** Responses such as "Does that answer your question?" or "Does that example give you the information you were asking about?" are good examples to start with here.

Remember this shorthand, five-prong formula for answering behavioral interview questions:

> **Understand**
> **Determine the competency**
> **Think**
> **Tell**
> **Confirm**

If the behavior-based question happens to be an experience you have dealt with, terrific. Tell your story using the C.A.R. approach (identify the Challenge or situation, your Action, then the Result).[189]

If the behavior-based question is not something you have dealt with directly, but you

---

189 Safani, "Tell a Story."

have an analogous situation, tell the hiring executive that you have not handled that situation directly, but you have handled a very similar situation and tell your story.

If you do not have a similar situation, has a colleague handled that situation or one like it? If so, indicate this to the hiring executive. Tell the story, then explain whether you agreed or disagreed with the way your colleague handled the situation. If you disagreed, describe how you would have done things differently.

Finally, if the behavior-based question is not something you have dealt with directly, you do not have a similar situation, and you are unaware of whether a colleague has handled the situation, then indicate that you have not handled the situation and offer to answer it in the hypothetical—describe what you would do. This form of an answer is not ideal, since the hiring executive believes it's an important question, but it is better than no answer at all.

It is inevitable that you will encounter behavioral interview questions. You will never be able to predict what behavioral questions you'll be asked, but you can prepare ahead of time with your prewritten success stories to defuse being put on the spot. This way, you will be able to answer smoothly when these types of questions come up. You can also ask for time to think of a response if you can't think of an answer right away—be sure to give an answer of some kind eventually, though. You don't want the employer thinking you only wanted to stall.

Common Competencies Covered by Behavioral Interview Questions

Below are some competency topics with sample behavioral-based questions. The style of the questions should give you a good idea of what behavior-based questions sound like and how they may be asked in an interview.

Communication Skills
- Describe a time when you made formal recommendations or a formal presentation to senior management.
- It's difficult at times to get others to try new and innovative ideas. Tell me about a situation in which you persuaded others to explore something new.
- Tell me about a time when you dealt with the poor performance of a subordinate. How did you go about communicating this fact to the subordinate?

Time Management, Organization, and Planning
- Have you dealt with any simultaneous distractions, interruptions, or unanticipated

events on the job? How did you resolve these situations when you found out about them?

- In the past, what types of far-reaching company goals have you set out to achieve? What has been your degree of success?

Management Skills

- Tell me about a situation in which you needed to raise the performance level of your group.

- Tell me about a time when you praised your group for a job well done. What did you do?

- Give me an example of a time when you dealt with an uncooperative subordinate who was disrupting your group. What did you do?

- Describe the last time you needed to terminate an employee. How did you go about that?

Problem-Solving

- Tell me about a serious on-the-job issue and how you worked through it.

- Think of a difficult decision you had to make. Explain what happened. If you could do it over, how would you do it differently?

- How would you describe your style or approach to solving problems? Give me an example.

Leadership

- Give examples that show how you influenced and led others.

- How do you delegate tasks at work right now?

- Describe a situation in which you assumed leadership duties and your method for doing so.

- What strengths of yours influence your leadership methods the most? Describe a situation in which you used them.

Your Interview Wardrobe

For professionals and executives, one word sums up your attire for an interview: conservative. Wearing traditional, professional business attire instantly communicates to the hiring executive that you are confident. It also gives you an advantage over other job seekers, using the persuasion principle of authority.

Looking sharp also has the added advantage of making you feel in control and sets the stage for a superior interviewing performance. As a result, the hiring executive and others will respond to your image of professionalism in a positive way.

When it comes to the specific dos and don'ts on what to wear, if you find yourself questioning whether or not to wear something to an interview . . . don't. Use conservative judgment and always err on the side of traditional, conservative corporate attire.

Interviews with Potential Peers or Subordinates

When interviewing with company employees that could be peers or subordinates, remember that they want to meet you and get to know you professionally. However, most likely they have two important, hidden issues:

1. Do I like this person? Does he/she fit in? Can I see myself working with or for this person?

2. Friend or foe? Could this person (you) represent a threat to my job or career at the company?

Ingratiate yourself by asking questions of these people. Try to remove barriers by answering their questions and showing interest in them, both professionally and personally, if possible. It is not uncommon for the candidacy of a job seeker to unravel as a result of internal political maneuvering by an employee who feels threatened.

Explaining a Job Termination in an Interview

The first thing to understand about a job termination is that it's not the end of your career or job search. Even if the termination was for cause, it does not necessarily mean that landing a fulfilling career position is forever gone. A glitch in your employment history is something you can and will overcome. In fact, many hiring executives have had the very same experience at one time in their careers as well. They may be more empathetic and understanding than you think. The key is handling a past termination with professionalism and grace. Here are some tips to help you:

Get your facts straight. Set any emotions you may have about your termination aside, and communicate with your former employer. Come to an understanding on what the circumstances were and what public statements will be made, should a background check be performed. With that information, you must align your explanation with that of your former employer. Otherwise, you jeopardize landing future opportunities.

Be honest. Employers appreciate and value honesty. You are always safe if you tell the truth and provide the honest reason for your termination. Be positive about your former employer, as well (similar to concepts earlier in this book about explaining unemployment). Say only what's necessary (over-explaining is a common mistake). Answer any questions and focus on the position (without dodging the questions).

Script a response. Word choice matters. Don't use "fired" or "terminated." Instead, soften the language and use "let go," "released," and if applicable, "laid off" or "my position was eliminated." Phraseology can put a more positive spin on your job search. Reorganizations, corporate layoffs, and downsizing are all accepted reasons for job terminations, and using those terms isn't as big of a negative as it was in the past.

Mention accomplishments in the position or since the termination. These can be ones you achieved in the position you were terminated from, or ones achieved since the termination. The key here is to match the needs of the open position. Moving the conversation toward those topics refocuses the discussion on how you can benefit the employer.

Know how to handle termination for cause. Explaining a job termination for cause involves many of the techniques already mentioned, plus a few others that can help overcome the concerns the hiring executive may have.

Be prepared to explain the circumstances. If applicable (and only if applicable), indicate that the company was right to terminate you. Indicate that you still respect your former employer as a company. Make it clear you have learned from the events that resulted in your termination. Accept your share of the responsibility and tell the hiring executive that it will not happen again. **This is important: this hiring executive must be convinced that the circumstances that led to your termination for cause will not happen again.** The hiring executive does not want to knowingly hire a problem employee.

Put the employer at ease. A termination is a red flag that puts the hiring executive on alert to a potential hiring mistake. It is your goal to alleviate that concern the best you can through your honesty, accountability, and past accomplishments.

Explaining Employment Gaps or Long-Term Unemployment

If you have employment gaps in your job history or a long stretch of unemployed time, accept the reality that a hiring executive will ask about it. Many of the techniques from the previous section on handling job termination (never disparage a former employer, be honest, accept responsibility, acknowledge the circumstances and what you've learned) work here as well.[190]

As part of your explanation, inform the employer about what you have been doing during this gap time to stay current with your industry or to enhance your skills and knowledge. This can include activities previously mentioned, such as consulting, working toward an industry designation, and so on.[191]

Another approach is to mention you are being selective with your next career move and not looking for just any job.[192] With this approach, be able to list at least two or three criteria that you are looking for in your next position (to validate your selectivity claim). If you have turned down any offers, mention them (as further proof of selectivity). A severance package, if you received one in your last position, also supports the notion that you are looking for the right career fit.[193]

You can also mention that you underestimated the difficulty of finding a suitable position. But in response, you intensified your efforts and now have several opportunities in play (as long as it's true, of course). This approach may heighten the urgency to pursue you because the hiring executive knows you have increased your efforts and have other opportunities you are pursuing.

Finally, at the end of your explanation, ask a probing question about the position, preferably addressing an area where you possess a particular strength. This question

---

190 Pongo, "How to Explain Work History Gaps in the Interview," *The Pongo Blog,* https://www.pongoresume.com/blogPosts/372/how-to-explain-work-history-gaps-in-the-interview.cfm (accessed February 16, 2016).

191 Jill Kempka, "Resume FAQ: How Do I Handle Employment Gaps?" *Career Coach* (blog), *Manpower,* January 25, 2013, manpowergroupblogs.us/manpower/career-coach/2013/01/25/resume-faq-how-do-i-handle-employment-gaps/ (accessed February 16, 2016).

192 Biron, "How to Explain Employment Gaps in a Job Interview," *Career Sidekick* (blog), December 9, 2013, http://careersidekick.com/how-to-explain-employment-gaps-in-a-job-interview/ (accessed February 16, 2016).

193 For Dummies, "Answering Interview Questions About Job History Gaps," Dummies.com, www.dummies.com/how-to/content/answering-interview-questions-about-job-history-g0.html (accessed February 16, 2016).

directs the interview away from the gap and back to the position, where you can showcase your qualifications.

What if the employer does not ask about the employment gap? Do you proactively bring it up? Possibly. Doing so indicates you have nothing to hide, are willing to address concerns, and you prepared for this situation. However, bringing up the gap may not be appropriate—use your judgment. If you do address it, simply asking if there are any concerns about your employment gap is all that's needed to start this conversation.

When you do answer questions about gaps or extended unemployment, be confident. Part of the evaluation will be how you handle questions. And remember, employers today "are more understanding of employment gaps" than they once were.[194] Many job seekers with employment gaps have overcome employers' concerns and landed fulfilling career positions.

Explaining Job Hops in an Interview

As a general rule, employers begin to view a job seeker as a job hopper if they've held more than four to five jobs in ten years[195] or had a series of employments in a compressed period of time. Realizing that hiring is both time-consuming and expensive, employers view job hoppers as risky hires. From an employer's view, job hops reflect instability and give the impression of someone who gets easily dissatisfied or many other negative conclusions.

If your work history has job hops, address them in an interview with the same formula as employment gaps (anticipate that employers will ask, explain the circumstances without giving extreme detail, and ask a probing question about the position to shift focus away from the moves and back to you and your qualifications).

There are also several explanations specific to job hops that you can use (if they apply to you). One is demonstrating a strategic plan for your job moves (even if they did not work out). Another explanation is that in order to be more well-rounded for executive positions you took a position with a higher level of responsibility or in a new area (for example, out of sales and into operations).

A third approach is to admit to the job hops, accept your share of responsibility, mention some lessons you learned, then emphasize that you are looking for stable long-term employment. You can't afford another short stint. Your plan is new employment that

---

194 CareerBuilder, "Employers Share Encouraging Perspectives."

195 Lisa Amstutz, "Survey of HR Managers: How Many Job Changes is Too Many?" (blog), *Robert Half*, January 17, 2014, http://www.roberthalf.com/finance/blog/survey-of-hr-managers-how-many-job-changes-is-too-many?hsFormKey=06a77aee09a564eca4467cf5525e3c15 (accessed June 9, 2015).

will last several years. Finally, you can inform the employer that you have reevaluated your career and focused your efforts toward a particular career path or position type(s). You must be logical and convincing if you choose this approach.

Job hops are not a death knell to a satisfying and fulfilling career. However, establishing tenure and a track record of success with a single employer is always the preferred goal.

Handling the Money Question

Never bring up the topic of compensation during screening interviews. You want to establish a match for the position and build rapport with the employer. Bringing up the topic too soon sends the wrong message.

However, there is a growing trend among employers to inquire about compensation early in the interviewing process. In fact, according to a CareerBuilder survey, nearly half (48 percent) of employers now ask about compensation in their first talk with a job seeker.[196]

What if the employer asks you about compensation? The question can be viewed two ways: it could be a standard question asked of all candidates, so the employer can look for the price tag. Or, it could be an expression of interest, and a classic buying sign. The problem is there is no way to know for sure, unless you ask the hiring executive(s), which could create an awkward moment in your interview. Try to avoid that.

If asked about money, here is a response that works well:

> *"I'm currently earning $_____. But, I'm sure if you extended an offer to me, that offer would be fair, in light of my past accomplishments and future potential with (the company). And based upon this position's qualifications and expectations, I see my talents contributing to your organization's success by (list ways you can contribute)."*

This response allows you to address the question and leverage the situation into an opportunity to sell yourself.

If you are uncomfortable disclosing your compensation, this response can work well also:

> *"I'm glad you brought that up. All I'm going to ask is the compensation for this position be fair and competitive and I'm sure we will arrive at a fair number once we have thoroughly discussed the position and my qualifications."*

---

196 CareerBuilder, "Forty-Nine Percent of Workers Do Not Negotiate Job Offers, Finds CareerBuilder Compensation Survey," news release, August 21, 2013, http://www.careerbuilder.com/share/aboutus/pressreleasesdetail.aspx?sd=8/21/2013&id=pr777&ed=12/31/2013 (accessed June 2, 2015).

This response puts the hiring executive at ease about compensation and invites further discussion about the position and your qualifications.

Closing the Interview

Closing an interview persuasively can be among the most important moments in an interview. It can differentiate you from other candidates. If done well, you can move closer to a job offer.

Provide a Summary Statement of your Qualification.

Analogous to the closing argument of an attorney to a judge or jury, try to close the interview with a brief summary of how your skills and background match the position and how being hired will benefit the company. This is a great technique to remind the hiring executive of your qualifications for the job.

Ask to Proceed or Ask for the Job.

If you have a sincere and earnest interest in the position and the company, make sure to express your interest in the proceeding in the interviewing process.

Should your interview be the final step in the process, and you want the job, ask for it. Doing so removes the mystery for the hiring executive and could be exactly what he or she wants to hear. Don't be coy. If you want the job, say so.

Ask about Timing

Make sure you get some commitment on the timing of a decision (the persuasion principle of consistency and commitment). This could be a decision for the next step or the final hiring decision. Then, to control your own expectations, add one week. Discussions like these just seem to take longer than anticipated.

General Interviewing Tips

Some general suggestions to remember about interviews:[197]

- Arrive ten to fifteen minutes early. Being late is never excusable. If you are going to be late, call the hiring executive.

- Smile. Maintain good eye contact with the hiring executive. If you don't, the hiring

---

197 Portions adapted from Claycomb and Dinse, *Career Pathways*, Part 8.

executive may draw a conclusion that you are being dishonest or have something to hide.

- Get the hiring executive to describe on-the-job responsibilities early so you're able to match your qualities, achievements, and experience to those requirements. This is an effective interview tactic.

- Try to avoid answering questions with a simple yes or no. Whenever possible, mention an accomplishment or success story.

- Stick to the facts and be genuine when discussing personal strengths or achievements with the hiring executive. Remember: only you are responsible for selling yourself to the hiring executive. Make the hiring executive realize the company *needs* you in the organization.

- Take extra copies of your resume. You may meet with others you did not know about. Don't be caught unprepared.

- Do not exaggerate (or lie). Answer questions truthfully.

- Never be negative regarding current or past employers. If you are, it conveys to the employer that you hold a grudge or may have an attitude problem.

- Do not over-answer or give long-winded responses. Give appropriate and responsive answers, but keep them brief. There is anecdotal evidence that more job seekers advance in the interview process and receive more offers when the hiring executive talks more in the interview than the job seeker.[198] Answer questions, but be sure to listen.

- Do not ask about perks (paid time off, compensation, performance increases, and so on) in any first interview(s) unless the hiring executive mentions them first. If he or she requests a salary figure, refer to the script from the Handling the Money Question section in this chapter.

- Behave as if you want to be hired for the position you're interviewing for, but be open to different opportunities. Being able to choose from multiple offers is more advantageous than having just one.

---

198 "Understanding the Employer's Perspective," Internships.com, http://www.internships.com/student/resources/interview/prep/getting-ready/understand-employer (accessed July 10, 2015).

- Ask questions throughout the interview—without interrupting the hiring executive—not just when the hiring executive is finished. An interview should be a mutual exchange of information, not a one-sided conversation. Frequently, you will be evaluated based on the questions you ask.

- If you feel the interview is going badly or realize you've been passed over, do not let your discouragement show.

Debrief Yourself

After every interview, take a few minutes to reflect upon how it went. This self-debriefing is designed to help you collect your thoughts on what *you* liked or disliked about the company, opportunity, people, office environment, products, services, and so on. It is also an opportunity for you to reflect upon your interview performance and make necessary changes.

Ask yourself these questions:

1. *How long did the interview last?* As a general rule, the longer an interview lasts, the better. Remember that approximately 60 percent of all successful hires are based on personal chemistry.[199] The longer the interview, the more rapport is built.

2. *What things did I do well?* Praise yourself for those things you did well in the interview(s). Write them down.

3. *Was I unprepared for any questions?* Write them down and craft an answer. There's always the chance you'll be asked that question again.

4. *What important issues were mentioned in the interview?* Use these items as part of your thank-you letter.

5. *What did I learn during my research and interview that appeals to me?* List the positive things about the company, opportunity, people, and so on.

6. *Identify any concerns and negatives.* This is different from identifying unanswered questions. Items that go here are red-flag areas (e.g., the company is about to file for bankruptcy).

7. *Rate the opportunity on a scale of one to ten.* This is an emotional, gut feeling. How

---

199 DiResta, interview by Canters, "How to Blitz."

do you *feel* about it? You are looking for an opportunity that not only seems right, but feels right too.

8. *Was compensation discussed?* You will not bring up the topic of compensation, especially during initial interviews. However, if the hiring authority broaches the topic, it could be a sign of interest. Write down what was said.

9. *How was it left?* Were the parting comments simply a description of the interview process or was there a definite indication that you would be asked back for more interviews? Obviously, you want an expression of continued interest.

10. *How do I rank this opportunity against others I am pursuing?* Keep track of the opportunities and how they compare to each other. If an opportunity is not for you, notify the hiring executive and release yourself from the interview process.

11. *Was there anything I could have done better or differently?* Honestly assess your performance. Make note of those things you would do differently or better.

Write a Thank-You Letter

You need to thank the hiring executive for their time. See Chapter 6, Cover Letters and Other Written Communications.

- Immediately following the interview, write down key issues discussed. Think of the qualifications and perhaps professional traits the employer is looking for and match your strengths to those.

- Send the letter (email or snail mail) no later than twenty-four hours following the interview.

- If there's no communication in one week's time, call to let the employer know you are still interested and want to move forward in the process.

Second and Home-Office Interview Strategies

Second interviews (as well as home-office interviews) are conducted to clarify information;

dig more deeply into your background, skills, and experience; secure additional input from others; and ensure you are a fit with company culture and personality. Planning and preparation are keys to a successful second interview.

The following tactics will help you achieve success at a second interview—hopefully leading to a job offer:

1. **Get an agenda that identifies your interviewer(s).** Once you have it, research their backgrounds, tenure with the company, promotions, previous employers, schools, and so on.[200] Look for something you share in common with them, and before the interview mention that you've read about them. Most executives will be impressed you took the time to research them (especially if you offer a sincere compliment). All of this taps into the persuasion principle of liking and personal chemistry.

2. **Review your notes from the first interview.** Try to decipher what about your qualifications, professional skills, and qualities scored enough points to earn you a second interview. Also, determine where you might be weak. Emphasize your strengths, and compensate with assets to offset weaknesses.[201]

3. **Prepare questions.** Focus on the company, position, and each of the hiring executives you will meet. Make sure your questions are focused on their area of responsibility. A good general question is, "What is the number one issue or challenge you are facing in the (Name of Department)?"

4. **Be ready for in-depth conversations.** Fully engage every hiring executive in deep discussions about your skills. Remember the UPAC method for answering general interview questions and showcasing yourself. In-depth interviews are normally where behavioral questions come up. Remember the process of handling those kinds of questions. Keep in mind you are being evaluated on your overall fit within the company as well as your ability and skill set.[202]

5. **Ask for concerns.** This is the same tactic as with screening interview(s). Try to defeat the concern and emphasize a compensating asset.

6. **Close (and, when appropriate, ask for the job).** As the second round of interviews

---

200 Hansen, Katharine, PhD. "Do's and Don'ts for Second (and Subsequent) Job Interviews," *Quintessential Careers*, http://www.quintcareers.com/second-interviewing-dos-donts/ (accessed February 16, 2016).

201 Ibid.

202 Ibid.

winds down, close by telling the hiring executives that you *want the job, and ask for an offer*. This is especially true if this is a final home-office visit. Be ready to discuss compensation should the employer bring it up.

7. **One final thought: get a good night's sleep.** Second or home-office interviews can be long, especially if your day is comprised of a series of interviews.[203]

Common Interviewing Mistakes

There are a plethora of mistakes that can be made during an interview. Many are common sense, such as don't chew gum in an interview. However, lesser known are the verbal and nonverbal mistakes that job seekers make.

This is a big deal. Research indicates that over 98 percent of hiring executives base much of their hiring decisions on both verbal and nonverbal communication skills.[204] Below is a list of the most notable mistakes job seekers make:

- Not listening.[205] This includes interrupting the hiring executive.

- Not making eye contact.[206]

- Being careless about appearance and hygiene. Wearing unprofessional attire (including accessories). Wearing too much perfume or cologne. Having bad breath.

- Failure to provide a coherent and organized response to the question asked.[207] Failing to articulate.

- Giving rambling responses. Providing needless information. Boring the hiring executive. Not staying on topic.[208] Being long-winded.

- Lacking enthusiasm about the position or company.

---

203 Ibid.

204 Peterson, Marshalita Sims. "Personnel Interviewers' Perceptions of the Importance and Adequacy of Applicants' Communication Skills," *Communication Education* 46, no. 4 (1997): 287–291, quoted in Kurtzberg and Naquin, *Essentials*, p. 31.

205 Kurtzberg and Naquin, *Essentials*, p. 31.

206 Ibid.

207 Ibid.

208 Ibid.

Not Getting the Job: Handling the Rejection

Accept this fact: you will be rejected. For some, one of the most emotionally difficult things to endure is a rejection after progressing through the interviewing process for a job. It can come verbally, by email, or by written letter. It can be disheartening . . . all of your time and effort for nothing. Well, not exactly. Take some time and review and analyze the interviewing experience with this employer. After you receive the news, decompress for a while, and then evaluate the entire interviewing process with that employer. Think through it step by step. What did you do well that got you into the process? What did you do well during the process? What did you learn? Now, what could you have done better (if anything)? Realize that hiring decisions are often subjective. There may have been nothing else you could have done. Regardless, take it apart and perhaps write things down. Reinforce in yourself what you do well and keep doing that. Learn from any mistakes and make adjustments. You don't want to make the same mistake again. Ask the hiring executive (or someone in the process) for candid feedback. Many employers resist doing this for fear of possible litigation—some even have company policies prohibiting the giving of feedback. If you get feedback, learn from it.

Finally, after sending a thank-you letter, move on. Your future (today) is not with that company, but some other employer. It's up to you to persevere and move forward. Your next career position is out there waiting for you.[209]

Hiring Timeline: a Longer Process

Hiring practices have changed over the last several years. Most notably, the interview process for many professional-level positions has gotten longer.[210] There are a multitude of reasons for this. Here are some common ones:

1. **The business climate or priorities have changed.** Slowed sales, legislative threats, financing, product and service issues, or any one of a number of other business issues

209 See also, Simpson, Cheryl, 10 Healthy Ways to Cope with Job Search Rejection, https://www.linkedin.com/pulse/10-healthy-ways-cope-job-search-rejection-chery. March 27, 2017 (accessed March 29, 2017).

210 Weber, Lauren, and Rachel Feintzeig. "Why Companies Are Taking Longer to Hire," *Wall Street Journal*, September 1, 2014, http://www.wsj.com/article_email/companies-are-taking-longer-to-hire-1409612937-lMyQjAxMTA1MDIwMjEyNDIyWj (accessed February 16, 2016).

may take a higher priority than filling the position.[211]

2. **A change or review of company strategy.** A senior-management or board of directors can change or review the business necessity for the position. These high-level meetings can also bring into review the hiring profile or job description of the professional background needed to fill the position. If these meetings get scheduled or are in the near future, the hiring process will wait until decisions are made.[212]

3. **Economic fear.** Delay in hiring can be an indication of lack of confidence in economic conditions, because a slow economy and hesitation about hiring reinforce each other.[213]

4. **Scheduling issues of the hiring executive or someone necessary to the process.** Business trips, client meetings, off-site strategy meetings/retreats, vacations, illness, family issues, and so on can prolong the process. Until schedules can be reconciled, the process stalls.[214]

5. **Scheduling issues of other job seekers.** Employers will accommodate the scheduling needs of well-qualified job seekers. While these schedules are worked out, you wait.[215]

6. **Courting passive candidates.** When employers recruit currently employed candidates, this can often extend the hiring process. Courting employed candidates can take longer than hiring those who are actively seeking new employment.[216]

7. **Fear of making a hiring mistake.** According to a CareerBuilder study, "The vast majority of employers admit that making a bad hire is far more costly than leaving a position open."[217] A mistake can also blemish the hiring executive's track record with the company, which scares the executive.

As a defense mechanism against making a hiring mistake, many employers have

---

211 Joyce, "After the Interview."

212 Ibid.

213 Weber and Feintzeig, "Why Companies Are Taking Longer."

214 Joyce, "After the Interview."

215 Ibid.

216 Weber and Feintzeig, "Why Companies Are Taking Longer."

217 CareerBuilder, "2015 Candidate Behavior Study."

elevated the requirements for a qualified candidate and put elaborate interview processes in place. This includes adding several other executives into the process, using personality profiles and other tests more often,[218] and employing industrial psychologists, among other mechanisms (hence creating perceived safeguards against a bad hire and shared risk if the hire does not work out). As a result, you will interview with more people and "jump through more hoops" as you go through the interview process.

You need to accept the reality that many interview processes will take longer than you expect. Accepting this fact will help you control your expectations and make it emotionally easier to deal with.

There are a couple of things you can do to avoid getting frustrated about these elongated interview processes. First and foremost, continue your job-search efforts unabated. Don't stop. Find new opportunities with other employers.[219]

Stay in routine contact with the hiring executive. Put the hiring executive at ease that you are a good hire (and not a hiring mistake waiting to happen). Through your communications, continue to match your background to the needs of the company. Stress your accomplishments. Use your best judgment on what other kinds of information to provide (see the list in the Drip Marketing section in Chapter 10).

Another way is to inform the hiring executive of another pending offer. Only use this tactic if the other offer is real. Sometimes this can motivate an employer to move forward. With others, it won't.

There are a couple of hiring "excuses" you may hear that you should be aware of:

"We want to make sure we hire the 'right' person for the job."

If this were true about you (from their perspective), you would be progressing in their interview process.

"We've decided to put the position on hold."

Seldom does an on-hold position resurface anytime soon.

If you should hear these phrases, take those opportunities off your active list. It is highly improbable they will result in further interviews and a job offer.

Eventually these long interview processes will shorten once employers begin to lose out on enough desirable candidates. Forward-thinking companies that are more aware of the hiring market will catch on quicker and change, as opposed to those companies that seek the perceived comfort of process and time. Until that happens, you will have to contend with longer interview processes.

---

218 Jena McGregor, "Interviewing for a Job."

219 Joyce, "After the Interview."

Chapter 12

Unique Tactics That Create Differentiation

Gather in your resources, rally all your faculties, marshal all your energies,
focus all your capacities upon mastery of at least one field of endeavor.
— John Haggai[220]

Differentiation has been mentioned numerous times in this book. It is pivotal to your job search to persuade the hiring executive that you are special. Creating differentiation in the mind of the employer is powerful because it taps into the persuasion principle of scarcity.

The following techniques will help further differentiate you from other job seekers. Each requires time, effort, and thoughtful preparation. To be effective, each tactic must be a substantive and well-presented package or document. Otherwise, they distract from your candidacy. Weigh how these tactics would be received by the hiring executive when deciding to use them or not. Well-timed and properly used, these tactics can catapult your candidacy to top-contender status for the open position.

---

220 Tracy, Brian. *Eat That Frog!: 21 Great Ways to Stop Procrastinating and Get More Done in Less Time*, 2nd ed. (Buchanan, NY: ReadHowYouWant, 2008), p. 84.

★ Brag Book

One of the more impactful strategies to create differentiation is a brag book. It is a collection of bound documents supporting (and showcasing) the qualifications and accomplishments referenced in your resume. In a business context, think of a brag book as your marketing packet. It contains important information about your candidacy for the job. The brag book also differentiates you from other job seekers by demonstrating your initiative.

While it takes some effort, a brag book is also a confidence builder. There's something gratifying and self-esteem boosting about seeing your accomplishments in print.

The brag book should be bound in a presentation binder and can be discussed during an interview, left with the hiring executive, or both. The brag book's length is up to you, but keep it to a maximum of fifteen pages as a general rule.

Here are some suggested key documents to include in your brag book:

1. **Cover Page**—Include your name (in large print), the position you are interviewing for and the name of the company you are interviewing with.

2. **Table of Contents**—There will be groupings of documents. You can either number each page in the book or delineate by sections (for example, Resume, Letters of Recommendation, and so on).

3. **Resume**—When possible, customize the resume to the job you are pursuing.

4. **Awards**—These demonstrate that you have been recognized for your ability and expertise.

5. **Press Releases**—Press releases regarding any project or achievement that you were involved or named in.

6. **White Papers**—Portions of any significant business analyses or white papers you wrote.

7. **Graphs or charts**—Graphs or charts that demonstrate your performance.

8. **Job Performance Reviews/Summary**—Positive comments from job performance reviews (be careful not to include references that could be considered confidential or proprietary).

9. **Personality Profile Results**—Summary page or selected pages from a personality profile that you believe enhances your candidacy.

10. **Articles**—Articles written about you, especially from industry or trade publications. Articles (or portions thereof) that you have authored.

11. **Letters of Recommendation**—Letters from clients, former bosses, colleagues, and so on.

12. **Endorsements and Testimonials**—Gather positive things that have been said about you. These include "great job" emails and LinkedIn recommendations.

13. **Professional Organizations**—A list of these demonstrates that you are involved in your industry.

14. **Civic Involvement**—Any documentation regarding your civic and philanthropic involvement.

15. **References**—Provide a list of references that will attest to your ability, professional qualities, and personal character.

A brag book is a great topic of discussion during interviews or a leave-behind to remind the hiring executive of your abilities and accomplishments.

When to Present the Brag Book

There is no right or wrong time, just perhaps a good or better time, to present the brag book. It is a matter of reading the situation and choosing the moment that feels best. However, it is normally best to introduce the book early in the interview so the hiring executive can be impressed (the majority will be), and possibly talk about its contents during the course of the conversation.

A brag book's primary function is to showcase your credentials and demonstrate your interest in the position and company. It will also assure the employer that you have tangible proof of your abilities and accomplishments. Few people take the time to provide any sort of validation or proof of their abilities. A brag book shows potential employers you are serious—a high achiever who will put in extra effort now and on the job, which gives you a competitive advantage over other job seekers.[221]

---

221 Strankowski, Donald J. "Your License to Brag: The Brag Book," Ascend Career and Life Strategies, LLC, April 2005, http://www.ascendcareers.net/newsletters/April2005.html (accessed February 17, 2016).

★ Career Summary Sheet

A career summary sheet is usually a one-page document designed to intrigue, inform, and impress an employer. It summarizes your career experiences and focuses them specifically on an employer's particular need. When properly written and presented, the career summary sheet can be a notable differentiator and possible conversation starter. Use this as part of an interview where you want to make a brief presentation about your qualifications and understanding of the industry. Like a brag book, this can also be a leave-behind.

The most important consideration when contemplating whether or not to prepare a career summary sheet is the employer's receptivity.

A career summary sheet is not a restatement of your resume, although there could be information common to both. Unlike a resume that has standard sections (Professional Summary, Core Skills, Employment History, and so on), or a cover letter that has rules for proper formatting, a career summary sheet allows you to sell yourself in a persuasive manner. It is about you. Because of these unique characteristics, creating a career summary sheet can be difficult on the one hand, yet creative on the other.

In deciding whether to prepare a career summary sheet, first determine whether you can create an impactful, unique document. If you're unsure, don't pursue this tactic. If you do create a summary sheet and objective observers don't give you positive responses, reevaluate whether using one is right for you. If it isn't customized or unique to the employer and their needs, it's just another distracting piece of paper.

Some ideas for a career summary sheet include:

- Ask a question (to create intrigue); then answer it.

- Address a market trend.

- Use recommendations creatively.

- Reveal a professional insight using the first person ("I").

- Use your professional profile—similar to your resume's summary, but written differently.

- Emphasize an achievement with bar graphs.

- Reference any online information.

- Write a personal note at the bottom.

- Sign the document.

A career summary sheet is a blank canvas. Properly created, it can showcase your abilities, skills, and professional qualities. Format and present the summary sheet professionally. Make it consistent with your resume's formatting style, fonts, and so on.

In the following example, the job seeker knows the employer needs a senior-level sales professional with a demonstrated track record of success. He also learned that senior management had concerns about market shifts. He specifically targeted those issues in his career summary sheet.

Career Summary Sheet—Example

Jeff Holmes
123-456-7890
jeffxyz@yahoo.com
www.linkedin.com/in/jeffxyz

Do you need a proven sales and marketing professional on your team?

"Watching Jeff work with clients, media, markets, and more is a delight. His effectiveness in understanding and delivering the key messages to support our business goals is of the highest caliber."

— Peter Pumlin, Worldwide Vice President Sales, Big, Inc.

Are shifts in market trends impacting your business?

Having thrived through two major technology changes in two different industries, I have extensive experience with the effect of market shifts on organizations and business conditions. Throughout the economic slowdown and dozens of corporate downsizings, I have continued to exceed expectations. Regardless of the industry or the company maturity, I want to help a business maximize their results by leveraging my experiences and marketing capabilities with my successful selling skills.

Notable accomplishments

- First sales executive to ever negotiate an exclusive five-year single-supplier contract.
- Maintained 82 percent of sales revenue in single-supplier relationships.
- Mentored China sales team to achieve a 300 percent increase in sales for 2012.
- Consistently overachieved sales goals from 20XX–20XX with 105 percent to 200 percent performance.

- Managed an over $3 million project with global operations and teams spanning three continents.

- Grew segment customer base by 100 percent and capacity by 300 percent.

- Positioned flagship product to be chosen by 74 percent of professionals, marking a 34 percent increase.

- Increased attach ratio of segment-related products from 8 percent to 30 percent of divisional transactions.

- Improved Go-to-Market plan to reduce start-up time by two years and save $500,000.

Does your business need a results-oriented sales professional?

"Jeff is a dynamic business-to-business sales and marketing professional recognized for delivering results."

— Cindy Frene, CEO, Frene Consulting Group

Profile

I am a visionary sales and marketing executive with over twenty years corporate experience and ten years prior experience in private business. In my career I have worked with businesses of all sizes and scopes, from startups to international conglomerates. I have also sold and marketed everything from a $3 consumable to capital equipment in the $500,000 to $1M range. I have worked in both B2C and B2B environments, and recently have been developing business models in the evolving B2B2C markets. I have a track record of simultaneously exceeding sales goals and delivering customer satisfaction.

Capabilities

- Plans multimillion-dollar, capital-equipment sales campaigns.
- Delivers compelling sales presentations.
- Develops business and market concerns.
- Assesses landscape for competition.
- Exceeds sales and budget goals.
- Possesses local, national, and worldwide sales experience.
- Communicates comfortably with operational to C-level staff.

Videos
- Jeff Holmes sales presentation — YouTube
- Jeff Holmes interview 20XX — YouTube

★ Testimonial Sheet

A testimonial sheet is normally a one- to two-page document containing testimonial statements about you from former bosses, executives, and colleagues.

The document's persuasive powers (and potential for differentiation) come from the notion that others promoting you is more persuasive than you promoting yourself (the persuasion principle of social proof).[222] Therefore, the testimonial sheet must contain truly stellar statements—and enough of them—to convince the hiring executive that the statements are an accurate reflection of your performance and professional character.

There are a variety of sources for testimonials, including letters of recommendation; LinkedIn profile recommendations; statements contained in a job-performance review; complimentary emails from clients and colleagues; responses from quality-assurance questionnaires from clients; and even excerpts from speakers' notes from an awards banquet. Regardless of the source, the key is the testimonial or recommendation must be significant enough to impress the employer.

Identify the source of the testimonial by name, title, and company whenever possible, to ensure credibility. Inform your source that you are identifying them on the testimonial sheet. This is unnecessary with testimonials or recommendations from your LinkedIn profile, since that information is already in the public domain.

When to provide the testimonial sheet is a matter of professional judgment. Timing is important to ensure maximum impact. Other documents you plan to provide to employers could influence when you provide the testimonial sheet. It can become a matter of "which document when" during the interview process.

Consider withholding the testimonial sheet until mutual interest has been established in the interview and you sense the time is right to provide unique information that differentiates you from other candidates. Trust your professional judgment.

Here is an example of a testimonial sheet:

---

222 Matt, "Brag Book."

Tamara B. Mersmann, RN
84 Mashapaug Avenue ~ Boston, MA 01566
Home: 508-888-8990 ~ Cell: 508-888-6861 ~ tmersmann@charter.net

Colleague Testimonials 20XX–20XX

I have greatly enjoyed working alongside you. I also have the greatest confidence in you, and would hire you in a flash for any other sales role. I told Michael (CEO) that you have the purest motives/no agenda, i.e., get the job done, of anyone on his team. He agreed. As a person, you are the best! Great values, great faith, and great humanity all rolled into one.

Patrick Kahler
Senior Advisor, Strategy and Development
Acme Co.

I have had the privilege to work both as a management counterpart and direct report to Tammy. During both experiences, I was very impressed with Tammy's abilities. Tammy's style is very conversational with a get-it-done mentality. I would describe Tammy's management style as one that allows individuals to be empowered. Tammy is a listener not a teller, she does not try to mold you into her shadow, but wants you to bring new ideas and ways to be successful forward. Tammy sees the value in success for all, not just herself as a manager, which I believe why she is such a strong leader. Her view of a team, not a group with a leader, allows all to flourish and goals to be attained.

Stephan Wilkinson
Former Sales Executive
Fusion, LLC

Tammy is an asset to our company. She is a gifted individual who is able to blend her knowledge of operational and sales processes in betterment of revenue trends and team performance. She has turned a sub-performing infusion branch into a revenue leader.

Robert Enright
Chief Executive Officer

Fusion, LLCTammy's enthusiasm is wonderful. She has great initiative. She has hit the ground running and we are happy to have her as an employee.

Mischelle Murphy RN, MS
Vice President and Chief Operating Officer
Medical Management, Inc.
(excerpt taken from performance review)

An "energizing individual," a "power professional," "possessing a clear presence of mind in the face of difficult situations."

All of these and more are what is routinely spoken when one attempts to describe Tamara's work ethic, effectiveness, and true business savvy. I have personally witnessed Tammy emerge from some of the most challenging scenarios that one might meet in business today! Incredible!

Andrew Piper
Former Regional Sales Director
Hope Hospice

Tammy is truly a gifted sales professional, and I am happy to have had the opportunity to work with her. She is knowledgeable about the industry, works diligently, and focuses on tailoring solutions to meet customers' needs. In short order, Tammy was able to penetrate a new market, leveraging existing products and services, and create market demand. As a result of Tammy's efforts, TopInsurer was able to add new clients to its roster and generate revenue from nontraditional sources. Tammy is a great sales executive and I am happy to recommend her.

Jayson Andrewjeski
Former Vice President Operations
TopInsurer, Inc.

★ Action Plan

Another way to impress the employer and differentiate yourself from the competition is with an action plan, or a mini-business plan written specifically for the position you are pursuing. This is a tactic normally reserved for when you are advancing in the interview process with an employer.

From the first interview and your independent research, you should have a good idea about the job and the challenges facing the position or company. With this information in mind, write an action plan (thirty, sixty, or ninety days). You can go even further out if you want. The point is to demonstrate to the hiring executive you took the time to contemplate how you would begin performing the position's duties and responsibilities.

Consider some of these topics when formulating your action plan:

- Analysis of current market conditions

- Analysis of top competitors—strengths, weaknesses

- Analysis of products and services

- Any issues on distribution

- Analysis of any noteworthy regulatory compliance issues

- Any issue on delivery, implementation, client retention, technology, operations, and so on

- Any and all relevant topics related to your particular industry or position function

With an analysis of the topic (potential challenge), provide your proposed action steps followed by a reasonable prediction of the positive outcome (result). Think as if you are writing a success story using the CAR (Challenge, Action, Result) formula mentioned earlier.[223]

Overall considerations for the action plan include:

- Identifying needed or potential resources for your plan

- Identifying priorities and timing

- Determining how your plan would achieve the organization's potential goals

- Identifying which functional areas or company departments would need to be changed or engaged to achieve success

- Calculating how to measure success

There are a myriad of topics that could be addressed. Once you tap into your experience and critical-thinking abilities, the ideas and words will follow.

The action plan should be at least five pages in length, but no more than ten. Consider

---

223 Safani, "Tell a Story."

emailing the document to the hiring executive twenty-four to thirty-six hours prior to your interview so the document is read before you arrive. Be prepared to talk in-depth about its contents.

The action plan can also be in the form of a PowerPoint presentation. If you can borrow the design of the company's website as the background, do it. Keep the presentation reasonably short and focused on relevant topics.

For both written or PowerPoint action plans, don't get too detailed. Stay within your comfort zone of information. And make sure you make a statement early on that you are working from the limited information that has been shared in the interview process so far.

If it comes down to you and another candidate, your action plan differentiates you by offering the hiring executive insight into how you will do the job and provide results.

Advanced Techniques to Create Differentiation

The next techniques require additional time and commitment to be executed successfully.

Personal Website

There are several benefits of having a personal website when conducting a job search. According to Workfolio, an application development firm, just 7 percent of people looking for a job have their own website.[224] That means that 93 percent don't. By having a well-designed and informative personal website, you differentiate yourself from over 90 percent of all job seekers. In addition, creating a personal website demonstrates initiative. You took the time and effort to do something unique.

A personal website can create a positive first impression of you in a hiring executive's mind, often before your first face-to-face meeting. This is important, as "56 percent of all hiring managers are more impressed by a candidate's personal website than any other personal branding tool."[225] Starting the hiring process on that note is a significant advantage.

A personal website increases your "findability" and presence. Recruiters, HR, and hiring executives can find you online and view your site.

Naturally, a personal website is a great platform for job-search content. There is a lot of

---

224 Smith, Jacquelyn. "Why Every Job Seeker Should Have a Personal Website, and What It Should Include," *Forbes*, April 26, 2013, http://www.forbes.com/sites/jacquelynsmith/2013/04/26/why-every-job-seeker-should-have-a-personal-website-and-what-it-should-include/#73ae8b8a902e (accessed February 17, 2016).

225 Ibid.

job-search information you can put on your website. This includes your resume, contact information (make sure it appears in several places or is easily found), a personal bio, awards, recommendations, and so on (review the lists in the brag book and drip marketing sections for ideas). It is also a way to give a hiring executive insight into your personal life in addition to your professional experience. Just use good professional judgment on what information you disclose. And make sure that your resume, LinkedIn profile, and website information line up (employers, dates of employment, and so on).

Finally, a personal website is a great platform to communicate and advance your brand. Who you are and how you promote yourself is very important. When your branding message comes together with color and design on a website, you've created a message that can emotionally appeal to a hiring executive.

Before you start building your personal website, take some time and think through what kind of content you want to include, how you can differentiate yourself, and how you would like it to appear, among other considerations. Creating your website can be exhilarating. Take some time and do it right the first time. And remember, it doesn't have to be built in a day.

As for platforms and service providers, there are quite a few available. If you search for "The Top 10 Website Builders" on the Internet, you will get a list to choose from.[226]

A Blog

A blog is a place where you can write about your experiences, display your expertise on a topic, express opinions, comment on trends, etc. Frequently, a blogging feature is a part of your personal website. Blogging can help your job search in several ways.

Starting a blog is a clear differentiator. How many of your colleagues have a blog, especially for the purposes of a job search? Not many. Having a blog can certainly catch the attention of a hiring executive.

Tips on content: Write on topics you are comfortable. Research and read up on topics and issues. This keeps you mentally engaged in your industry and might even move you forward. Now, what's your opinion or insight on those topics and trends? It's fine to write a lengthy piece, but then break it down into small posts. Make it an eight-part series, for example. This way you are not constantly creating content. Try to be routine when posting—once a week on Tuesdays, for example.

---

226 See also, "The Best Website Builders 2016," Top10WebsiteBuilders, http://www.top10webbuilders.com/?s1-google/s2-us-search/s3-website-builder-p (accessed February 17, 2016).

The content of your blog can build upon and enhance your brand. It's a platform for you to express who you are and your expertise as a professional.

Your network will expand with a blog. It will start slowly, but as you post interesting information, the word spreads, both verbally and electronically. You can promote your blog through your LinkedIn account, Facebook, Twitter, and other social media venues. This can eventually lead to referrals, introductions, conversations, and job leads. But it takes time.

A blog can be an extension of an interview. Consider this: in the course of an interview a topic may come up that you have written about on your blog. If the conversation aligns with what you wrote, tell the hiring executive about your blog entry. That's not something a hiring executive hears often. Or, at the end of the interview, suggest to the hiring executive that he or she check out your blog (and personal website) for more in-depth information on you. If the hiring executive does, that amount of time spent on your blog is actually an extension of your interview.

Similar to personal websites (most are blogs), there are several service providers you can choose from. WordPress is often mentioned, but look at the same list referenced in the personal website section.

A word of caution: remember that blogging is a job-search tool. For some, it can become addicting. There are far more productive things to do to advance your job search than making blog entries—namely, networking and marketing your credentials. Don't fool yourself into believing that posting entries on your blog is significantly advancing your job search. It is clearly a differentiator, but it's not likely to be the driving force for job leads.

Infographic Resume

An infographic resume is a colorful, high-resolution document that visually presents your background and accomplishments by using pie charts, bar graphs, and time lines in creative ways. They can be particularly impactful when displaying notable achievements, high-level recommendations, and patterns of success, among other things.

The differentiating factor of an infographic resume comes from the fact that readers are drawn to colorful images. That attention can set you apart in today's crowded job market.[227] There's a tendency to remember things better when they are presented with images.

An infographic resume can, in limited circumstances, replace the traditional resume.

---

227 Pamela Skillings, "The Ultimate Infographic Resume Guide," *Big Interview* (blog), June 18, 2013, http://biginterview.com/blog/2013/06/infographic-resumes.html (accessed February 17, 2016).

This is most often the case in the creative fields like design, marketing, advertising, digital media, and so on.

However, for most, an infographic resume should be used as a supplement or differentiation tactic in conjunction with a traditional resume. Even then, its use is better suited for some positions (sales, for example) than others.[228] An infographic resume can be effective where your job search is concerned; just keep in mind these caveats.

There are advantages, disadvantages, and considerations for using an infographic resume in a job search. Let's start with a few advantages:

It differentiates you. Although the idea of an infographic resume has been around for a while, they are not widely used and therefore seldom seen by hiring executives in most industries. A well-thought-out, well-prepared, and well-presented infographic resume can make you stand out compared to other job seekers.[229]

It works well as a networking tool. You can use an infographic resume alongside (or instead of) your traditional resume and business cards when you network at an event or industry function.

One unique approach would be selecting your most persuasive achievements and creating an infographic handbill. Create a four-inch-by-six-inch infographic and put it on thicker paper or use it as a large business card. This is seldom seen; it's guaranteed to create conversation.[230]

It provides insight into your thinking and presentation skills. One interesting advantage to an infographic resume is it opens the door of insight into how you think and creatively present ideas and concepts. This can be persuasive if the position(s) you are pursuing require presentation skills.[231]

It vividly presents your professional background. Infographic resumes are colorful, high-resolution documents. Unlike your LinkedIn profile (which is an online template) and your resume (which has expected and accepted sections), an infographic resume is a blank canvas (similar to a career summary sheet, but different). It is a platform to creatively present your professional background and accomplishments any way you choose, using color and graphics.

---

228 See also, ibid.

229 Ibid.

230 See also, ibid.

231 Ibid.

Although the advantages of an infographic resume are attractive, there are considerations that may turn it into a disadvantage if not handled properly. These include:

How will it be received by hiring executives? This is a serious consideration. An infographic resume is a unique job-search technique and it can be intriguing. It can open your mind to all sorts of creative thoughts on how to present your information. This is especially true once you start viewing examples. However, it may not be the best strategy for every industry or position.[232] Only you can gauge the receptiveness and persuasive influence an infographic resume would have on hiring executives in your job search.

It must contain persuasive or unique information. If an infographic resume is not persuasive or is poorly constructed, it will hurt your job search. It can be a distraction, reflect negatively on your candidacy for the job, or eliminate you as a contender for the position.

It must look great. Not just good. Your final product must have a "holy cow this is really cool" factor. Otherwise, it will not have the persuasive and differentiating effect you are looking for. One interesting concept you could explore is creating an infographic section on your traditional resume. This would be a form of a showcase resume using color and graphics as your showcase section. Then, the resume information would follow in the usual style.[233]

A Few Final Thoughts about Infographic Resumes

It is highly recommended that you speak to professionals who create these documents. Seek their opinion as to whether you have the caliber of career information and accomplishments to have a persuasive and unique infographic resume (with the understanding that they will have the incentive to persuade you to buy their services). Set aside any negative thoughts about the infographic resume as an idea, and objectively seek out and evaluate examples of other infographic resumes from people with similar backgrounds to yours (if possible). Since creating the document on your own can take countless hours, hire a professional to do it for you. The time required to create an infographic resume is better spent pursuing other job-search activities—networking, marketing your professional credentials, and so on.

If you create an infographic resume (or have one created for you), get it out there. One easy thing to do is attach it to your LinkedIn profile. Obviously you want to have it with

232 Ibid.

233 See also, ibid.

you to hand out during networking events and as a supplement to interviews. Since you put the time, effort, thought, and money into this tactic, look for ways to leverage it in your job-search activities.

Caution: creating an infographic resume can be a distraction or become busywork stopping you from moving your job search forward. Be aware of your time and use it wisely. An infographic resume is a differentiator, but it will not get you a job all by itself.

Discovering examples of infographic resumes and professionals (vendors) who create them is as simple as conducting a Google search for "infographic resumes."

Chapter 13

References

The key to your universe is that you can choose. — Carl Frederick[234]

References often receive insufficient attention. They become an afterthought of the job-search process until suddenly they are needed.

References can have a significant influence on the hiring decision. Depending upon who you provide as a reference, the reference can appeal to the persuasion principles of authority and social proof.

Many employers never ask for references. Some ask simply to look at the list and decide whether they appear credible. And some call. Regardless, you must always be prepared to provide references. Put into a business context, references are your client testimonials.

As you think about your references, consider people that can attest to different aspects of your professional experience, professional skills (hard and soft), as well as your professional qualities. This can save you time when it comes to providing references. For example, let's say one of the themes of the interviewing process was technical skills and the professional quality of integrity. Who do you know that could speak, with examples or experience, to your technical skills? Who could attest to your professional integrity? It could be two different people.

---

234 "Carl Frederick Quotes," World of Quotes, http://www.worldofquotes.com/author/Carl+Frederick/1/index.html (accessed June 10, 2015).

References can play a vital role in getting a job, especially if the decision to hire comes down to two or three candidates. The recommendation from a solid reference can move the decision in your favor.

Choose Your References Wisely

A good reference is someone with firsthand knowledge of your ability, track record, and character. They can persuasively articulate your qualifications, experiences, strengths, and results to the employer. Choose someone you feel good about, who believes in you, wants you to succeed, and has your best interests at heart. Be sure to ask for permission to use them as a reference (as a professional courtesy), and ensure they will be positive about you. Also, touch base with your references regarding your job search, and notify them when you know (or have reason to believe) references will be checked. Prepare them with key information (details of the position, challenges the employer told you about, and so on), so your reference can showcase you to the employer.

References and a Secret Job Search

This can be tricky. You do not want the word getting out that you are exploring a career move because that could have negative ramifications. But, you need references. The key is approaching people you can trust. You may have to inform the hiring executive of your situation and indicate the sensitivity of your references. Most hiring executives will completely understand.

★ Unsolicited Third-Party Affirmation

This technique, if properly used, can be extremely persuasive. It can be used anytime during the interviewing process but can be most useful when a final hiring decision is about to be made. Here is how it works:

Ask one of your references, or someone that can vouch for you, to call the hiring executive, unannounced (it must be a phone call, not an email). The purpose is to speak with the hiring executive and provide persuasive information about you and your fit for the job (attempting to capitalize on the persuasion principle of social proof).

This technique works best when your reference does not mention that you asked them to make the call (leave that decision up to your reference). This technique's impact is further enhanced if the reference happens to know the hiring executive *and* that relationship is positive. Imagine the scenario. The hiring executive is at his desk. Hiring for that open position is in the back of his mind. His receptionist pages him and says there is a person on the line who would like to speak with him about you. He's curious. If he has a moment, he will take the call. Then, out of the blue comes this glowing recommendation. Calls like this do not happen every day. That call and the contents of the conversation will linger in the mind of the hiring executive and differentiate you, which is the desired effect. You may or may not get the job, but you can feel good that you gave one last shot at persuading the hiring executive in your favor.

Chapter 14

Evaluating and Negotiating a Job Offer

By fighting you never get enough, but by yielding you get more
than you expected. — Dale Carnegie[235]

One of the most important steps in your job search is navigating all the stages of a job offer, once one is received.[236] According to a nationwide survey conducted by CareerBuilder, nearly half (45 percent) of hiring executives wish to be flexible on a first offer. Negotiations are almost always an expected part of the process of receiving an offer, especially for "professional and business services workers."[237]

In employment negotiations, it is imperative that you be sensitive to your emotions as well as the employer's. Both parties must treat negotiations with respect and dignity so everyone feels good at the conclusion of the process.

In this chapter, we will discuss basic steps involved in successful negotiations so you can approach this process with knowledge, insight, and confidence. What follows are the top-tier guidelines of the art form that is negotiation.

---

235 Carnegie, Dale. *How to Win Friends and Influence People.* (New York: Simon and Schuster, 2010), p. 134.

236 Portions of this chapter adapted from Claycomb and Dinse, *Career Pathways*, Part 9.

237 CareerBuilder, "Forty-Nine Percent of Workers Do Not Negotiate."

Never Play Hardball

Never play hardball when negotiating a job offer. If you do this, one of two things will happen. One, the employer withdraws the offer. Two, the employer may take some form of reprisal later. Hardball simply has no place in employment negotiations. For example, many home buyers and sellers use these types of tactics when they negotiate.[238] It is a one-time transaction. This is why home buying has the potential to be such a confrontational and unpleasant experience. Do you want to start your new employment relationship under a dark cloud? Enough said.

Ten Steps for Evaluating and Negotiating an Offer: The WITS Approach™

Throughout the interview process, the employer has made a series of judgments as to whether you can make or save the company money;[239] whether you can do the job and do it well; and whether you are motivated to do the job and fit in culturally. All of this also influences your perceived value and ROI in the mind of the executive. The results of interviewing ultimately determine the decision to hire and any offer's monetary amount.

When an employer extends an offer of employment to you, it is easy to allow your excitement, emotions, or nerves to cloud your thinking. When that happens, you can make mistakes in judgment that may potentially be costly. According to a survey conducted by LinkedIn, 60 percent of job seekers rely on their own subjective judgment when negotiating compensation.[240] Relying on purely cosmetic factors to judge a job offer can cost you. That is not to say you shouldn't be excited—you should be. In fact, be ecstatic. An offer is the positive result of your hard work. However, this is the time to finish strong and make sure you evaluate the terms of the offer objectively and handle negotiations professionally.

The following ten-step methodology provides structure around evaluating, negotiating, and closing an offer of employment. You can call it the WITS Approach™: *Wait* before negotiating. *Investigate* the offer's terms. *Tally* and assess the terms both objectively and emotionally. *Settle* the negotiations. With these broad themes in mind, below are the intuitive steps for evaluating and logically negotiating a job offer:

---

238 Lisa Earle McLeod, "The Big Mistake People Make When They Negotiate," *Life on Purpose* (blog), *McLeod & More, Inc.*, March 26, 2014, http://www.mcleodandmore.com/2014/03/26/the-big-mistake-people-make-when-they-negotiate-2/ (accessed June 19, 2015).

239 Whitcomb, *Job Search Magic*, p. 274.

240 LinkedIn Talent Solutions, "2015 Talent Trends," p. 30.

1. Research
2. Preparation
3. Receiving the offer
4. Gathering all information
5. Evaluating
6. Negotiating (if necessary)
7. Reevaluating modified terms
8. Closing the negotiation and reaching an agreement
9. Accepting the offer
10. Getting the final offer in writing

And always remember: in a negotiation, keep your WITS about you.

Step One: Research, Research, Research

Before you can successfully evaluate and negotiate an offer of employment, it may be necessary to research the marketplace to discover how people with similar positions are compensated. Many job seekers already know this information using their skill set and experience as guidelines.

Sources

There are several websites that provide information on compensation for a variety of positions within an industry (www.salary.com, www.rileyguide.com). LinkedIn also provides salary information through its Salary Insight tool (www.linkedin.com/salary). This tool allows you to search by title and location. It also allows you to compare salaries based on education, experience, and company size, among others. To use the tool, you will need to share your salary information. Be mindful that information can be dated and is not always an accurate reflection of current compensation. However, the published information will give you some benchmarks to guide your thinking.

Another good method for determining a position's fair compensation is to contact colleagues with the same or similar positions. Presumably they will help you determine what is competitive in the market.

The final research method is to contact recruiters with whom you've already made contact. Who knows better than a recruiter about compensation being paid for various positions?

Step Two: Preparation

This is an area most job seekers either fall short in or neglect altogether.

Preparation brings together the information you have learned and received during your interview(s), and the research information you have discovered, and aligns it with your Target Opportunity Profile. Preparation also includes your assessment and insights on what you know and believe are the hiring executive's needs and wants in the open position. It is this insight—how the employer views his/her needs—that too often gets forgotten by job seekers at this stage of the process (review Understanding the Employer's Mindset in Chapter 3).

Thinking about, assessing, and understanding the hiring executive's point of view is critical when you are evaluating and negotiating a job offer. Any insight on how the hiring executive sees things or calculates the company's needs, wants, goals, and limitations is powerful, regardless of how imperfect your information is.

After you write down how the opportunity fits your Target Opportunity Profile, write down how you fulfill the needs and wants of the employer. Make note of any information you may want to mention or emphasize.

This preparation process will bring everything together, spark your thinking, and prepare you mentally to evaluate, engage, and negotiate a job offer.

Step Three: Receiving the Offer

Offers can be extended over the phone, by email, or face-to-face. Always express your appreciation and interest, but ask the hiring executive for some time to evaluate the offer.

It is not uncommon for an offer to have a deadline. However, most companies will give you at least twenty-four to forty-eight hours, and perhaps more, if necessary. The key at this juncture in the process is to make a well-informed decision. If you feel the need to buy time, this is when you can request more information, especially concerning benefits. Resist the impulse to negotiate at this time. Wait. You may not have all the information you need to evaluate the offer and make an informed decision.

Step Four: Gather All Information

Review the information about the offer and its terms. Remember to ask for and collect any missing information necessary to help you evaluate the offer fairly. Below is a non-exhaustive list of job-offer components:

- Salary

- Insurance—health, life, disability, dental

- 401(k)—retirement plan
- Bonus pay, structure, factors regarding how to earn bonuses
- Salary adjustments—timing of performance reviews and percentage
- Relocation expenses
- Tuition assistance
- Vacation or Personal Time Off (PTO)
- Commission structure
- Equipment—car, cell phone, computer, office equipment for home office, and so on
- Professional organization membership dues
- Stock options/stock grants
- Memberships (country club or fitness)
- Severance package

Step Five: Evaluate the Offer

When evaluating the offer, try to determine its total value in terms of compensation and benefits. Are there any trade-offs? Is there intangible value (less travel, shorter commute time)? If you are relocating, is there a cost-of-living adjustment that could positively or negatively affect the offer's value?

Judge the offer on professional and emotional terms. What are your feelings about working for the company? Or the hiring executive? Are there other emotional or logistical considerations?

How does this career opportunity line up with your Target Opportunity Profile?

Speak with a trusted, uninvolved friend or colleague—their objective insight may help clarify matters or bring up advantages or concerns you hadn't considered.

Determine your walk-away point on monetary compensation. Although you may not know exactly what your bottom-line amount is, you should have a good initial feeling of it. Negotiations have not begun, but have a sense of when to walk away. When it comes to negotiations, only you can assess the offer's terms to determine whether it will work for you. Assess whether you might be willing to negotiate away something in exchange for something else you want.

And there is always a chance that the offer is acceptable just as it is. If so, accept it—congratulations, you've landed a job.

Step Six: Negotiation: Establish a Tone of Cooperation and Justify Your Requests

Establish a Tone of Cooperation

If negotiations are necessary, call the hiring executive again and express your interest and enthusiasm about the opportunity. This next point is important: hopefully you have established good rapport with the hiring executive. Set the tone for the negotiations by indicating that you want the job, and by working together you should be able to reach a mutually beneficial agreement for the company, the hiring executive, and you. This step is important because it establishes the environment of cooperation. Inform the hiring executive that there are a few topics that need to be discussed, and once they are resolved, you would be in a position to accept the offer.

Justify Your Requests

Employers do not mind negotiating job-offer terms as long as the requests are reasonable and the negotiating process is done quickly. One of the most powerful negotiating techniques is providing logical and reasonable justification for a request. Research indicates that people have a deep sense of fairness.[241] Justification appeals to the hiring executive's sense of fairness. It doesn't always work, but it can help.

Begin the conversation on a positive note with those major items you agree upon. Then discuss points of negotiation, beginning with the most important. Frequently this will be compensation, although there can obviously be others such as benefits, PTO, and more.

If the point of negotiation is compensation and the salary is not high enough, ask whether it can be increased; state a specific number. Justify the increase based on your past earnings, qualifications, accomplishments, and so on.

There could be several reasons for a significant difference between what you are seeking and what the company is offering. The company may not have the budget for the difference between what you want and what they can offer. Another explanation is perhaps the company has a parity issue—in other words, there are other employees with the same position getting paid less. Hiring executives must be sensitive to these and other issues.

One way to handle this issue is to explore a title change that could put you in a different pay range or a customized title that justifies the compensation difference.

Another approach to increased compensation is to ask for a sign-on bonus or to have a job-performance review in three to six months. Perhaps you can negotiate higher incentive

---

241 Honck, Alan, with Gordon Orians. "Are We Born With a Sense of Fairness?" *Pacific Standard*, December 26, 2012, https://psmag.com/are-we-born-with-a-sense-of-fairness-edd2d2680c10#.ce304fxbb (accessed April 18, 2016).

compensation based on agreed-upon performance. These techniques can increase your total annual compensation.

However, another concept is to leave some money on the table. The idea here is this: if you negotiate higher compensation, the hiring executive may hire you, but since you were so expensive their expectations are heightened. The time line for a return-on-investment for hiring you may get shorter.

Silence Is Golden

One of the most difficult things to learn in negotiations is silence. Silence in negotiations is not a bad thing; in fact, it can be golden (literally).

For some job seekers, enduring silence can be hard, especially when you really want the job. You don't want to make the hiring executive uncomfortable or risk having the executive pull the offer altogether. That is very unlikely to happen. Just make your request and resist any urge you have to speak—bite your lip if you have to; it'll heal. The employer has the ball in his court. Do not interpret any silence as a rejection from the hiring executive. Give the hiring executive the time necessary to process your request. If you speak and break the silence, there is a high probability that you will not get your request (at least in the form you requested). The end result is you may have just negotiated against yourself.

Step Seven: Reevaluate Modified Terms

As negotiations proceed and terms are modified, reevaluate how you feel about the job, the offer's terms, and the opportunity. Are the modified terms moving you closer to what you feel comfortable accepting?

Step Eight: Close Negotiations and Reach an Agreement

Sometimes during negotiations, proposals and counter proposals will be exchanged between you and the hiring executive. New terms may be offered and other considerations may come into play. But when terms seem to be reaching a point of agreement, you need to close the negotiations by telling the hiring executive that if he/she can meet the points of negotiation, you will:

- Accept
- Resign from your current position (as applicable)
- Refuse a current employer's counteroffer (if offered)
- Discontinue discussion with other companies
- Start on an agreed-upon date

These closing statements finalize the negotiations. If the hiring executive accepts your requests, there are no more negotiations and you must follow through and accept.

Step Nine: Accepting the Offer—Be Timely

Always show appreciation for an offer of employment. Accept an offer immediately (or as timely as possible), especially if the terms have been negotiated and mutually agreed on. Doing so starts the employment relationship on the right foot, with optimism. Your excitement about the company and opportunity will also be communicated to the employer.

Step Ten: Obtain Final Offer in Writing

Ask for the final offer in writing and establish a start date. Start dates are generally negotiable if you have special circumstances that prevent you from starting when the hiring executive wants.

If Negotiations Fail

If negotiations cannot resolve the differences, close the negotiations professionally. Never burn bridges. You don't know when you will encounter or interact with the hiring executive again under different circumstances.

It is not uncommon for a hiring executive to approach you later with different terms. Things can change in a company to open the door for an opportunity. Closing negotiations professionally keeps that door open for the future. More on turning down an offer in the next section.

Declining an Offer of Employment

The key to declining an offer is to do so professionally and gracefully. The employer has put in hours of time and effort and concluded that you can add value to the company. However, for any one of a hundred reasons, the job is just not right for you.

Your decision to turn down the offer must be prompt. The employer has a position to fill, and needs to move forward with their process. Delaying your decision and notification is not fair to the employer.

It is always best to verbally tell the employer of your decision. It's the mature and professional way to handle the situation. Also, follow up your call and conversation with a brief email declining the offer.

In your communications, always show your appreciation for the hiring executive's time and interest. Pay a sincere compliment to the hiring executive, the company, its future, and so on.

Provide a reason for your decision. It can be general or reasonably specific depending upon the circumstances. Never state a negative reason.

If you are not already connected to the hiring executive on LinkedIn, extend a *customized* invitation. This creates a line of communication for future employment opportunities.

Below is a letter that contains the important points mentioned above, which can function as an outline for your call to the hiring executive as well:

> *Thank you so much for the offer of the assistant manager position. I am flattered to be chosen. I do appreciate your time and consideration. ABC Company is a dynamic organization with innovative products and services. Its future is bright.*
>
> *However, after careful consideration, I have decided to pursue another opportunity that I believe is a better fit for me at this stage of my career.*
>
> *It has been a true pleasure getting to know you and the other members of your team.*
>
> *Sincerely,*

Although the hiring executive will likely be disappointed, you want him or her to come away from the engagement with good feelings about you, as a candidate and a professional.

Negotiation Mistakes

In addition to failing to establish a tone of cooperation, not justifying requests, and negotiating against yourself by speaking when you should be silent, here are other common negotiating mistakes:

1. **Not preparing for job-offer negotiations.** Compile all the information you have about the company and opportunity, how it fits your needs, and—most importantly—how you solve the employer's hiring need.

2. **Misrepresenting yourself or any of the facts involved in the negotiations in any way.** If you lie and get caught, you lose big. The offer will go away and your reputation will be tarnished.

3. **Overemphasizing salary.** Avoid doing that. Compensation is important, but it should not be the sole determining factor in negotiations. Instead, evaluate the total offer inclusive of benefits and the non-tangibles (living in Charlotte, shorter commute, and so on). It is also important to evaluate the opportunity and how it can benefit your career path.

4. **Over-negotiating.** Use your discretion and professional judgment. Pick the item(s) of most importance and negotiate on those topics, falling back on less important topics if needed. It is one thing to be respected for your good, professional negotiation ability. Being viewed by the hiring executive as "gimme, gimme, gimme," is entirely different. That raises doubts in the employer's mind about whether he or she is making the right decision and your fit with company culture.

Final Thoughts on Successful Negotiation

Negotiation measures both your and the hiring executive's views, with an acceptable outcome for both parties being the preferred goal. Ideally, each of you will be willing to accept what the other is willing to give.

Remember, the ultimate goal is for both parties to feel comfortable with the offer's final terms.

How to Buy Time with a Job Offer

Receiving a job offer is normally great news. It's the successful culmination of all your hard work. Unless, you are in the midst of the interviewing process with other employers and you want to see if something better or more interesting comes through. How can you "buy some time" with the company that offered you a job while exploring your other opportunities? Your approach depends on whether you need a few days or a few weeks.

Be appreciative. Regardless of the amount of time you need, always show your appreciation for the offer. The employer has expended their time and resources and concluded that you can add value to their organization. Be appreciative.

Ask for needed information. If you need just a few days to see if another offer is going to be extended, ask questions or ask for information from the employer extending the offer. Frequently, asking questions about benefits or requesting information for unanswered questions about the position can get you a few days.

Ask for time. You can request that the employer give you a specific amount of time (a few days to maybe a week) to consider the offer. Most companies will allow for this. This must be handled professionally and with finesse because you don't want to leave the impression that their offer is second choice.

If you need several weeks. If you need an extended period of time (like several weeks), things get trickier. The request for an extended length of time to contemplate an offer is a clear indication that you want to consider other opportunities, while keeping their offer in your pocket. The best approach is to be honest and appeal to the employer's sense of understanding (empathy). Here is a script (which can be converted into an email, depending upon your circumstances) that will get you thinking in the right direction:

> *Thank you for your offer. I sincerely appreciate you selecting me for the position. I am very interested in <Company Name> and the contribution I can make.*
>
> *As you know, I am proactively exploring my career options. This is an important decision for me and it needs to be the right move. I hope you understand. I am asking for a few weeks to give you a decision. I intend to make a final decision on or before <give a specific date if you can>.*
>
> *It's my hope that you can understand my situation and if the roles were reversed you would want this level of consideration as well. Please do not interpret my request as any lack of interest. It is not. It is simply a request of time so I can make a well-informed career decision that not only affects me but my family as well.*

The employer is under no obligation to grant you this extension of time. However, the emotional appeal may get you some time to see if other offers materialize.

A hardball response. If the employer refuses your request for time and gives you a hardball response, pause and take serious note of it. Depending upon the circumstances, it could be a red flag. A poor outcome would be accepting the offer and discovering a difficult company culture that results in another job change.

Strategic use of the extended offer. It is acceptable to inform other employers that you have a pending offer. This could include the time limitations on that offer, if you believe that it could be a strategic advantage to release that information. Occasionally, this information can speed up the decision-making process if you are a preferred candidate. Using this technique can give you some insight regarding a company's interest in you. If they pick up the pace and move you quickly through the interviewing process, you are likely a top candidate (there could still be other top candidates as well). On the other hand, if they do not, you may not be a preferred candidate or the company is bound by its process and cannot expedite your candidacy.

What not to do. Do not accept an offer of employment *with the intention* of leaving when that better offer comes through. This is grossly unfair to the employer and will burn bridges within that company and potentially tarnish your reputation in your professional network.

Do not leave an employer that has offered you a job in the dark. If you have been granted time for your decision and opted not to accept to position, professionally decline the offer.

Chapter 15

Resignation and Counter Offers

The apprenticeship of difficulty is one which the greatest of men have had to serve. — Samuel Smiles[242]

Resignation

Resigning from a position must always be done with the utmost professionalism. Avoid resigning and departing on bad terms or under a cloud of misgivings.[243] The world is small, and how you handle your resignation and departure could impact your future, especially for those in a niche industry or smaller market. Although resigning is awkward, if you use the following recommendations, it will be smoother.

First and foremost, do not resign until you have an acceptable and unconditional offer of employment from your new employer. Although you may have (and signed) a written offer letter, that offer might depend on background or drug checks, and/or reference

---

242 Smiles, Samuel. *Character*, new ed. (London: John Murray, 1876), p. 350.

243 Alison Green, "How to Resign Your Job Gracefully," *On Careers Blog, U.S. News & World Report*, July 28, 2008, money.usnews.com/money/blogs/outside-voices-careers/2008/07/28/how-to-resign-your-job-gracefully (accessed February 17, 2016).

verification. After all that, then the offer is "live," but not before. Check with your new employer's HR department to confirm that contingencies are satisfied and you are cleared to resign.

Check the employment documents and policy and procedures manual of your current employer, understand the requirements, and tender your resignation to comply with them. Normally, two weeks' notice is standard, but some employers require more.[244] Don't risk losing pay or benefits by not following procedure.

If possible (and frequently it is not possible), wait to resign so there's no issue about retaining any pensions or other time-dependent bonuses you're entitled to.

The actual act of resignation can be tense. You are about to deliver unexpected news. Script or list talking points and practice them before meeting with your boss.

Realize resigning is the culmination of a negotiation—one your boss did not know he was in. Your resignation could reflect poorly upon him. To gain an understanding of what has just happened, your boss may seek a time-out, usually by asking you not to make any rash or final decisions. Your boss is buying time to figure out what to do. This might be followed by an invitation to discuss company problems, your career path, or any one of a number of topics to sway your decision, including a counteroffer.

Be prepared. Your boss will likely ask why you are leaving. You have choices to make. Your professional judgment and discretion will guide your decisions. Provide honest answers. Occasionally, providing your reasoning could give your current employer information and insight your own boss may not be aware of. It can be valuable to the employer. However, if your honest answers would create turmoil, burn a bridge, or simply be inappropriate, opt for a generic reason ("a better opportunity," "a different direction I want to go in my career," "a different role," and so on).[245]

It is not uncommon for a boss to inquire about the new employer. Revealing the name of your new employer may depend on the kind of relationship you have with your boss. It is entirely your decision whether or not to release this information, and there are reasons to withhold it. For example, your boss (and others at your current employer) could use the information to tell you about all the bad things they've ever heard about the new company. In fairness, however, you should inform your employer of the nature of your new employer's business. If your new employer is a competitor, your employer should know this. Some companies have policies of immediate discharge when an employee accepts employment with a competitor.

---

244 Ibid.

245 Ibid.

Assume that, upon resignation, you will be asked to leave immediately. This may or may not happen, but be emotionally prepared either way. Consider taking steps to remove your personal property from your office before officially resigning—and only your own property. Be absolutely certain you don't take any private or patented company items with you.[246]

Prepare mentally for some emotion, including your boss's reaction. He or she will probably be surprised, disappointed, and maybe even angry. Make your resignation clean and professional.

Don't procrastinate or make things take longer than needed. And don't entertain a conversation about circumstances that would change your mind. If your boss asks that you not announce your resignation to your coworkers, comply with that request, as they likely need to make adjustments and business arrangements before formally announcing your resignation. Once the resignation meeting is complete, professionally end the conversation and walk away. Removing yourself from your boss's office (or from the call, depending on the circumstances) ends the engagement and allows you to breathe a sigh of relief. It's over, and you can move forward.

Always resign in writing and, whenever possible, in person. If you happen to be an off-premises or remote employee, a telephone call is fine. Do not send your resignation by email. If resigning by phone, speak with your boss first and tell him you will send a formal resignation letter.

Offer to assist in any transition of projects and work to others. This is a professional gesture and will leave your employer with a favorable last impression of you. Stay engaged in your job if your employer asks you to work your full resignation period. Come in on time, do your job, and don't leave early. Finish strong and be professional to the end.[247]

Some odds and ends to consider:

- Inform important contacts both inside and outside your organization of your resignation.[248]

- Confer with your boss about when it would be appropriate to inform others.

---

246 Calvin Sun, "10+ Things You Should Do When You Resign," *10 Things* (blog), TechRepublic, March 17, 2008, www.techrepublic.com/blog/10-things/10-plus-things-you-should-do-when-you-resign/ (accessed February 17, 2016).

247 Green, "How to Resign."

248 Sun, "10 Things."

- Ask your boss about changing your voice mail greeting or creating an email auto-response regarding your departure (if appropriate).[249]
- Provide your employer with all passwords.[250]

Finally, consider sending a thank-you note to your boss about a week after you leave the company. Express your appreciation for the opportunity, experience, and so on. Convey your best wishes for their continued success. Send a similar note of appreciation to appropriate contacts higher on the organizational chart. This classy move can pay real career dividends later.

Writing a thank-you note is a differentiator for you as a professional. You are building bridges for the future and enhancing your professional reputation. This is especially true for niche-industry workers, or those in a small city. Your former boss and other people from your former employer could become:

- A future employee of your new employer (future colleague)
- A customer of your new employer
- An advocate for you and your new employer
- A referral source

Below is a sample resignation letter that is simple and direct:

Name
Address
City, State ZIP

Subject: Voluntary Resignation of (Your Name)

Dear (Name of Supervisor):

Please consider this letter effective notice of my resignation from (Name of Company). The date of my final day is (month/day/year—do research so this date is correct based on your employer's HR policies).

I am very grateful for the opportunities made available to me while being associated

---

249 Ibid.

250 Green, "How to Resign."

with (Company Name). I've decided to resign after careful, deliberate thought, and to take advantage of an opening with another employer. This, I believe, will enable me to further my career.

Please be aware my choice reflects a sincere desire and is final.
Sincerely,
(Your Name)

Counteroffers

The longer I live, the more I am certain that the great difference between men—between the feeble and the powerful, the great and the insignificant—is energy, invincible determination—a purpose once fixed, and then—death or victory!

— Sir Thomas Fowell Buxton[251]

A counteroffer is any effort designed to entice you to ultimately withdraw your resignation and continue employment.[252] There are four types of counteroffers:

1. **Financial**

2. **Promotional**

3. **Emotional**

4. **Preemptive**

---

251 "Thomas Fowell Buxton Quotable Quote," Goodreads, http://www.goodreads.com/quotes/891186-the-longer-i-live-the-more-i-am-certain-that (accessed June 10, 2015).

252 Love, Scott. "Counteroffer—Should I Entertain a Counteroffer?" The Vet Recruiter, http://thevetrecruiter.com/important-information-about-recruiters-for-job-seekers/counteroffer-should-i-entertain-a-counteroffer/ (accessed June 11, 2015).

Financial

This is the most common form of counteroffer. It is normally an increase in your compensation through salary, bonus rate (or potential), commission structure, stock options or grants, and so on.

Promotional

This form of counteroffer could be a change in title (sometimes with a modest increase in salary), change in duties and/or responsibilities, or a move to a different department. Too frequently this kind of counteroffer ends up having less substance than represented.

Emotional

This form of counteroffer borders on dirty pool. It is delivered to appeal to your loyalty. Statements like "It just won't be the same around here without you" are standard fare. Promises of improvements, promotions, or any other sentiment designed to invoke a feeling that "you'll really miss out if you leave now" is an emotional counteroffer. So is any statement designed to elicit guilt or play on your emotions, such as "How will Ben ever finish that project with you gone?" Beware.

Preemptive

This type occurs prior to your resignation. It is an improvement in your employment situation that miraculously happens, unexpectedly, while you are exploring and interviewing for a new position. How lucky can you get, right? If any bells of suspicion start ringing in your head due to this timing, trust your instincts. Something is up.

Here's how a preemptive counteroffer comes about: while you are interviewing, on the premises of a potential employer, or offsite at a coffee shop, someone recognizes you with an executive of another company. That person tells someone else, and the news gets repeated until your boss finds out. Not to be outflanked, your boss improves your employment situation with the desired effect of having you discontinue your job-search activities. It's sneaky and it can work. You are left guessing whether the improvements are a sincere gesture from your employer or a counteroffer tactic.

Career Hazards of Accepting a Counteroffer

Receiving a counteroffer can be flattering and a boost to your professional ego. However, virtually all career experts agree that you should not accept one.[253] Understand this next point very clearly: the time, cost, and effort in recruiting and training a new employee are substantial for any employer and far outweigh the cost of offering you a counteroffer.[254] A counteroffer is a business decision (a cost calculation) and seldom a sudden awakening to your worth or company issues.

Realize that your current employer has an investment in you through your training, experience, and expertise. They do not want to lose that investment to another company (especially to a competitor). Again, the extension of a counteroffer is a business calculation.

When you prepare to resign, realize that a counteroffer may come, and remember the reasons why you wanted to make a job change in the first place. Think about the excitement of going to your new employer. Company culture, practices, policies, and a host of other factors seldom change, and if they do, it's gradual. The events that inspired you to move on from this employer will likely happen again.

If you accepted the new offer to pursue an entirely different avenue in your career, a new challenge, or a passion, accepting a counteroffer will delay or prevent you from accomplishing those goals.

When you accept a counteroffer, you burn bridges with the prospective employer who offered you a new job.[255] They most likely won't consider hiring you again. Accepting a counteroffer also calls into question your loyalty and motives with your current employer, and you will be scrutinized. Internal relationships that you have with your boss, other managers, peers, and subordinates could change.[256]

Accepting a counteroffer can slow your career growth and advancement. Once your loyalty and motives are brought into question, promotions will be much more difficult to come by (if ever). You may be passed over for advanced training. Your employer will hesitate to invest in you.

253 Love, "Should I Entertain"; Lankford, Kim. "Should You Take That Counteroffer?" Monster, http://career-advice.monster.com/in-the-office/leaving-a-job/should-you-take-that-counteroffer/article.aspx (accessed June 11, 2015); Alison Green, "Why You Shouldn't Take a Counteroffer," *On Careers Blog, U.S. News & World Report*, March 26, 2012, http://money.usnews.com/money/blogs/outside-voices-careers/2012/03/26/why-you-shouldnt-take-a-counteroffer (accessed June 11, 2015).

254 Love, "Should I Entertain."

255 Green, "Counteroffer."

256 Love, "Should I Entertain."

All companies face difficult times that could require cutbacks and staff reductions. When that happens, your boss may choose to honor your resignation after the fact by laying you off.

Where is the money for a financial counteroffer coming from? Has your next raise merely been moved up?[257] Is it coming from another department's budget (if so, have you raised the angst of another department head)? All companies have wage and salary guidelines that create strained budgets and parity issues with others. This could backfire and create animosity toward you.

For all of these reasons (and others unique to the company and circumstances), accepting a counteroffer creates a high probability you will leave or get fired within one year.[258] Some career experts say that "statistically, four out of five employees who accept a company's counteroffer end up leaving that company within 6 to 9 months anyway."[259] Accepting a counteroffer is not a good long-term career strategy—it's a short-term fix at best.

Detachment: a Technique to Defuse the Emotions of Resignation

When you resign, wisely assume you will receive a counteroffer, either immediately or shortly after the resignation conversation. Here is an excellent technique that has helped others in this situation: mentally detach yourself and become a student of your boss's reaction. Is it surprise (likely), disappointment, or anger? Does he call time-out and ask you to delay your decision? Does she extend a financial, emotional, or promotional counteroffer? Or nothing at all? This detachment technique significantly reduces the situation's inevitable emotional charge. You will see the situation from an objective (or perhaps academic) perspective. The resignation and counteroffer are easier if you employ this approach.

Can accepting a counteroffer ever be a good career move? Yes. However, it is very . . . very . . . very (catching the emphasis here?) . . . very rare.

Aside from limited circumstances, the ultimate truth about counteroffers is they don't work. Accepting one is more of a quick fix, and you will be conducting a job search sooner than you think.

---

257 Ibid.

258 Green, "Counteroffer."

259 "Counter Offers," Cybercoders, http://www.cybercoders.com/home/counteroffer/ (accessed June 11, 2015).

Chapter 16

Covenants-Not-To-Compete and Non-Solicitation Agreements

Disclaimer: *The contents of this chapter are not legal advice. They are for educational purposes only. None of the information provided should be construed, interpreted, or acted upon in any way in determining a course of action. If you have or believe you may have a legal restriction on your employment, seek legal counsel. Do not rely on the information contained in this chapter or book.*

Our doubts are traitors, and make us lose the good we often might win,
by fearing to attempt.
— William Shakespeare, Act I, Scene IV, *Measure for Measure*[260]

Covenants-not-to-compete and non-solicitation agreements can have a significant impact on your job search. In some industries, they are deemed unnecessary and therefore seldom used. In others, they are an ingrained business practice.

The purpose of this chapter is to give you a general understanding of these agreements and the potential effects they can have on your job search.

---

260 "William Shakespeare Quotes Measure for Measure," http://www.william-shakespeare.info/quotes-quotations-play-measure-for-measure.htm (accessed June 11, 2015).

Definitions of a Covenant-Not-to-Compete and a Non-Solicitation Agreement

Setting aside true legal definitions, the following definitions will guide our discussion:

- **Covenant-Not-to-Compete:** a contractual agreement forbidding a job seeker from obtaining employment with a competitor of a former employer.

- **Non-Solicitation Agreement:** a contractual agreement forbidding a job seeker from soliciting business from a client (vendor, supplier, and so on) of the job seeker's former employer.

A covenant-not-to-compete has significantly more impact on a job seeker's search. Depending upon the terms, this can be an inconvenience (a short and mild restriction) or a career-changing event (lengthy and highly restrictive). These agreements hamper your ability to obtain employment in the field or industry of your former employer.

A non-solicitation agreement can be less problematic, allowing you to work in the field of your choice with a competitor, with the understanding that you will not approach or solicit the clients (vendors, suppliers, and so forth) of your former employer.

Where They Appear

These agreements generally appear in three places:

- As part of a written offer of employment
- A separate agreement, normally supplied with the offer letter
- Employer handbook

Determining Which Kind of Agreement You Have

As you read the appropriate documents, look for this kind of language (or similar):

Covenant-Not-to-Compete

"During the period of time that the Employee is employed by the Company and for a period of two (2) years after the termination or cessation of such employment for any reason (both periods of time, taken together, being referred to hereinafter as the "RESTRICTED PERIOD"), the Employee shall not, anywhere in the United States, directly or indirectly, whether individually or as an officer, director, employee, consultant, partner, stockholder (other than as the holder of not more than one percent (1%) of a publicly held corporation), individual proprietor, joint venturer, investor, lender, consultant, or in any other capacity whatsoever, develop, design, produce, market, sell, or render (or assist any other person in developing, designing, producing, marketing, selling, or rendering) products or services competitive with those developed, designed, produced, marketed, sold, or rendered by the Company at any time during the Restricted Period."[261]

Non-Solicitation Agreement

"During the Restricted Period, the Employee shall not, directly or indirectly, whether individually or as an officer, director, employee, consultant, partner, stockholder, individual proprietor, joint venturer, investor, lender, consultant, or any other capacity whatsoever: (a) solicit, divert, or take away, or attempt to solicit, divert or take away, the business or patronage of any clients, customers or accounts, or prospective clients, customers or accounts, of the Company or (b) hire, retain (including as a consultant), or encourage to leave the employment of the Company any employee of the Company, or hire or retain (including as a consultant) any former employee of the Company who has left the employment of the Company within one (1) year prior to such hiring or retention."[262]

Enforceability

You must understand that these agreements are enforceable. Only by application of law do they become unenforceable.

These agreements are interpreted by state law. Each state handles these agreements its own way. California has outlawed covenants-not-to-compete as a legislative concern.[263] There are a few other states that have as well. You will need to determine whether your state of residence enforces such agreements (most states will).

Reasonable in Scope, Space, and Time

For a covenant-not-to-compete to be enforceable it must be reasonable—an issue to be

---

261 Non-Compete Agreement—Art Technology Group Inc. and Joseph Chung, http://contracts.onecle.com/art/chung.noncomp.1998.08.18.shtml (accessed March 16, 2016).

262 Ibid.

263 Izzi, Matthew. "California Ban on Covenants Not to Compete," LegalMatch, http://www.legalmatch.com/law-library/article/california-ban-on-covenants-not-to-compete.html (accessed June 11, 2015).

determined by the facts and the courts. Generally speaking, a covenant-not-to-compete must be reasonable in scope, space, and time, which usually breaks down this way:

Scope: what you are forbidden from doing.

Space: where you cannot do it, geographically.

Time: how long you cannot do it.

There are a myriad of factors that influence what is reasonable in scope, space, and time that will be tied directly to your specific situation.

Generally, if a covenant is deemed unreasonable in any of the three criteria, the whole agreement fails. There are exceptions to this generalization. The most notable is some courts will rewrite unreasonable provisions to make them reasonable under the circumstances. This practice is called "blue lining."[264] In essence, the court takes a blue pen and will rewrite the provision. However, many courts will stick to the facts to determine enforceability.

Employer's Reactions to Breaches of Agreement

Employers respond differently to violations of these agreements. They can do or have done the following:

- Nothing
- Send a threatening letter, normally by certified mail
- Have a lawyer send a threatening letter, normally by certified mail
- Send a copy of your agreement to your new employer (yes, some have done this)
- Seek a preliminary injunction—this is a legal maneuver preventing you from working for about ten days
- Seek a permanent injunction, which would stop you from working completely until the issue is resolved
- Seek active litigation—file a lawsuit

Sometimes employers will growl and bark but not bite, stopping short of legal action. Do not assume this is true for every employer. If they have the grounds to pursue you for

---

264 Broadcasting and the Law, Inc. "Employment contracts—'blue line' rule." Abstract. *Broadcasting and the Law* (1997). http://www.readabstracts.com/Mass-communications/Employment-contracts-blue-line-rule-Noncommercial-stations-underwriting-announcements.html (accessed June 11, 2015).

breach of the agreement, they have the right to do so. Sometimes it's a matter of how much of a threat you are to their business.

Right-to-Work States

Some job seekers believe that restrictive agreements are not enforceable because they live in a right-to-work state. This is generally not true. The right-to-work statutes of a particular state seldom have any bearing on the legal enforcement of these agreements (unless some language relevant to these agreements is buried within the statute).

Practical Application—Effects of These Agreements on Your Job Search

As a practical matter, non-solicitation agreements are less concerning than covenants-not-to-compete. You simply need to avoid the prohibited clients (vendors, suppliers, and so on) for the restricted period of time. You are permitted to obtain employment in your field of choice and with a competitor if you choose.

Covenants-not-to-compete, on the other hand, can significantly impact your job search by restricting your field of options. This bears repeating because many do not take these implications seriously enough. Careful consideration must be made regarding how you choose to proceed, and you should prepare yourself for the possibility that you may not be able to find work in your industry for months or years, depending on the terms of your agreement.

Always advise a potential employer that you have a restrictive agreement. Failure to do so raises fidelity issues in the employer's mind, such as, "What else didn't he (or she) tell us?"

One approach to consider is to obtain a waiver from your employer, which protects you from legal action if you accept employment that could violate your agreement. This is a good tactic if the new employer's products and services are less important or not as widely known as your current employer's products are. Generally, a waiver will be a written letter from an executive with the authority to waive a potential violation. It is a way to sleep at night if you wish to eliminate concerns you may have.

Chapter 17

How to Relaunch a Stagnant Job Search

Every champion was once a contender that refused to give up.
—Rocky Balboa[265]

You're engaged in a job search and things have slowed to a crawl. You've done everything you know to do, and still have no results. Don't panic. There are practical steps you can take to get back on track. These are:

Learn something new. This may not sound like a tactic to reignite a job search, but it is . . . and it's a big one. You need to stimulate your mind with new information. Identify a professional designation and start the work to achieve it. If you need to improve your technology skills, now is the time to do it. Whatever you learn stimulates the mind and when completed, can differentiate you from other job seekers.

Many job seekers find they feel renewed and have a more optimistic outlook on a stale search when they begin learning new things. You feel better knowing you are doing something to move your job search forward.

---

265 "Rocky Balboa Quotable Quote," Goodreads, http://www.goodreads.com/quotes/3228059-every-champion-was-once-a-contender-that-refused-to-give (accessed April 12, 2016).

Another approach to learning something new is to seek out information about job searching. This could be through LinkedIn groups, podcasts, or blogs that focus on job searching. Accessing this information may give you nuggets of information that you had not thought of that could improve the effectiveness of your job search.

Help someone. This will improve your attitude and help shake off the disappointments of the past. As you go about your day, look for opportunities to help others. This could be passing along a job lead to another job seeker or simply holding the door open for someone. Becoming others-focused shifts your mindset and gets you out of yourself and focused on service. This can give you a daily dose of purpose, value, and accomplishment. Becoming service oriented will improve your attitude and make you feel better. Today is a new day. You're going to change your activities and be more productive.

If your circumstances permit, consider volunteering. Depending upon the organization, it could present networking opportunities. According to LinkedIn, many employers consider volunteering equivalent to employment.[266] In addition to the job-search advantages, there are a host of positive emotional and physical benefits to volunteering as well.[267]

Revamp your resume. Does it present you persuasively? Be honest. If you wrote your resume yourself, seriously consider contacting a professional resume writer and have it evaluated. Could improvements in content and formatting be worth the cost to have it redone? Having a new resume is a change that can improve your confidence during your search. (Don't forget, any changes to your resume should also be reflected on your LinkedIn profile.)

Refresh your LinkedIn profile. Like your resume, critically evaluate your LinkedIn profile. Is it as complete as it could be? Is it optimized for maximum exposure when a hiring executive or recruiter searches for a person like you? Are your keywords placed in the optimal sections of your profile (headline, summary, career experience, and so on)?[268] Is it compelling (using accomplishments)? As a general rule, are you getting at least twenty profile-views a week?

Improve your attitude. You have reason to be optimistic. Things are about to change because you are going to use new strategies to create job-search activities. It will be work, but the

266 Dougherty, "16 Tips to Optimize."

267 "Volunteering and its Surprising Benefits," HelpGuide.org, http://www.helpguide.org/articles/work-career/volunteering-and-its-surprising-benefits.htm (accessed February 17, 2016).

268 See also, Frasco, "11 Tips."

results will be different. And it all starts with your attitude. Get positive. Be positive. Do what needs to be done (with a smile, despite momentary setbacks) and you will experience positive results.

Increase your networking activities. You've likely networked as a part of your search. To reignite your networking efforts, start making new connections, especially on LinkedIn. Focus on new connections to people you believe may be able to help or hire you. For every two new connections (or LinkedIn invitations extended), reach out to an existing networking contact and bring them up to speed on your job search (or any other relevant topic). For all new connections, wait a few days and then communicate with them. Going through this process will expand your network and lead to new conversations with new contacts while touching base with your existing network.

Are you on the telephone, reaching out to people voice to voice? And making a minimum of twenty outbound calls a day to current, but more importantly, *new* contacts? If you can get on a roll making calls, that's great. This requires planning and some research for telephone numbers. Do that later in your day and use the morning to generate calls. The more calls you make, the quicker your job search will end successfully. Remember to network face-to-face as well. Don't curl up in a ball—get out and meet people. Attend industry gatherings, whether local or national, or get together with friends and neighbors. This can be a bonanza of networking opportunities. People will help you if they can and if you give them the opportunity to do so.

Use job alerts more strategically. If you have not been using job alerts, do so now (Indeed. com, SimplyHired.com, LinkedIn, or job boards). If you have been using them, review them and include other jobs you are interested in and qualified for. Get a new flow of information on opportunities in the market.

Proactively market your professional credentials. The mantra here is: don't think in terms of a job—look for a company you'd like to work for.[269] Once you identify companies that are (or could be) interesting to you, hunt in the Hidden Job Market by reaching out directly to the likely hiring executive and presenting your professional credentials. This technique requires effort, but you will find jobs and job leads that you otherwise would not find.

Exercise. There are a few reasons why exercise is a technique to reignite your job search. The first is, it's healthy. Perhaps you have a few pounds you could live without. It can improve your appearance. Secondly, exercising routinely gives you a sense of accomplishment. When

---

269 Whitcomb, *Job Search Magic*, p. 273–274.

tough days happen, at least you got your exercise in. And finally, exercise can improve your mindset due to the natural release of chemicals in your body.

Focus on differentiation. What in your background and accomplishments makes you different, unique, and/or valuable to an employer? Think hard about this. Are you making these factors apparent to employers? If not, showcase them. Now is not the time to be humble.

Seek out a career-transition coach. A coach is an objective source who can help you in many ways—to empathize with you, as well as challenge, educate, counsel, and encourage you. Simply having a professional to talk to (and be accountable to) who is experienced in career transition can open your mind intellectually, help you deal with the many emotions that accompany a job search, and more. If you choose to go down this path, evaluate a coach to ensure they have the insight necessary to benefit and guide you. There are organizations that list credentialed career-transition and career coaches. They include: International Coach Federation (www.coachfederation.org), The Academies (www.theacademies.com), Career Directors International (www.careerdirectors.com), among others.

Think through these techniques. Find the ones that apply to you and implement them. All it takes is one of these techniques (but more likely a combination) to reignite your search and land job offers.

Chapter 18

Required Job-Search Skills for Long-Term Career Employment

You miss one hundred percent of the shots you don't take. — Wayne Gretzky[270]

Statistically, professionals entering the job market today could have ten to fifteen jobs during their career. Sound like a lot? Let's do some math.

On average, most professionals stay in their current employment between four and five years,[271] then change jobs (or positions), either by choice or otherwise. Employment trends indicate that people are working longer before retiring, either by choice or necessity.[272] This employment "life span" can now last forty to fifty years. If the statistics hold true, more than ten jobs (or positions) during a career is quite possible.[273]

---

270 "Wayne Gretzky Quotable Quote," Goodreads, http://www.goodreads.com/quotes/4798-you-miss-one-hundred-percent-of-the-shots-you-don-t (accessed July 13, 2015).

271 Bureau of Labor Statistics, "Employee Tenure Summary," news release, September 18, 2014, http://www.bls.gov/news.release/tenure.nr0.htm (accessed May 29, 2015).

272 Woods, "Working Longer."

273 Bureau of Labor Statistics, "Number of Jobs Held, Labor Market Activity, and Earnings Growth Among the Youngest Baby Boomers: Results from a Longitudinal Survey," news release, March 31, 2015, http://www.bls.gov/news.release/pdf/nlsoy.pdf (accessed May 29, 2015).

Consequently, and as a result of these statistics, it is now *imperative* that you learn job-search skills to ensure long-term career employment. Mastering these skills is not hard (especially since you have this book) but it is necessary. Today's professional must understand:

1. **How to compose an effective, professional resume.** You don't need to know the mechanics of how to actually write a persuasive resume (font use, graphic design, etc.), just understand the contents of the various components. Chapter 4.

2. **How to create and maintain an online professional profile.** This is most notably, LinkedIn. Chapter 5.

3. **How to write effective job-search communications.** This includes emails, letters, thank-you notes, follow-ups, and so on. Chapter 6.

4. **How to create, nurture, and leverage personal, and, more importantly, professional networks.** Being connected and in touch with those that can help you or hire you in a job search. Chapter 7.

5. **How to match/relate your background to the needs of the employer and sell yourself through accomplishments.** This is knowing how to interview to get a job offer. Chapter 11.

6. **How to effectively execute a job-search strategy.** Knowing how to start a job search from a dead stop and move it forward to job offers. Conceptually, this includes every chapter in this book.

Is understanding these job-search skills that important? Think of it this way: job-search skills are those skills that allow you to market your professional abilities so you can earn an income and have a fulfilling career experience. You decide.

Chapter 19

A Personal Letter to You about Career Management

A bold heart is half the battle. — Dwight D. Eisenhower[274]

I wanted to write the final chapter of this book differently from the others. For this chapter, I want to offer advice so you will never again be unemployed, or, if you do find yourself without a job, to have as brief of an unemployment period as possible.

Do you remember when I listed six career tenets that will add clarity, understanding, and perspective to your career? Here's the list—it's worth repeating:

1. I am solely responsible for my career success.

2. It is my responsibility to enhance my value proposition. To achieve this, I must find opportunities to learn, improve, and expand upon my skills.

3. I must deliver an ROI to my employer through the value my function brings to the company.

4. I am responsible for my work-life balance. Wherever I determine to spend my time and place my priorities, they are ultimately in my control.

---

274 Maxwell, John C. *The Maxwell Daily Reader: 365 Days of Insight to Develop the Leader Within You and Influence Those Around You*. (Nashville, TN: Thomas Nelson, 2011), p. 227.

5. It is my responsibility to stay informed about the financial health and well-being of my employer and the industry in which I work.

6. Change is inevitable in my career. How I respond to change is completely within my control. Change often creates opportunities that can be capitalized upon given perspective, knowledge, a positive attitude, and focused effort.

If you'll notice, each tenet has its own message but at the foundation of each is personal responsibility. The success of your career is your personal responsibility . . . and no one else's.

I want to give you twelve tips—pieces of advice, really—that will not only prepare you for new career opportunities, but also help you rebound more quickly from an unexpected job loss.

Create a rainy day fund.

In my opinion, this first point doesn't seem like it has much to do with career management at all. But it does. Many job searches can take four to six months, sometimes longer. Save your money to cover living expenses for at least six months.

With this strategy, if you lose your job unexpectedly, you won't panic. You can engage in a self-motivated job search with purpose and strategy and find the right career opportunity, not just a job to pay the bills.

The rainy day fund also gives you resources to invest in job-search tools and services. This could include a resume-writing service, business cards, wardrobe necessities, a career coach, or other services. The rainy day fund has emotional benefits as well, allowing you to pay the bills, prevent feelings of desperation, and keep fear at bay.

Keep your resume current.

As you progress through your career, it is easy to let your resume grow stale. That's understandable—you are busy doing your job. But you're not managing your career. It takes precious little time to keep your resume up-to-date. Whenever something positive happens in your career or at least once a year—use your annual job performance review as a reminder—update your resume. Or, at minimum, put an update at the end of the resume and handle it later. The point is to jot it down, with a date, so you don't lose track.

Keep your LinkedIn profile current too.

The same line of thinking applies to your LinkedIn profile (and any other professional online profiles). Keep it as vibrant as possible. As you know, your LinkedIn profile is pivotal to a job search and equally important for career management. Your LinkedIn profile is how opportunities will often find you. It is imperative that your online presence is up-to-date.

Stay informed and in tune with your employer, industry, and the value of your job.

There is a lot to talk about here. When I speak with candidates who have lost their jobs, a sizable number noticed warning signs of trouble to come. Either they ignored the red flags and hoped they would be saved from any layoffs or thought the situation would blow over. As you now know, you are personally responsible for your career. There are a few times when a candidate lost their job without warning, but this is rare.

Be aware of how your employer is doing financially. Is there talk about mergers, acquisitions, or IPOs? Significant governmental or regulatory threats? Ask yourself: How does this information positively or negatively affect my career? Evaluate the information, assess the situation, do research, communicate with others, make a determination, and judge timing. Use your business knowledge and trust your instincts. Then act if needed.

The same kind of analysis applies to your industry as well. It is important to be knowledgeable and aware of its overall health. Industry shrinkage by market forces or governmental intervention should cause a moment of pause and evaluation of career choice. It is always better to move away from an industry in decline to one that is growing and expanding, if in fact your transferable job skills permit.

Finally, stay acutely aware of the value of your role in a company. Do you, in your job and function, make or save the company money? If the value of your job is fading, seriously consider making a career move.

Plan your career path.

You must allow yourself to dream and explore what you want to do and where you want to take your career. This could be anything from climbing the corporate ladder to starting your own business. Where do *you* want to go?

For any plan to be effective, you must write it down. It is remarkable how writing something down solidifies a plan and creates a sense of self-accountability. Start with one-, three-, and five-year plans. In my experience, going much further is not realistic. Too many things can change . . . interests, opportunities, setbacks. In other words, life happens.

Write down the specific actions and steps to move you forward. Add time lines. It's been said that "a goal is a dream with a deadline."[275] This exercise is very similar to "Profiling Your Next Career Opportunity" with a broader scope and longer time line. You might want to review that part of the book (Chapter 2) and its concepts with a self-motivated career management point of view.

Network.

Network actively. Build contacts within and outside your company. Review the Networking chapter and focus on strategies most relevant to you. Ask yourself this question: If I lost my job today, do I have ten inner-circle contacts (a Cabinet) that I could reach out to that would help me? This should be the minimum number of "go-to" networking contacts.

The power that professional networking can have on your career is remarkable. Remember that in networking, those who give, get.[276] When the time is right, networking can propel your career to heights and a level of professional satisfaction that you might not have thought possible.

Stay sharp and develop new skills.

One of the keys to long-term employment and career management is to become indispensable. I don't think this can be completely achieved in most companies, but you want to get as close to it as you can. At a minimum, you want your employer to perceive you in such a way that it will hurt the company if they should ever lose you.

To me, this is achieved by enhancing your current skill set and developing new skills. Attend workshops, seminars, and conventions. Stay informed about emerging trends and technology or products.

I highly recommend that you earn an industry designation. This adds credibility to your name and your brand (more on that in a moment). Getting a certificate of completion from a one-day seminar is not what I mean. Rather, pursue those industry designations that take effort and have substantive meaning both in content and with your peers. It may take time and effort, but the knowledge and differentiation you gain with your current employer and for future employment opportunities makes it well worth it.

Many candidates have told me that pursuing an industry designation rejuvenated them. New learning opens the mind and can keep you creative and sharp, growing, and vibrant.

275 "Napoleon Hill Quotable Quote," Goodreads, http://www.goodreads.com/quotes/244859-a-goal-is-a-dream-with-a-deadline (accessed June 11, 2015).

276 Vlooten, "The Seven Laws."

Nurture your brand.

Good career management encompasses brand management. Review this book's Branding section (Chapter 3). Stay aware of your value proposition, ROI, and differentiation factors. These create your brand, which must be nurtured and guarded, like your professional reputation.

To nurture your brand, ask yourself a two-part question: What am I known for? And, is that getting communicated to those that matter? Assess, evaluate, and make adjustments if you don't like the answers.

Ensure your visibility at work and in your industry.

Closely tied to branding is the concept of visibility. Work to get known within your company and your industry, in ways that support your brand. It could be as simple as some internal networking—but don't become a politician. You can be subtle to get your work noticed. Or, you could speak at an industry conference. Visibility is easier via LinkedIn and its Groups feature, by starting discussions, or contributing insightfully to existing ones. If you are not sure, don't post it. Ask a colleague to double-check the idea. Visibility can work for you, but if mishandled, it can work against you.

I suggest finding a dynamic professional association that piques your interest. Find a way to get involved. Your involvement does not have to be time-consuming. The point is to contribute and become known. It will enhance your networking efforts.

Be aware of opportunities in the market.

Although you may be content, challenged, and fulfilled in your current position, it is incumbent upon you to be aware of new opportunities that can enhance your overall lifetime career experience. LinkedIn has ways for you to be alerted about opportunities that would interest you or be your next progressive step in your career. Use them.

Return calls and emails from recruiters and others; listen to opportunities they present. The bottom line is this: whether you stay with your current position or pursue a new opportunity, ultimately, it is your choice. You are proactively managing your career. What a great position to be in.

Consider getting a mentor or career coach.

I want to draw a distinction between a mentor and a career coach, though both can serve similar purposes regarding your career management. A mentor, as I am using the word, is normally a person in your field that you know and respect. You want to emulate this person. It is someone with whom you have established a good relationship.

A career coach, on the other hand, is a paid professional who coaches and advises others on career matters.

A mentor will be guiding you based largely on personal experience. For most mentors, this is an opportunity to share relevant past experiences, insights, and hard-earned wisdom. Many mentors feel they are passing along a piece of their legacy as a result of the relationship. They give, but they also receive good feelings from the relationship.

A career coach is paid. Evaluate a coach to ensure they have the insight necessary to benefit and guide you. While a mentor will give advice based largely on past experience, a career coach can draw from the experiences of scores of professionals that the coach has worked with. Also know that a mentor will "tell" in guiding you, while a true coaching professional will ask more questions to help you explore potential answers. It will be a different kind of relationship.

Whether you choose a mentor or coach, it is important to define and mutually agree on what is expected from both to make the relationship work. Notably, the frequency of communication should be discussed, even if it is on an as-needed basis.

The most important thing for you to remember about a mentor or coaching relationship is to engage in conversation but also be able to listen and learn. Be able to quiet yourself. Frequently, you will receive not only valuable insight and knowledge, but also wisdom. This information can have a profound impact on your career.

It's a matter of attitude, introspection, and perspective.

Over the course of my career, I have reviewed the career paths of thousands of people. One frequent theme is common to most: your career will be an unpredictable journey.

Regardless of the twists and turns, I highly encourage you to always maintain a positive outlook and attitude. Consider it an invaluable career-management strategy. Want proof? "Nearly 88 percent of the 3,785 senior-level executives surveyed by ExecuNet said they would rather enhance their team with that individual who possesses a good attitude, even if he or she does not perform to the highest level or have top qualifications."[277] This statistic directly applies to internal promotions as well as external job opportunities. Having a positive attitude will enhance your career opportunities.

Another related career-management concept is introspection. I have spoken to professionals who have developed in their careers and wake up one morning regretting

277 ExecuNet, "Senior-Level Business Leaders Say Positive Attitude is the Key to Getting the Job," news release, March 25, 2013, http://www.execunet.com/m_releases_content.cfm?id=4812 (accessed June 11, 2015).

the ways their career reshaped them. I remember one candidate shared he had become irritable, impatient, and overly consumed with thoughts about money, among other things. He wanted a change from the demands of his current job so he could return to a less stressful career existence and back to the person he truly was.

Career management means remaining true to who you are, and being comfortable with the fit between you and the demands of your job. When they do not match close enough, you—and your family—will likely experience outward signs of the internal friction (irritability, reclusiveness, impatience, and so on). Good career management requires times of introspection to examine you for who you are (or are becoming) as a result of your career. The outcome of that introspection may be motivation for a career move.

Tied to introspection is the concept of perspective. Introspection is an internal evaluation while perspective is an external evaluation. Perspective, as I am using the word, frequently comes to the surface with tenured career professionals. They begin to ask themselves these kinds of questions:

"What is the purpose of what I do?"

"Am I helping anyone?"

"Do I provide any value?"

Or, in a grander sense . . .

"Why am I on this earth?"

These are deep questions and ones that are perfectly normal to ask. From my experience, the key is to discover and name at least one, and hopefully more, redeeming qualities that makes your work valuable to others, directly or in conjunction with coworkers or others.

The naming process identifies and solidifies the value of your work in your mind (intellectually) and your heart (emotionally). What your heart and mind hold onto will bring feelings of professional worth. It's a great feeling that your heart and mind know your work matters.

Let's tie this all together: attitude, introspection, and perspective. Working backward: when you genuinely feel your work matters, you have professional self-worth. When your job is consistent with who you are as a person, there is internal peace and a match with you and your career. Both affect your attitude in a very significant and positive way. Having a positive attitude is a career strategy and leads to more career opportunities, which is a component of proactive career management. I love it when it all comes together!

I hope these twelve tips, based on my experience and the experience of others, impart valuable insight on proactively managing your career. It is my heartfelt and sincerest hope that you experience the most successful and emotionally fulfilling career you possibly can!

Best Wishes Always,
Brian E. Howard

Appendix A

Success Story Worksheet and Samples

Success Stories

Employer:

Your Position:

When:

Skill/Competency:

Challenge (Situation/Task):

Action:

Result:

Success Story—Example #1

Employer: XYZ Insurance Company

Position: Vice President of Product Development and Contracting

When: 20XX

Skill/Competency: Creativity, Critical Thinking, and Analysis

Challenge: While working at a large national insurance carrier (use the actual name in your story), their workers' compensation product portfolio was missing an ancillary product line/division. This was causing us to miss out on a potential revenue stream and the opportunity to compete against those companies providing these products as a stand-alone service.

The theory was that by adding ancillary services, we would add revenue, increase customer retention, and promote long-term loyalty from our existing client base.

Action: We developed a new line of contracts for ancillary providers. We established a list of providers in multiple fields, i.e., DME,[278] O and P, home health, and so on. With these providers, we contracted and negotiated pricing. Once we had 80 percent of the contracts signed, we began marketing the new product offerings through conferences, seminars, and email blasts to existing and potential clients. At the same time, we developed a fully insured product that provided us with a one-stop-shop ability to service existing and potential clients.

Result: The end result of this effort was our ability to grow the bottom-line revenue by 27 percent in the first year after the network was up and running. This product division stands today and continues to grow.

---

278 Durable medical equipment; see "Durable Medical Equipment (DME) Center," Centers for Medicare & Medicaid Services, http://www.cms.gov/Center/Provider-Type/Durable-Medical-Equipment-DME-Center.html (accessed July 13, 2015).

Success Story—Example #2

Employer: ABC Company

Position: COO/Legal Counsel

When: 20XX

Skill/Competency: Communication, Presentation, and Relationship/Trust Building

Challenge: With hundreds of legal actions pending against the company because of a product that admittedly entices litigious behavior, the task was to alleviate the anxieties of current and prospective clients.

Action: Focus client attention on the product's results, not on what could or might happen. There were more than one hundred filings against the company, but less than 5 percent resulted in a hearing, and more than half of those settled prior to the actual hearing date. When there was a hearing, only a handful resulted in the client paying full bill charges.

Result: As a result, when netting the entire portfolio of a client's book of bills, the company would save 40 percent or more off the allowable charges. Once the message changed from trying to minimize the risk, to acknowledging the risk, and then aggregating the impact of the entire book of bills, clients were able to put it in perspective. The odds of a lawsuit that resulted in a hearing and the client having to pay bill charges were similar to driving a car and anticipating an accident. Tens of thousands of people drive cars each day and arrive safely at their destination. Furthermore, we chose to indemnify clients for any expenses so that their greatest risk would be to pay total bill charges, which was what they were asked to pay in the first place. As a result, clients not only stayed with the company, but we were able to add numerous high-profile clients. The net growth of the business was seven times the initial revenue with incredibly generous margins in excess of any industry standard.

Success Story—Example #3

Employer: National Company

Position: Senior Vice President of Sales

When: 20XX

Skill/Competency: Creativity, Analytical Thinking, and Problem Solving

Challenge: The firm had experienced four years of flat or declining revenues. As a result, the owner despised salespeople, as he was not seeing a return on investment. He refused to spend the requisite resources to secure the talent needed to compete in the marketplace. I was brought in to reverse the revenue trend and add more staff at a lower-than-competitive market rate of compensation.

Action: Not having resources to secure the talent to compete on an individual basis, and not having a corporate reputation to help recruit talent, I chose a slightly different strategy. I convinced the owner that I was going to secure top-tier talent using cumulative budget dollars. In essence, I hired two people with the money that had been allocated for three new hires.

Additionally, I had to focus existing resources on the market segments where they could win business. The high-powered talent was directed at large national opportunities and the existing talent was redirected to regional opportunities. I helped both national and regional colleagues target and secure value-added resellers. The resellers created a one-to-many relationship and once we worked out the economics, these resellers approached clients they already had and created a revenue stream for them and us.

Result: The result was a 14 percent growth rate for the business by the end of year one. We were able to capture some very competent sales talent as the reps began to earn healthy commissions compared to other regional and national colleagues selling the same services.

Appendix B

Sample Resumes

The following resumes are examples of the three most common resume formats. Some follow the advice of the resume section, and some do not. They are for illustrative purposes only.

Example 1: Traditional Reverse Chronological Resume

Example 2: Functional Resume

Examples 3 and 4: Showcase Resumes

For an in-depth discussion on resumes, check out *Motivated Resumes and LinkedIn Profiles*. The book is unlike any resume book ever written. It gives you unprecedented insight and advice from over a dozen credentialed, experienced, and award-winning resume writers in the industry. With over 188 pieces of advice quoted throughout the book on how to write a resume, you will learn how these writers create impactful resumes that stand out.

Motivated Resumes and LinkedIn Profiles has over 80 sample resumes, 40 sample cover letters, and other job-search written communications. You can view the works of these industry-leading resume writers in a portfolio format, learn about them, and even contact them if you choose to have your resume professionally written.

Example 1—Traditional Reverse Chronological Resume

Jack Johanson
1234 State St., Kansas City, MO 64066
816-555-4444 • jjohan@ymail.com

PROFESSIONAL PROFILE

A results-oriented and driven senior insurance sales, marketing, and business development executive with a distinguished reputation for profitable new business growth, prospect identification, pipeline development, product promotion, and creative sales and marketing strategies. Extensive expertise in customer-needs analysis with a consultative approach to C-level insurance products, services sales, and account retention. Repeated success guiding sizeable, cross-functional teams in the design, development, and roll-out of innovative solutions driving record-setting sales. Expert presenter, negotiator, closer, and businessperson able to forge solid relationships and build partnerships across multiple organizational levels.

- National Sales Strategy
- Key Performance Indicators
- Data Analytics/Predictive Modeling
- Product Line Growth and Profitability
- Home Office Coordination
- Claims Cost Reduction
- Technology-Driven Solutions
- Branding and Market Positioning
- Market Share Analysis
- Client/Account Development
- Team Building/Coaching
- Customer Service

PROFESSIONAL EMPLOYMENT HISTORY

20XX–Present **THERAPY AND REHAB, CO.**
Vice President National Accounts—Wausau, WI

Business development executive in charge of identifying and developing new markets and innovative insurance products to increase revenues and open new channels to expand market presence.
- Successfully implemented nationwide new markets strategy and

action plan for developing new sources of business including brokers, reinsurers, captives, self-insured associations, assigned risk plans, guarantee funds, and managing general agencies.
- Created and led development, design, and roll-out of nationwide regional sales expansion plan.
- Top salesman bringing on eight national accounts and increasing revenues by 33 percent.

20XX–20XX   LIABILITY INSURANCE COMPANY
Sales Executive—Chicago, IL

Regional manager leading company's Midwest expansion into a retail agency distribution model for selling property and casualty products and services.
- Grew premium and expanded customer base by 40 percent.
- Appointed forty-five new agencies in fifteen states.
- Introduced Agency Growth Action Plan and reporting tools.

20XX–20XX   MEDICARE COMPLIANCE CORPORATION
Director Sales and Marketing—Minneapolis, MN

Director of Sales and Marketing for nationwide insurance consulting operations, including managing all aspects of the $30M, five-region, twenty-five-member sales and marketing organization, and the growth and development of its 550 carrier, third-party administration, self-insured, state funded, and broker clients.
- Top architect of nationwide sales and marketing expansion plan leading to the increase in overall revenues to $30M from $1.5M and market position to #2 from #31.
- Top salesman for both 2008 and 2009. Increased Midwest region revenues by 875 percent (from twenty clients and $400,000 to 180 clients and $3.5M) during that period.
- Introduced web-based claims auditing program to show extra cost-savings opportunities for clients.

19XX–20XX   ALL RISKS INSURANCE CO.
Vice President—New York, NY

Vice President in charge of twenty-five employee, $40M property and casualty (excess and surplus lines) wholesale brokerage and managing general agency operation. Worked with over two hundred retail agents.

- Redesigned sales and brokerage units leading to revenue growth of 22 percent.
- Successfully negotiated three new carrier contracts for new program op-portunities.
- Introduced agency automation training program.

19XX–19XX   REECE INSURANCE GROUP, INC.
Chief Operating Officer—Atlanta, GA

Executive in charge of four-office, fifty-employee, $42M multistate property and casualty (excess and surplus lines) wholesale brokerage and managing general agency operations. Sold services nationally to over 250 retail agencies and brokers.

- Led merger of two newly acquired operations resulting in 30 percent expense reduction.
- Expanded agency base by 30 percent and successfully negotiated five new carrier contracts for new program opportunities.

19XX–19XX   NICHOLS HOLDINGS, LLC
Manager, Product Development—Baton Rouge, LA

Director of new product development initiatives for the national rating organization's seven hundred insurance carrier affiliates. Consultant in charge of emerging issues and trends practice.

- Led the design and development of online Underwriting Workstation, Pricing Analysis Tool, and PricePoint projects.
- Heavy emphasis on e-commerce strategic planning, claims benchmarking, and actuarial analysis.

Education   Top Flight University
BSBA, Management and Marketing

Example 2—Functional Resume

Kelsey Owen

890 Cedar Street • Sunset, NM 12345 • H: 123-456-7890 • C: 861-123-4567
kowen@nomail.com

Specialty Pharmaceutical Sales

Energetic professional dedicated to developing business relationships for revenue growth. Driven health care professional with entrepreneurial experience developing business referrals through hard work and relationships. Transitioning to sales career to deliver sales results through business development, marketing, and strategic planning. Successfully leverages core strengths and connections across the region to develop new business.

Core Strengths

√ Cold Calling	√ Sales Presentations	√ Networking
√ Negotiations	√ Relationship Cultivation	√ Marketing Tactics
√ Business Retention	√ Operations Management	√ P and L Experience
√ Vendor Relations	√ Compliance	√ Employee Relations

Career Skills

Sales—Utilized a solution-based sales approach to successfully gain an audience, assess needs, recommend solutions, negotiate terms, and close sales.

Networking—Established a referral network and created a steady stream of clients.

Consultation—Educated client-patients on the validity and effectiveness of physical therapy, which resulted in a profitable business enterprise.

Product Development—Created new services in response to market demand and patient needs.

Operations/Entrepreneurship—Took start-up of a rehab and physical therapy health care clinic to profitability in just three yearS.

Professional Experience

Co-Owner/Sports Therapist, The Sports Rehab Center, Sunset, NM, 20XX–20XX:
Built a start-up rehab clinic; established and maintained a profitable business for eight years.

Rehabilitation Director, Pinnacle Therapy, Sunset, NM, 20XX–20XX

Rehabilitation Therapist, Ferguson Chiropractic Center, Sunset, NM, 19XX–20XX

Education, Licenses, and Certifications

BS, Kinesiology, Stretch University, Muscle, AZ
New Mexico Board-certified Rehabilitation Specialist • Certified Sports Therapist

Example 3—Showcase Resume Focused on Business Relations and Product Knowledge

Contact Information:
danevans@nomail.com
8526 Glenwood Street
Somewhere, OR XXXXX
Cell: (503) 123-4567

Professional Positions Held:

Independent Consultant (Current) SNL
(20XX–20XX):
VP of Sales

HMO Consulting Inc.
(20XX—20XX):
President

D&E Corporation
(20XX–20XX):
Director of Opera-tions, Sales and Marketing

Big 6 Consulting
(20XX–20XX):
Senior Manager

Hooligan Consulting
(19XX–20XX):
Senior Manager

A+ Consulting
(19XX–19XX):
Project Manager

GPS (19XX–19XX):

Dan Evans

Summary:

Currently an independent consultant serving the payer and provider health care community. Business development, marketing, opera-tions, and product executive with over twenty years of experience in leading consulting, cost containment, and technology organiza-tions in the health care industry, focusing on various payer and provider clients. Successful track record working with leading health care executives to help reduce costs, increase revenues, im-plement technology, and create efficiencies to improve overall or-ganizational growth. Over the past eight years, major focus has been on business development, leading two separate organizations to over 30 percent annual growth in overall revenue.

Industry Experience:

SNL: A national leader in cost management for out-of-network claims re-imbursement. Products were rolled out as a revolutionary product in 2009 as a cost-based data and transparent solution to determine a rational reim-bursement of claims for payers, providers, and consumers. General re-sponsibilities and accomplishments include:

- Leading business development for the innovative repricing methodol-ogy to the market. The product is transforming the industry for reimbursement of out-of-network claims, determining a rational reimbursement to providers based on actual cost plus a fair margin, as opposed to a discount off an inflated billed charge. Impactful outcomes include:

  - New sales efforts helped lead the company to an over

Client Manager

Products:
- Claims Repricing
- Claims Audit
- Bill Review
- Claims Adjudication
- Claims Clearinghouse

Sample Clients:
- BCBS Western Pennsylvania
- BCBS Florida
- BCBS Michigan
- BCBS Massachusetts
- BCBS Louisiana
- Blue Cross of California
- Capital Blue Cross
- Empire BCBS
- HCSC (BCBS IL, OK, TX, NM)
- WellMark
- Various Other Blues Plans
- Aetna
- CIGNA
- Coventry
- United Health Care
- Mutual of Omaha
- Fortis Health/Fortis Benefits
- Over Twenty Various Health Plans
- Over Fifty Various TPAs

Education:

Bachelor of Science
Minnesota State University

30 per-cent revenue growth for each of the past two calendar years, virtually doubling the overall company revenues

- Increasing the overall group health payer client base by over 25 percent, which included third-party administrators, as well as large insurers Cigna and Coventry

- Entering the organization into two new sales markets—workers comp and the government health sector

- Delivering hundreds of sales presentations to clients, pro-spects, payers, employer groups, industry leaders/think tanks, associations, health-care conferences, and govern-ment officials

HMO Consulting: Incorporated independent consulting firm to conduct several initiatives within health care, including:

- Leading a tactical strategy within Blue Cross Blue Shield of Florida to boost the EDI rates within the Florida Provider Network

- Acting as a liaison between Blue Cross Blue Shield of Florida and the Florida provider community to implement a successful conversion to the National Provider Identifier, as legislated by the HIPAA man-dates

- Working with the product development team to develop and roll out innovative cost-based methodology to payers.

D&E Corporation: A health-care-transaction clearing-house and profes-sional services organization that provides technology and services to payer, provider, and employer organizations to transmit and process claims and other health care transactions. General responsibilities and accomplish-ments included:

Continuing Education at the School of Computer Technology
Pittsburgh, PA

Other Areas of Interest:

Director of Basketball Operations: St. Michael Parochial School

Prior President of the Total Board of Education—St. Michael School

Leader of various charitable organizations including United Way, Urban Educa-tion Service,

Athletic coach for Elementary School, Junior High, and YMCA

Former Board Member of St. Michael Parish Council

- Leading the business development, operations, IT, and product de-velopment of all clearinghouse activities, which included over 80 percent of the corporation's overall revenue

- Growing the revenue base by 30 percent in the first calendar year of the leading product—Medicare Claims Crossover that sent claims from CMS to secondary payer organizations for supplemental cov-erage—that interfaced with over seventy payer clients, including twenty different Blue Cross Blue Shield organizations

- Increasing the revenue of the EDI Clearinghouse for providers in the Midwestern states for all HIPAA-related transactions

Big 6 Consulting: Provides strategic advisory and technology experts to help deliver integrated solutions to optimize business performance. General responsibilities and accomplishments included:

- Identifying all record retention requirements—legal and business—for large payer organizations

- Conducting an assessment of a hospital's strategic initiative to out-source their supply chain operations, from distribution to point of use

Hooligan Consulting and A+ Consulting: Two of the world's largest management consulting firms that work with national and international corporations to deliver strategy, operations, and technology solutions. General responsibilities and accomplishments included:

- Leading engagements on business transformation activities for two large Blue Cross Blue Shield organizations. This included claims system selection and implementation, developing process and system interfaces, and determining impacts on organization and HR

- Managing overall impact and implementation of HIPAA for several Blue Cross Blue Shield organizations in both the technology and business operational areas, as well as overall corporate strategic planning

- Implementing many additional projects for large payer organizations including imaging/workflow, producer compensation reengineering, and consolidation of HMO organizations

GPS: A national leader in technology services including infrastructure, ap-plications, and business process outsourcing. General responsibilities and accomplishments included:

- Leading effort on corporate strategy for two large Blue Cross Blue Shield plans to merge the existing claims and membership legacy systems that impacted many significant areas including claims, pre-mium billing and membership, customer service, and human re-sources, managing the electronic commerce department in charge of the development and implementation of a managed–care, electronic network for a major East Coast Blue Cross Blue Shield plan

- Implementing large-scale technology initiatives for many Blue Cross Blue Shield claims systems impacting all areas of the organizations

Example 4—Showcase Resume Using a Chart

Beverly Hopkins

90210 State Way ▪ Somewhere, TX 76001 ▪ cell (817) 123-4567 ▪ bhopkins@goglobal.net

Senior Vice President of Sales and Business Development
Sales Leadership ◊ Strategic ◊ Passionate

Performance Summary

Dedicated sales professional with twenty-plus years of success generating revenue and securing high-profile clients and brokers for industry leaders, such as Fish-fil-A, Martens International, Barton, Wells Fargo, Cohans, and Yates, with excellent client retention. Experienced in every aspect of launching new startup companies. Seasoned veteran with sales experience in multiple industries.

Core Competencies

√ Training	√ Presentations	√ Closing
√ Large Account Prospecting	√ Account Management	√ Client Retention
√ Regulatory Compliance	√ Sales Operations	√ Product Development
√ Budget Management	√ Problem Solving	√ Business Development
√ Negotiations	√ Relationship Building	√ Push-Pull Marketing

Revenue Growth

Maintained consistent, year-over-year pattern of increasing revenues through robust and downturn economies, from $20M to $35M as illustrated below:

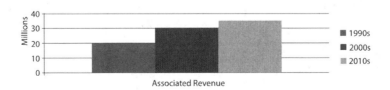

Professional Experience

RIP Consulting Group   **20XX–Present**

Start-up company that is a distributor/wholesaler of aggregate and spec and aggregate self-funded group health plans.

President, Health Division

Manage the sales and marketing for the company, including direct sales and broker-channel management, interface with underwriting, compliance, and investors.

- Added fifteen new accounts through direct and broker sales in a new market.

Last Decade Healthcare   **20XX–20XX**

Leading company in the limited-benefit medical plans industry.

Vice President of Sales and Business Development—*Promotion*   **20XX–20XX**

Responsible for hiring and training of five staff members (three of whom were area vice presidents) and assisting them in achieving sales goals, interfacing with carrier underwriting to design plan, and adjusting rates for a competitive plan offering. Maintained and grew broker contacts and client business, negotiated major client renewals and contracts, and analyzed vendors. Redeveloped the western region broker channel.

- Maintained 100 percent of all large clients negotiating multi-year contracts.
- Grew revenue from $21M to over $30M in two years.
- Negotiated profit-sharing agreement that resulted in an additional $200,000 in net profit.
- Wrote over $4M in new business.

Regional Vice President—*Promotion*   **20XX–20XX**

Managed five AVPs and trained new staff, responsible for sales in southwestern, south-central, and western regions. Controlled regional budget and those of direct staff.

- Generated over $8.5M in gross sales while remaining under budget.
- Won Fish-fil-A account, resulting in $2.8M in revenue.
- Implemented "Push-Pull" marketing strategy resulting in increased market penetration.

Area Vice President   **20XX–20XX**

Changed industries, and hired to grow revenue and open a new market in the Central Region.

- Grew regional revenue from zero to $1.5M in fourteen months.

American Printing   20XX–20XX

Multimillion dollar global company, leader in the wide format printer industry.

Sales Executive, Display Division   Responsible
for account development and the direct sales of printers in TX, OK, LA, and AR. Greatly improved customer satisfaction among existing client base.

- Increased top-line revenue growth by 27 percent.

The Pique Company   19XX–20XX

The Pique Company is centered on disruptive technologies and breakthrough solutions for the product-goods-packaging, graphic-communications, and functional-printing industries.

Account Manager, Southern Zone   20XX–20XX

Developed a channel for printers in the South-Central Region. Responsible for working in tandem with distribution partners to grow the market share. Prospected for large direct accounts and supported nine account executives.

Account Executive   20XX–20XX

Trained dealers on new digital products and worked with system integrators to generate digital portrait studio sales.

- Reached 143 percent of year-to-date goal in seven-state territory.
- Built photography business from zero to $20M in three years.

Specialist, Systems and Solutions   19XX–20XX

Acted as racing segment manager, worked with Pensky Racing to evaluate profitability targets of event photography of NASCAR and other venues.

- Ranked as top producer for three-year tenure.
- Exceeded revenue goals every year while remaining under budget, 165 percent of quota.

Education and Licensing

Northern Minnesota University—Somewhere, MN
Bachelor of Science in Marketing, concentration sales and management

Appendix C

Sample Letters

Letter of Application

Street Address
City, State ZIP Code
Phone Number

Date

George Heisler
XYZ Company
87 Delaware Road
Hatfield, CA 08065

RE: Senior Systems Engineer

Dear Mr. Heisler,

I am a senior level systems engineer and in the last four years I have designed and implemented one of the first large-scale, virtual desktop deployments used in education. I am writing to apply for the senior level systems engineer position advertised in the *Times Union*.

The opportunity presented in this listing is very interesting, and I believe that my strong technical experience and certifications will make me a competitive candidate for this position. The key certifications that I possess for success in this role include:

- VMware Certified Professional, Data Center Virtualization
- VMware Certified Professional, Desktop Technologies
- EMC Information Storage Associate
- EMC Implementation Engineer, VNX Solutions Specialist
- Cisco Certified Entry Networking Technician

In 20XX, I accepted the Computerworld Honors Program Laureate Award in Washington DC for designing and implementing virtual desktops. I believe my above certifications and past experiences qualify me to orchestrate your virtual desktop software.

As requested, I am enclosing a completed job application, my certifications, my resume, and three references. I will contact you by next week to discuss this opportunity with you further. I can be reached anytime via email at john.donaldson@emailexample.com or my cell phone (909) 555-5555.

Thank you for your time and consideration. I look forward to speaking with you.

Sincerely,
(*Signature in blue or black ink*)

John Donaldson

Letter of Inquiry

Street Address
City, State ZIP Code
Phone Number

Date

George Gilhooley
XYZ Company
87 Delaware Road
Hatfield, CA 08065

RE: Information Technology Department

Dear Mr. Gilhooley,

For the past two years, I have been working as an engineer on a cloud-based system that supports over 450 virtual desktops in ten states. I am inquiring about job opportunities in your IT department.

I am certified in:

- VMware Certified Professional 4 and vSphere 5
- IBM Certified Advanced System Administrator—Domino 7.x
- Cisco UCS
- Windows Servers

In addition to the above certifications I am proficient in Cisco switches, EMC and Equallogic SANs, and Commvault. I have worked in varied environments from small businesses to international corporations, and this has prepared me to excel with your company's cloud-based systems software. Because of my past experiences and accomplishments, I believe I am qualified for your IT department as a systems engineer.

Enclosed is my resume for your review and consideration. XYZ Company has a reputation for excellence. I would like to use my talents to advance your software. I will call you to further discuss my talents and how I can benefit your company. If you prefer, you may reach me in the evenings at (555) 555-5555.

Thank you for your time. I look forward to meeting you.

Sincerely,

(*Signature in blue or black ink*)
John Donaldson

Enclosure: resume

Response to a Job Posting

Director, Operations (Mail Order)

Job Description

Based on the extensive growth of our corporation, we are looking to add an accomplished professional to join our growing team as we are expanding our mail order pharmacy services and scope. We are a financially stable and fundamentally sound corporation experiencing tremendous success based on our corporate model as well as our delivery methods for the patient populations which we service.

Position Purpose:

Oversee pharmacy mail order operations (inventory, shipping, fulfillment, and customer service), ensuring timely and accurate processing of related activities.

Position Responsibilities:

- Develop operational plans and implement new programs related to the processing of pharmacy mail orders
- Oversee the supporting functions for mail service fulfillment, including customer service, product fulfillment, inventory management, shipping, and general facility management
- Oversee new client implementation and transition of new business, including managing the IT infrastructure and web strategy
- Design and implement new processes for automation and streamline operations by incorporating cost-saving programs
- Evaluate and implement mail service pharmacy procedures to ensure compliance with all related laws, regulations, and executive orders

Send your resume to: Bjohnson@emailaddress.biz

EMAIL RESPONSE

Dear Brenda Johnson:

Would you like to increase the efficiency and revenues of your pharmacy mail orders by 20 percent? If so, I am the Director of Mail Order Pharmacy you need.

With nine years of experience managing the $3.5M mail order division of *Drugs For You*, I have had the following successes:

- Led creative team to define strategic goals and design company's first pharmacy mail order services.
- Set up software team to develop home page on the Internet for online ordering. This distribution channel increased sales by 20 percent.
- Supervised twenty-five employees in all departments, including finance, design, and purchasing to realize 100 percent of deadlines.
- Reorganized ordering processing procedures, which increased customer satisfaction by 25 percent.

I am passionate about process improvement. When I look at departments, internal processes, and protocols, my mind immediately asks whether there exists a better, more efficient, or profitable way. This way of thinking has both saved money and generated new revenue sources in the past.

I believe you will find my skills beneficial to XYZ. I will follow up with you in a few days to discuss this opportunity with you further.

Sincerely,

Joe Jones

(Contact Information)

Job-Match Cover Letter

Street Address
City, State ZIP Code
Phone Number

Date

George Gilhooley
XYZ Company
87 Delaware Road
Hatfield, CA 08065

RE: Chief Sales Officer position

Dear Mr. Gilhooley,

I am an Executive Vice President of Sales. For the past fifteen years, I have been leading the sales division and have served over one thousand existing clients nationwide. I am a qualified candidate for your Chief Sales Officer position, as I have illustrated below.

Position Requirements	Qualifications of (Your Name)
Team Building	Transformed the sales team to Insight Selling. Achieved 103 percent of sales plan in 20XX.
Product Development	Created Beyond-Check. Introduced to existing clients. Currently 122 percent of goal.
Budgeting/Forecasting	Due to company-wide budgetary realignment, implemented a variable workforce and reduced spending by $1M.
Mentoring/Development	Led a business development team that achieved 162 percent of plan.

In addition to the above qualifications, I led a sales team of six market managers and forty-two account executives to successfully retain and gain new business and managed $200M in sales for this year.

Enclosed is my resume for your review and consideration. XYZ Company has a reputation for excellence. I would like to use my talents to advance your sales. I will call you to further discuss my talents and how I can benefit your company. If you prefer, you may reach me in the evenings at (555) 555-5555.

Thank you for your time. I look forward to meeting you.

Sincerely,
(Your Name)

Marketing Email Example #1

Subject Line: #1 Work Comp Sales Professional

Mr. Johnson:

I am a **top-producing Workers' Compensation Cost Containment Sales Professional** that ranked as the #1 sales representative among my peers for 20XX and 20XX. I played an instrumental role in the growth of my former employer. I am exploring a career move.

My sales achievements include:

1. Consistently **exceeded sales quota** for the last four years.

2. **Ranked #1** in sales in 20XX and 20XX of twenty reps nationally. **Sales Representative of the Year.**

3. **20XX—Account Coordinator of the Year Award.**

Click *here* for a one-minute bio video.

I sold pharmacy services, transportation, translation, home health, physical therapy, durable medical equipment, and other services in the workers' compensation and auto insurance industries. Territory includes the Great Lakes area, calling on nurse case managers, claims managers, and adjusters, among others. I have no travel restrictions.

If you have an interest or a need for a sales professional with a consistent track record for new business sales, please reply or call me.

Best Regards,

Your Name

Phone Number

Marketing Email Example #2

Subject Line: Operations and Business Development Executive

Mr. Johnson:

Congratulations on the recent launch of your ProDent claims platform.

I am an operations and business development executive with a proven track record of building and managing profitable organizations in the health care industry. I recently built a health and dental claims clearinghouse **from scratch to over ten million** transactions per year.

I am looking to make a career move into a key leadership role with either an emerging health care organization, or a division of a larger company that needs operational efficiency, development, and sales growth.

My achievements include:

1. Built a dental managed-care organization **from zero to two hundred thousand members** in two years.

2. Negotiated and acquired large blocks of business ranging from **$2M to $120M** for a national health and dental organization.

3. Generated **$40M in new business revenue** while at the same time reducing the cost of sale by 10 percent.

My experience includes working in both turnaround and early stage growth environments. I can make difficult—yet informed decisions, and I am not afraid to roll up my sleeves. I've led companies and divisions with over $200 million in revenue and managed multiple departments with staff ranging from fifteen to three hundred professionals. I also have extensive knowledge in government and regulatory affairs.

I am driven to achieve. Throughout my career I have always maintained a passion to grow businesses, create efficiencies, and improve revenues.

If you have an interest in an accomplished senior health care executive, please reply or call me.

Best Regards,

Your Name
Phone Number

Thank-You Letter/Response

Issues Brought up in Conversation

- Company has just restructured its accounting department
- Department is in the midst of automating various accounting procedures
- Got the feeling that the place is in chaos
- Indicated employee morale was down, which has adversely affected efficiency of office

January 15, 20XX

Mr. Randy Jones, Vice President of Accounting
EFD Corporation
12345 Main Street
Baltimore, MD 23654

RE: Our recent conversation

Dear Mr. Jones:

Thank you for the time spent with me on the phone yesterday. I understand your department is undergoing some major transitions. I am confident that my accounting systems conversion experience and skills would help get your department up and running in your stated goal of six months.

As we discussed, I spent seven years at Martinsen Company, managing its accounting and finance department. During this period, I accomplished the following:

- Converted manual reporting systems to computerized operations, which led to a cost savings of $60,000 per year, and increased efficiency by 40 percent.

- Participated in the downsizing process, which cut my staff from thirty to twelve.

- Implemented motivational programs to increase employee morale and keep productivity constant throughout this six-month period.

- Created a financial operating plan to fully fund banking services of $250,000.

- Execution of this plan resulted in generating earnings in short-term reserves, while contributing 7 percent of revenue to long-term reserves.

In the transitional time you are experiencing, there is nothing more important than communicating effectively with your personnel and organizing the group to reach common goals. While with Martinsen, I completely reorganized accounting procedures following the downsizing. As you can imagine, there was a lot of resistance from the staff. I was able to take that resistance and turn it around. Within two weeks, I had each team member up and running on the new system with smiles on their faces. I attribute this to my team-oriented focus, clear communication style, and organizational skills.

I believe you will find my management, organizational, and systems skills are what you need during this transitional period. I will call you next week, as you suggested, to speak further with you about future opportunities.

Sincerely,

Peter Fabin
Phone Number

Job-Match Thank-You Letter

Street Address
City, State ZIP Code
Phone Number

Date

Robert Chalfant
XYZ Company
12734 Johnson Dr.
Sometowne, MI XXXXX

RE: Senior Software Engineer

Dear Mr. Chalfant,

Thank you for taking time today to speak with me about the senior software engineer opportunity. Based on our conversation, your requirements for the position and my background match.

You stated that you needed someone with:

Position Requirements	Qualifications of (John Smith)
Degree in Computer Science	Graduated cum laude with a degree in Computer Science
Five-plus years' exp. C#.NET	Eight years' experience with C#.NET
Five-plus years' exp. JavaScript, JSON	Ten years' exp. with JavaScript, JSON
Cisco certified a plus	Cisco certified since 20XX

I have solid client-facing skills, having participated in numerous presentations. As you may recall, I received a letter of commendation from my vice president of technology for my client presentation abilities. I am able to balance the technology needs with the business and budget constraints of a client.

I am a strong fit for the senior software engineer position. I would like to work for (Company Name) and would welcome an opportunity to discuss how we could move the process forward to an offer. You can reach me anytime on my cell number: (555) 555-5555.

Sincerely,
John Smith

Thank You Letter

Issues Brought up in Interview

- Last person in position did not take initiative in starting new projects
- Company is facing the problem of finding substitute products as the supply of raw materials decreases
- Hiring executive liked my leadership abilities and innovative strategies
- I feel I am competing against an individual with five to seven more years of experience than myself; this could be a concern of the hiring executive

Date

Jane Whittington, President
PPI Corporation
98765 Main Street
Milltown, PA 17896

RE: Vice President position

Dear Ms. Whittington:

Thank you for the opportunity to interview for the vice president position with your company. After finding out more about the responsibilities of the position, I know my leadership skills and use of innovative strategies will benefit PPI significantly.

In my last position with DFG Company, I accomplished the following, which I can repeat for your organization:

Took the initiative to research new markets and opportunities. Upon penetrating two new markets, our company increased revenues by 16 percent in nine months.

Worked with engineering and manufacturing teams to develop substitute products using recycled aluminum. Using these products allowed the company to save 15 percent in manufacturing costs, while offering a superior product to our customers.

While in my position at DFG, I took my company from number eight in the industry to number two.

I believe my proven ability will allow me to lead PPI to the top of the industry. Jane, I will contact you next week to see where you are in the decision process, as you suggested.

Sincerely,

Stanley Snyder

Thank-You Letter When Not Selected for the Job—Email

Subject Line: Thank you—from (Your Name)

Mr. Jefferies,

I received a communication today informing me that I was not selected for the senior account management position. I want to express my appreciation for your consideration. (Company Name) is a dynamic company with strong products and services. I'm sure it will continue to succeed in the future.

I remain interested in (Company Name) and should another opportunity become available, please reach out to me.

Best Regards,

Your Name

Networking Follow-Up Letter

Date

Mr. John Baker
President
BFO Company
1200 Market Boulevard
Whitewater, Michigan 19117

RE: Our lunch on Tuesday.

Dear Mr. Baker:

Thank you for meeting me for lunch on Tuesday. It was a pleasure getting together with a fellow Lambda Chi alumnus. When I came across your name in the alumni directory, I never realized we would have so much in common. It was such a coincidence that you know Brian Klein and Mike Allen, my "brothers" from the University of Nebraska. What a small world.

As we discussed, the plastics industry has changed dramatically over the last five years. It is an exciting time. I know I have the skills and experience needed to help a company make the changes necessary to become a player in today's marketplace. As I pointed out, some of my most recent accomplishments have been:

- Assisted plant manager with implementation of comprehensive safety program, which resulted in zero time-loss accidents in 20XX.

- Led engineering team to overhaul manufacturing process, which increased production by 40 percent.

- Reengineered department to increase efficiencies and cut labor costs by $100,000 per year, while maintaining productivity.

I appreciate your advice and the contacts you supplied me with. I will be reaching out to those individuals this week. In the meantime, please feel free to call me at (123) 555-4567 if you hear of any opportunities that may fit my background.

John, if there is anything I can do to return the favor, please just pick up the phone. Thanks again.

Sincerely,

Dustin Jasien

Introductory Email to a Search Firm

Subject Line: #1 Work Comp Services Sales Professional

Mr. Johnson:

I am a **top-producing workers' compensation services sales professional** that ranked as the number one sales representative amongst my peers for 20XX and 20XX. I played an instrumental role in the growth of my former employer.

My sales achievements include:

- Consistently **exceeded sales quota** for the last four years.
- **Ranked number one** in sales in 20XX and 20XX of twenty sales reps nationally. **Sales Representative of the Year**.
- **20XX—Account Coordinator of the Year Award**.

Click to watch a brief <u>one-minute bio video</u>.

I sold pharmacy services, transportation, translation, home health, physical therapy, durable medical equipment, and other services within the workers' compensation and auto insurance industry. Territory includes the Great Lakes area calling on nurse case managers, claims managers, and adjusters, among others. I have no restrictions on travel.

If there is a possible fit with one of your clients, I would like to speak with you about that opportunity. Alternatively, if I am a candidate that fits your specialty, please keep me in mind for future opportunities.

I have attached a resume for review.

Best Regards,

Your Name

Contact Information

Bibliography

Introduction and Chapter 1: Things to Know about Your Job Search

See also, Beshara, Tony. The Job Search Solution: The Ultimate System for Finding a Great Job Now! 2nd ed. (New York: AMACOM, 2012), Chapter 13, "Looking for a Job When You Have a Job."

Byrne, Donn Erwin. The Attraction Paradigm. (New York: Academic Press, 1971), quoted in Kurtzberg and Naquin, Essentials, p. 35.

Cialdini, Robert B. Influence: Science and Practice, 4th ed. (Needham Heights, MA: Allyn & Bacon, 2001), quoted in Kurtzberg and Naquin, Essentials, chapter 5, p. 94–101.

Cialdini, Influence, p. 204–205, and chapter 7, "Scarcity: The Rule of the Few," quoted in Kurtzberg and Naquin, Essentials, p. 94–101.

Cialdini, Influence, p. 180–185, and chapter 9, "Authority: Directed Deference," quoted in Kurtzberg and Naquin, Essentials, p. 94–101.

Cialdini, Influence, p. 53, and chapter 3, "Commitment and Consistency: Hobgoblins of the Mind," quoted in Kurtzberg and Naquin, Essentials, p. 94–101.

Cialdini, Influence, p. 144, 161, and chapter 5, "Liking: The Friendly Thief," quoted in Kurtzberg and Naquin, Essentials, p. 94–101.

See also, Cohen, Elizabeth, Blaming others can ruin your health, The Empowered Patient, August 18, 2011, http://edition.cnn.com/2011/HEALTH/08/17/bitter.resentful.ep/index.html (accessed March 28, 2017).

"David Ogilvy Quotable Quote," Goodreads, http://www.goodreads.com/quotes/262108-don-t-buntaim-out-of-the-ballpark-aim-for-the (accessed May 28, 2015).

DiResta, Diane, interview by Christina Canters, "Episode 29—How to Blitz Your Job Interview—Secrets of Executive Speech Coach Diane Diresta," DesignDrawSpeak, podcast audio, June 12, 2014.

Frasier. "Goodnight, Seattle: Part 2," first broadcast 13 May 2004 by NBC. Directed by David Lee and written by Christopher Lloyd and Joe Keenan.

"In the same way, faith by itself, if it is not accompanied by action, is dead" (James 2:17, NIV).

Joyce, Susan P. "Job Search Success Strategy: PROactive vs. REactive Job Search," Job-Hunt. org, http://www.job-hunt.org/article_proactive_job_search.shtml (accessed July 14, 2015).

Kanfer, Ruth, and Charles L. Hulin. "Individual Differences in Job Searches Following Lay-off."

Abstract. Personnel Psychology 38, no. 4 (December 1985): 835–847, http://www. researchgate.

net/publication/227749499_INDIVIDUAL_DIFFERENCES_IN_SUCCESSFUL_JOB_ SEARCHES_FOLLOWING_LAYOFF (accessed July 9, 2015); Moynihan, Lisa M., Mark V. Roehling, Marcie A. LePine, and Wendy R. Boswell "A Longitudinal Study of the Relationships Among Job Search Self-Efficacy, Job Interviews, and Employment Outcomes." Abstract. Journal of Business and Psychology 18, no. 2 (2003): 201–233, http://link.springer. com/article/10.1023%2FA%3A1027349115277 (accessed July 3, 2015).

Kaufman, Wendy. "A Successful Job Search: It's All About Networking," National Public Radio, February 3, 2011, http://www.npr.org/2011/02/08/133474431/a-successful-job-search-its-all-about-networking (accessed June 2, 2015); "Developing Job Search Strategies," University of Wisconsin, https://www.uwgb.edu/careers/PDF-Files/Job-Search-Strategies.pdf (accessed June 3, 2015).

Kurtzberg, Terri R., and Charles E. Naquin. The Essentials of Job Negotiations: Proven Strategies for Getting What You Want. (Santa Barbara, CA: Praeger, 2011), p. 18.

"Lincoln's Advice to Lawyers," Abraham Lincoln's letter to Isham Reavis, November 5, 1855, Abraham Lincoln Online, http://www.abrahamlincolnonline.org/lincoln/speeches/ law.htm (accessed May 27, 2015).

"Malachy McCourt Quotes," Goodreads, http://www.goodreads.com/author/quotes/ 3373.Malachy_McCourt (accessed February 5, 2016).

"Proactive Career Planning at Any Age," Aequus Wealth Management Resources, http:// www.aequuswealth.com/newsletter/article/proactive_career_planning_at_any_age (accessed July 10, 2015).

Thompson, Stacey A. "6 Virtues to Practice for Job Search Success," Virtues for Life, http:// www.virtuesforlife.com/6-virtues-to-practice-for-job-search-success/ (accessed June 1, 2015).

"Using LinkedIn to Find a Job or Internship," LinkedIn, https://university.linkedin.com/ content/dam/university/global/en_US/site/pdf/TipSheet_FindingaJoborInternship. pdf (accessed June 7, 2015); Kimberly Beatty, "The Math Behind the Networking Claim,"

Jobfully Blog, July 1, 2010, http://blog.jobfully.com/2010/07/the-math-behind-the-networking-claim/ (accessed June 11, 2015); Steven Rothberg, "80% of Job Openings are Unadvertised," College Recruiter (blog), March 28, 2013, https://www.collegerecruiter.com/blog/2013/03/28/80-of-job-openings-are-unadvertised/ (accessed June 11, 2015).

Varelas, Elaine, "How Long Will My Job Search Take?" The Job Doc (blog), The Boston Globe, June 12, 2013, http://www.boston.com/jobs/news/jobdoc/2013/06/how_long_will_my_job_search_ta.html (accessed June 4, 2015).

Varelas, Elaine, "How Long Will My Job Search Take?" The Job Doc (blog), The Boston Globe, June 12, 2013, http://www.boston.com/jobs/news/jobdoc/2013/06/how_long_will_my_job_search_ta.html (accessed June 4, 2015).

Widener, Chris. "Life Rewards Action," http://chriswidener.com/life-rewards-action/ (accessed May 27, 2015).

Woods, Jennifer. "Working Longer—Whether You Want to or Not," CNBC.com, December 23, 2014, http://www.cnbc.com/id/102264601 (accessed June 9, 2015).

Chapter 2: Profiling Your Next Career Opportunity—the Target Opportunity Profile

Berra, Yogi, "Yogi Berra Quotes," Baseball Almanac, http://www.baseball-almanac.com/quotes/quoberra.shtml (accessed May 27, 2015).

Cherry, Kendra. "What Is Flow? Understanding the Psychology of Flow," Verywell.com, last updated May 6, 2016, https://www.verywell.com/what-is-flow-2794768 (accessed May 10, 2016).

Claycomb, Heather, and Karl Dinse. Career Pathways—Interactive Workbook. (1995), Part 1, "Career Assessment"; Whitcomb, Job Search Magic, p. 478.

Whitcomb, Job Search Magic, p. 34.

See also, Yate, Martin John. Knock 'em Dead—The Ultimate Job Search Guide. (Avon, MA: Adams Media, 2014), p. 23–25.

Chapter 3: Essential Job-Search Topics and Tools

Andrew, Victoria, "The Power of a Positive Attitude," (blog), Kavaliro Employment Agency, May 23, 2013, http://www.kavaliro.com/the-power-of-a-positive-attitude (accessed June 8, 2015). See also, Jobvite Recruiter Nation Report 2016, http://www.jobvite.com/wp-content/uploads/2016/09/RecruiterNation2016.pdf (78% of recruiters cite enthusiasm as most likely to influence a hiring decision), accessed March 15, 2017.

Ayres, Leslie, "Why You Need a Resume Business Card," Notes from the Job Search Guru: A Career Advice Blog, March 16, 2009, http://www.thejobsearchguru.com/notesfrom/why-you-need-a-resume-businesscard/ (accessed November 4, 2015).

Ayres, "Resume Business Card."

Bergdahl, Michael. What I Learned From Sam Walton: How to Compete and Thrive in a Wal-Mart World. (Hoboken, New Jersey: John Wiley & Sons, 2004), p. 39.

Collamer, Nancy. "The Perfect Elevator Pitch To Land A Job," Forbes, February 4, 2013, http://www.forbes.com/sites/nextavenue/2013/02/04/the-perfect-elevator-pitch-to-land-a-job/ (accessed May 28, 2015).

"Doing What's Necessary, What's Possible, and What Seems to be Impossible," The Recovery Ranch, http://www.recoveryranch.com/articles/necessary-possible-impossible/ (accessed May 27, 2015).

Employee Retirement Income Security Act; see "Frequently Asked Questions About Retirement Plans and ERISA," US Department of Labor, http://www.dol.gov/ebsa/faqs/faq_consumer_pension.html (accessed July 8, 2015).

Hansen, Randall S., PhD. "Networking Business Cards: An Essential Job-Search Tool for Job-Seekers, Career Changers, and College Students When a Resume Just Won't Do." Quintessential Careers, http://www.quintcareers.com/networking-business-cards/ (accessed November 4, 2015).

Hansen, Randall S., PhD, and Katharine Hansen, PhD. "What Do Employers Really Want? Top Skills and Values Employers Seek from Job-Seekers," Quintessential Careers, http://www.quintcareers.com/job_skills_values.html (accessed May 27, 2015).

"Jarod Kintz Quotable Quote," Goodreads, http://www.goodreads.com/quotes/1234580-the-onlypeople-who-don-t-need-elevator-pitches-are-elevator (accessed May 28, 2015).

Nsehe, Mfonobong. "19 Inspirational Quotes From Nelson Mandela," Forbes.com, December 6, 2013, http://www.forbes.com/sites/mfonobongnsehe/2013/12/06/20-inspirational-quotes-from-nelsonmandela/ (accessed May 27, 2015).

Safani, Barbara. "Tell a Story Interviewers Can't Forget," TheLadders, http://www.theladders.com/career-advice/tell-story-interviewers-cant-forget (accessed May 29, 2015).

Tilus, Grant, "Top 10 Human Resources Job Skills Employers Want to See," (blog), Rasmussen College, July 29, 2013, http://www.rasmussen.edu/degrees/business/blog/human-resources-job-skills-employerswant-to-see/ (accessed July 10, 2015).

"Unleashing Your Genius," Quotes from the Masters, http://finsecurity.com/finsecurity/quotes/qm121.html (accessed May 27, 2015).

Walters, Secrets of Successful Speakers, p. 59.

"10 Ways You're Building a Fantastic Brand," Design Aglow (blog), February 3, 2015, http://designaglow.com/blogs/design-aglow/16728432-10-ways-youre-building-a-fantastic-brand (accessed May 28, 2015).

A process that resolves problems while reducing costs; see "What is Lean Six Sigma?" Go Lean Six Sigma, https://goleansixsigma.com/what-is-lean-six-sigma/ (accessed July 8, 2015).

Chapter 4: Impactful Resumes

Bucknell Career Development Center, "Creating an Effective Resume," Bucknell University, http://www.bucknell.edu/documents/CDC/Creating_An_Effective_Resume.pdf (accessed February 19, 2016).

CareerBuilder, "Employers Share Encouraging Perspectives and Tips for the Unemployed in New CareerBuilder Survey," news release, March 21, 2012, http://www.careerbuilder.com/share/aboutus/pressreleasesdetail.aspx?id=pr684&sd=3/21/2012&ed=12/31/2012&siteid=cbpr&sc_cmp1=cb_pr684_ (accessed February 19, 2016).

Claycomb and Dinse, *Career Pathways*, Part 3.

"Earnings before interest, taxes, depreciation, and amortization"; see Arline, Katherine. "What is EBITDA?" *Business News Daily*, February 25, 2015, http://www.businessnewsdaily.com/4461-ebitda-formula-definition.html (accessed February 19, 2016).

Guest Author (Bob Bozorgi), "Qualifications Will Get You an Interview, But They Won't Get You Hired," *The Undercover Recruiter* (blog), http://theundercoverrecruiter.com/qualifications-will-get-interview-wontget-hired/ (accessed May 29, 2015).

O'Brien, Matthew. "The Terrifying Reality of Long-Term Unemployment," *The Atlantic*, April 13, 2013, http://www.theatlantic.com/business/archive/2013/04/the-terrifying-reality-of-long-termunemployment/274957/ (accessed February 19, 2016).

"Quotes on Perseverance," *The Samuel Johnson Sound Bite Page*, http://www.samueljohnson.com/persever.html (accessed June 2, 2015); "Rasselas: A Word of Caution," *The Samuel Johnson Sound Bite Page*, http://www.samueljohnson.com/rasselas.html (accessed June 2, 2015).

See also, Safani, "Tell a Story."

"Self-Limiting Beliefs," *Quotes from the Masters*, http://finsecurity.com/finsecurity/quotes/qm103.html (accessed May 28, 2015).

Whitcomb, *Job Search Magic*, p. 274.

Yate, *Knock 'em Dead*, p. 45–46.

Chapter 5: LinkedIn

"About LinkedIn," *LinkedIn Newsroom*, https://press.linkedin.com/about-linkedin (accessed May 29, 2015).

Arruda, William. "Is LinkedIn Poised To Be The Next Media Giant?" *Forbes*, March 8, 2015, http://www.forbes.com/sites/williamarruda/2015/03/08/is-linkedin-poised-to-be-the-next-media-giant/ (accessed June 5, 2015).

Ayele, Daniel, "Land Your Dream Job in 2015 with These Data-Proven LinkedIn Tips," *LinkedIn Blog*, January 29, 2015, http://blog.linkedin.com/2015/01/29/jobseeking-tips/ (accessed June 9, 2015).

Bell, Karissa, LinkedIn will now help you secretly tell recruiters you want a new job, October 6, 2016, http://mashable.com/2016/10/06/linkedin-tell-recruiters-you-want-a-new-job.amp. (accessed November 7, 2016).

Dougherty, Lisa. "16 Tips to Optimize Your LinkedIn Profile and Your Personal Brand," *LinkedIn Pulse*, July 8, 2014, https://www.linkedin.com/pulse/20140708162049-7239647-16-tips-to-optimize-your-linkedinprofile-and-enhance-your-personal-brand (accessed November 11, 2015).

Foote, Andy, Maximum LinkedIn Character Counts for 2016, December 10, 2016 https://www.linkedin.com/pulse/maximum-linkedin-character-counts-2016-andy-foote. (accessed November 22, 2016).

Foote, Andy, Why You Should Complete Your LinkedIn Profile, (December 7, 2015). https://www.linkedinsights.com/why-you-should-complete-your-linkedin-profile/ (accessed November 22, 2016).

Frasco, Stephanie, "11 Tips To Help Optimize Your LinkedIn Profile For Maximum Exposure and Engagement," *Convert with Content* (blog), https://www.convertwithcontent.com/11-tips-optimize-linkedin-profilemaximum-exposure-engagement/ (accessed June 10, 2015).

General Limits for LinkedIn Groups, https://www.linkedin.com/help/linkedin/answer/190/general limits-for-linkedin-groups?lang=en (accessed November 23, 2016).

Geoff, "Top LinkedIn Facts and Stats [Infographic]," (blog), *We Are Social Media*, July 25, 2014, http://wersm.com/top-linkedin-facts-and-stats-infographic/ (accessed May 29, 2015).

Isaacson, Nate. "Professional Designations Are Great But They Are Not A Part of Your Name,"

LinkedIn Pulse, April 14, 2014, https://www.linkedin.com/pulse/20140414223601-23236063-professional designations-are-great-but-they-are-not-a-part-of-your-name (accessed July 16, 2015); Hanson, Arik. "Should You Put MBA Behind Your Name on Your LinkedIn Profile?" *LinkedIn Pulse*, May 29, 2014, https://www.linkedin.com/pulse/20140529131058-18098999-should-you-put-mba-behind-your-name-on-your-linkedinprofile (accessed July 17, 2015).

Jobvite Recruiter Nation Report 2016, http://www.jobvite.com/wp-content/uploads/2016/09/

RecruiterNation2016.pdf (41% of recruiters believe that seeing a picture of a candidate before meeting them influences their first impression) (accessed March 15, 2017).

Jobvite Recruiter Nation Report 2016, http://www.jobvite.com/wp-content/uploads/2016/09/

RecruiterNation2016.pdf (accessed March 15, 2017).

Jobvite 2016 Recruiter National Survey www.jobvite.com (accessed February 4, 2017).

Jobvite 2016 Recruiter National Survey www.jobvite.com (accessed November 17, 2016).

Knyszweski, Jerome. "How to Use LinkedIn as a Student—And Nail That Dream Job," *LinkedIn Pulse*, April 28, 2015, https://www.linkedin.com/pulse/how-use-linkedin-student-nail-dream-job-jerome-knyszewski (accessed May 28, 2015).

See, Kolowich, Lindsay, What is a White Paper, June 27, 2014 http://blog.hubspot.com/marketing/whatis-whitepaper-faqs#sm.0000lbm5cb9ke7e11nu1h1l4e63aj (accessed November 22, 2016).

LinkHumans, "10 Tips." See also, Smith, Craig, DMR, "200+ Amazing LinkedIn Stats" (Last Checked/Updated October 2016) http://expandedramblings.com/index.php/by-the-numbers-a-few-importantlinkedin-stats/. (downloaded November 28, 2016). This source indicates that 65% of job postings on LinkedIn require a bachelor's degree.

Matt, "Brag Book."

Oswal, Shreya, "7 Smart Habits of Successful Job Seekers [INFOGRAPHIC]," *LinkedIn Blog*, March 19, 2014, http://blog.linkedin.com/2014/03/19/7-smart-habits-of-successful-job-seekers-infographic/ (accessed June 9, 2015).

Pearcemarch, Kyle, SEO for LinkedIn: How to Optimize Your LinkedIn Profile for Search (March 19, 2015) https://www.diygenius.com/how-to-optimize-your-linkedin-profile-for-search/ (accessed November 22, 2016).

PhotoFeeler. "New Research Study Breaks Down The Perfect Profile Photo," PhotoFeeler, May 13, 2014 https://blog.photofeeler.com/perfect-photo/. (accessed November 7, 2016).

Pollak, Lindsey, "How to Attract Employers' Attention on LinkedIn," *LinkedIn Blog*, December 2, 2010, http://blog.linkedin.com/2010/12/02/find-jobs-on-linkedin/ (accessed June 4, 2015).

See, Practices to Avoid When Optimizing Your Profile For LinkedIn Search. https://www.linkedin.com/help/linkedin/answer/51499/practices-to-avoid-when-optimizing-your-profile-for-linkedinsearch?lang=en (accessed November 23, 2016).

Reynolds, Marci. "How to Be Found More Easily in LinkedIn (LinkedIn SEO)," *Job-Hunt.org*, http://www.job-hunt.org/social-networking/be-found-on-linkedin.shtml (accessed June 4, 2015).

Smith, Jacquelyn. "Here's What To Say In Your LinkedIn 'Summary' Statement," *Business Insider*, December 19, 2014, http://www.businessinsider.com/what-to-say-in-your-linkedin-summary-statement-2014-12 (accessed July 9, 2015).

Smith, Jacquelyn. "The Complete Guide To Crafting A Perfect LinkedIn Profile," *Business Insider*, January 21, 2015, http://www.businessinsider.com/guide-to-perfect-linkedin-profile-2015-1 (accessed June 4, 2015).

Smith, Craig. "133 Amazing LinkedIn Statistics." Last updated November 17, 2016, http://

expandedramblings.com/index.php/by-the-numbers-a-few-important-linkedin-stats/. (accessed November 28, 2016). See also, Smith, Craig, DMR, "200+ Amazing LinkedIn Stats" (Last Checked/Updated October 2016) http://expandedramblings.com/index.php/by-the-numbers-a-few-important-linkedin-stats/. (downloaded November 28, 2016).

Smith, Craig, DMR, "200+ Amazing LinkedIn Stats" (Last Checked/Updated October 2016) http://expandedramblings.com/index.php/by-the-numbers-a-few-important-linkedin-stats/. (downloaded November 28, 2016).

"10 Tips for the Perfect LinkedIn Profile," LinkHumans, SlideShare, published July 1, 2014, http://www.slideshare.net/linkedin/10-tips-for-the-perfect-linkedin-profile   (accessed November 11, 2015).

Uzialko, Adam, LinkedIn's Open Candidates: How to Search for a New Job, Quietly, October 6, 2016, http://www.businessnewsdaily.com/9468-linkedin-open-candidates.html (accessed November 25, 2016).

Vaughan, Pamela, "81% of LinkedIn Users Belong to a LinkedIn Group [Data]," *Hubspot Blogs*, August 11, 2011, http://blog.hubspot.com/blog/tabid/6307/bid/22364/81-of-LinkedIn-Users-Belong-to-a-LinkedIn-Group-Data.aspx (accessed June 8, 2015).

See, Whitcomb, Susan Britton. *Job Search Magic: Insider Secrets from America's Career and Life Coach*. (Indianapolis, IN: JIST Works, 2006), p. 68.

Whitcomb, *Job Search Magic*, p. 68.

Yate, *Knock 'em Dead*, p. 86.

Chapter 6: Cover Letters and Other Written Communications

Accountemps, "Farewell to the Handwritten Thank-You Note? Survey Reveals Email, Phone Call Are Preferred Methods for Post-Interview Follow-Up," news release, June 14, 2012, http://accountemps.rhi.mediaroom.com/thank-you (accessed July 9, 2015).

"Do Employers Expect a Job Interview Thank-You Card?" CVTips, http://www.cvtips.com/interview/do-employers-expect-a-job-interview-thank-you-card.html (accessed July 10, 2015).

Franklin, Benjamin [Richard Saunders, Poor Richard, pseud.]. *The Way to Wealth*. July 7, 1757, *American Literature Research and Analysis*, http://itech.fgcu.edu/faculty/wohlpart/alra/franklin.htm (accessed May 27, 2015).

"Give Thanks or Your Chance For That Job Could be Cooked," *TheLadders*, http://cdn.theladders.net/static/images/basicSite/PR/pdfs/TheLaddersGiveThanks.pdf (accessed June 5, 2015).

Hanson and Hanson, "What Do Employers *Really* Want?"

Helmrich, Brittney. "Thanks! 20 Job Interview Thank You Note Tips," *Business News Daily*, June 23, 2015, http://www.businessnewsdaily.com/7134-thank-you-note-tips.html (accessed July 9, 2015).

See also, Safani, "Tell a Story."

"Thank-You Note Etiquette," CareerBuilder, http://www.careerbuilder.com/JobPoster/Resources/page.aspx?pagever=ThankYouNoteEtiquette (accessed July 9, 2015).

Chapter 7: Professional Networking

Arruda, "Is LinkedIn Poised."

Ayele, "Land Your Dream Job."

"Constitutional Topic: The Cabinet," U.S. Constitution Online, http://www.usconstitution.net/consttop_cabi.html (accessed November 10, 2015).

Get Hired Fast!: Tap the Hidden Job Market in 15 Days by Brian Graham, *Cracking the Hidden Job Market: How to Find Opportunity in Any Economy* by Donald Asher, and others.

Kaufman, "A Successful Job Search."

Konnikova, Maria. "The Limits of Friendship," *The New Yorker*, October 7, 2014, http://www.newyorker.com/science/maria-konnikova/social-media-affect-math-dunbar-number-friendships (accessed November 10, 2015).

LinkedIn, "Using LinkedIn to Find a Job"; Beatty, "The Math Behind the Networking Claim"; Rothberg, "80% of Job Openings."

Moynihan et al., "A Longitudinal Study," quoted in Kurtzberg and Naquin, *Essentials*, p. 30–32.

"Operational Unit Diagrams," United States Army, http://www.army.mil/info/organization/unitsandcommands/oud/ (accessed November 10, 2015).

See also, Phillips, *Guide to Professional Networking*, p. 50–51; Pete Leibman, "9 Keys on How to Email a New Networking Contact During a Job Search (written by Career Expert, Pete Leibman)," *CareerMuscles* (blog), January 6, 2011, https://careermuscles.wordpress.com/2011/01/06/9-keys-on-how-to-email-a-newnetworking-contact-during-a-job-search-written-by-career-expert-pete-leibman/ (accessed November 10, 2015).

"Quotes on Initiative," *Leadership Now*, http://www.leadershipnow.com/initiativequotes.html (accessed May 28, 2015).

"Ralph Waldo Emerson Quotable Quote," Goodreads, www.goodreads.com/quotes/60285-do-the thing-you-fear-and-the-death-of-fear (accessed May 28, 2015).

Townsend, Maya. "The Introvert's Survival Guide to Networking," *Inc.com*, http://www.inc.com/mayatownsend/introvert-networking-guide.html (accessed November 4, 2015).

Vlooten, Dick van. "The Seven Laws of Networking: Those Who Give, Get," *Career Magazine*, May 7, 2004, http://sciencecareers.sciencemag.org/career_magazine/previous_issues/articles/2004_05_07/nodoi.1275810282259244595 (accessed June 16, 2015).

Williams, Armstrong. "A Few Simple Steps to Building Wealth," *Townhall*, June 13, 2005, http://townhall.com/columnists/armstrongwilliams/2005/06/13/a_few_simple_steps_to_building_wealth/page/full (accessed May 28, 2015).

Weiss, Tara. "Find Your Job by Going to a Conference," *Forbes*, March 24, 2009, http://www.forbes.com/2009/03/24/conference-job-seeking-leadership-careers-networking.html (accessed July 10, 2015).

Chapter 8: Social Media: Twitter and Facebook

"Basic Privacy Settings & Tools" https://www.facebook.com/help/325807937506242/?ref=contextual Facebook Help Center (accessed March 17, 2017).

CareerBuilder, "Number of Employers Using Social Media to Screen Candidates Has Increased 500 Percent over the Last Decade," news release, April 28, 2016, http://www.careerbuilder.com/share/aboutus/pressreleasesdetail.aspx?ed=12%2F31%2F2016&id=pr945&sd=4%2F28%2F2016 (accessed March 16, 2017).

"Character Limit and Changing your username" https://support.twitter.com/articles/14609 Twitter Help Center, (accessed March 14, 2017).

Facebook "Pages" https://www.facebook.com/help/282489752085908/?helpref=hc_fnav.

McDonnell, Amy "60% of employers are peeking into candidates' social media profiles" April 28, 2016 http://www.careerbuilder.com/advice/60-of-employers-are-peeking-into-candidates-social-media-profiles

The Muse, "Job Seekers: Social Media is Even More Important Than You Thought" by Brooke Torres https://www.themuse.com/advice/job-seekers-social-media-is-even-more-important-than-you-thought.

Pine, Joslyn. Ed., *Book of African-American Quotations*. (New York: Dover Publications, 2011), p. 51.

PRC, "Searching for Work in the Digital Era" http://www.pewinternet.org/files/2015/11/PI_2015-11-19-Internet-and-Job-Seeking_FINAL.pdf.

2016 Recruiter Nation Report fka Social Recruiting Survey http://www.jobvite.com/wp-content/uploads/2016/09/RecruiterNation2016.pdf.

"Setting up and Customizing Your Profile" https://support.twitter.com/articles/127871 Twitter Help Center, (accessed March 14, 2017).

Undercover Recruiter, "List of 140 Employers Posting Jobs on Twitter" by Jorgen Sundberg, http://theundercoverrecruiter.com/list-employers-posting-jobs-twitter/ (accessed March 16, 2017).

Chapter 9: Working with Search Firms

DISYS, "Top 5 Reasons to Use Staffing Firms as Your Primary Hiring Strategy," http://www.disys.com/top-5-reasons-to-use-staffing-firms-as-your-primary-hiring-strategy/ (accessed June 19, 2015); "Get Help With Hiring . . . And More: Working With Staffing Firms: What's in It for Me?" CareerBuilder, http://www.careerbuildercommunications.com/staffing-firms/ (accessed June 19, 2015).

"Don't Do That!—Mistakes To Avoid When Working With Recruiters," *True Source* (blog), November 2012, http://www.true-source.com/2012/11/dont-do-that-mistakes-to-avoid-when-working-with-recruiters/ (accessed June 9, 2015).

"Employment and Recruiting Agencies in the US: Market Research Report," IBISWorld, March 2015, http://www.ibisworld.com/industry/default.aspx?indid=1463 (accessed June 11, 2015).

"Johann Wolfgang von Goethe Quotable Quote," Goodreads, http://www.goodreads.com/quotes/316359-just-begin-and-the-mind-grows-heated-continue-and-the (accessed June 11, 2015).

Chapter 10: Proactively Marketing Your Professional Credentials

"Bonus Programs and Practices," *WorldatWork*, June 2014, http://www.worldatwork.org/adim

Link?id=75444 (accessed June 1, 2015).

See also, Claycomb and Dinse, *Career Pathways*, Part 5, "Phone-phobia."

Cornerstone Coaching LLC, "What Winston Churchill Can Teach Us About Inevitable Success," (blog), February 26, 2014, http://www.cornerstoneadvisoryservices.com/blog/what-winston-churchill-can-teach us-about-inevitable-success (accessed May 28, 2015).

DiResta, interview by Canters, "How to Blitz."

Hill, Paul. *The Panic Free Job Search: Unleash the Power of the Web and Social Networking to Get Hired*. (Pompton Plains, NJ: Career Press, 2012), p. 203.

Jobvite Recruiter Nation Report 2016, http://www.jobvite.com/wp-content/uploads/2016/09/RecruiterNation2016.pdf (64% of recruiters report awarding monetary bonuses to incentivize referrals into their organizations.) (accessed March 15, 2017).

Roosevelt, Theodore, "The Strenuous Life," (speech, The Hamilton Club, Chicago, IL, April 10, 1899), http://www.bartleby.com/58/1.html (accessed May 28, 2015).

Whitcomb, *Job Search Magic*, p. 273–274.

Chapter 11: Interviewing

Amstutz, Lisa, "Survey of HR Managers: How Many Job Changes is Too Many?" (blog), *Robert Half*, January 17, 2014, http://www.roberthalf.com/finance/blog/survey-of-hr-managers-how-many-job-changesis-too-many?hsFormKey=06a77aee09a564eca4467cf5525e3c15 (accessed June 9, 2015).

"Ball at Impact," Golfswing.com, http://www.golfswing.com.au/139 (accessed February 15, 2016).

Biron, "How to Explain Employment Gaps in a Job Interview," *Career Sidekick* (blog), December 9, 2013, http://careersidekick.com/how-to-explain-employment-gaps-in-a-job-interview/ (accessed February 16, 2016).

Bricker, Eric, "How to Ace Your Video Interview," *On Careers Blog, U.S. News & World Report*, July 11, 2013, http://money.usnews.com/money/careers/articles/2013/07/11/how-to-ace-your-video-interview (accessed December 1, 2015).

Bureau of Labor Statistics, "Number of Jobs Held, Labor Market Activity, and Earnings Growth Among the Youngest Baby Boomers: Results from a Longitudinal Survey," news release, March 31, 2015, http://www.bls.gov/news.release/pdf/nlsoy.pdf (accessed May 29, 2015).

CareerBuilder, "2015 Candidate Behavior Study."

CareerBuilder, "Employers Share Encouraging Perspectives."

CareerBuilder, "Forty-Nine Percent of Workers Do Not Negotiate Job Offers, Finds CareerBuilder Compensation Survey," news release, August 21, 2013, http://www.careerbuilder.com/share/aboutus/pressreleasesdetail.aspx?sd=8/21/2013&id=pr777&ed=12/31/2013 (accessed June 2, 2015).

Portions adapted from Claycomb and Dinse, *Career Pathways*, Part 8.

"Cognitive scientists say it can take up to two hundred times the amount of information to undo a first impression as it takes to make one," Zack, Devora. "10 Tips for People Who Hate Networking," Careerealism, May 4, 2015, http://www.careerealism.com/hate-networking-tips/ (accessed July 17, 2015).

DiResta, interview by Canters, "How to Blitz."

For Dummies, "Answering Interview Questions About Job History Gaps," Dummies.com, www.dummies.com/how-to/content/answering-interview-questions-about-job-history-g0.html (accessed February 16, 2016).

Hansen, Katharine, PhD. "Do's and Don'ts for Second (and Subsequent) Job Interviews," *Quintessential Careers*, http://www.quintcareers.com/second-interviewing-dos-donts/ (accessed February 16, 2016).

Jamal, Nina, and Judith Lindenberger. "How to Make a Great First Impression," *Business Know-How*, http://www.businessknowhow.com/growth/dress-impression.htm (accessed June 2, 2015).

Jobvite Recruiter Nation Report 2016, http://www.jobvite.com/wp-content/uploads/2016/09/

RecruiterNation2016.pdf (accessed March 15, 2017).

"Jose N. Harris Quotable Quote," Goodreads, http://www.goodreads.com/quotes/415120-to-get something-you-never-had-you-have-to-do (accessed June 22, 2015).

Joyce, Susan P., "After the Interview, What is Taking Them SO Long?" *Work Coach Café* (blog),

September 17, 2012, http://www.workcoachcafe.com/2012/09/17/after-the-interview-what-is-takingthem-so-long/ (accessed February 15, 2016); "2015 Candidate Behavior Study," CareerBuilder, http://careerbuildercommunications.com/candidatebehavior/

(accessed February 15, 2016); Jena McGregor, "Interviewing for a Job is Taking Longer Than Ever," *On Leadership* (blog), *Washington Post*, June 18, 2015, http://www.washingtonpost.com/blogs/on-leadership/wp/2015/06/18/interviewing-for-a-job-is-takinglonger-than-ever/ (accessed February 15, 2016).

Kempka, Jill, "Resume FAQ: How Do I Handle Employment Gaps?" *Career Coach* (blog), *Manpower*, January 25, 2013, manpowergroupblogs.us/manpower/career-coach/2013/01/25/resume-faq-how-do-ihandle-employment-gaps/ (accessed February 16, 2016).

Kurtzberg and Naquin, Essentials , p. 31.

McGregor, Jena, "Interviewing for a Job."

OfficeTeam, "Survey: Six in 10 Companies Conduct Video Job Interviews," news release, August 30, 2012, http://officeteam.rhi.mediaroom.com/videointerviews (accessed June 5, 2015).

Peterson, Marshalita Sims. "Personnel Interviewers' Perceptions of the Importance and Adequacy of Applicants' Communication Skills," *Communication Education* 46, no. 4 (1997): 287–291, quoted in Kurtzberg and Naquin, *Essentials*, p. 31.

Pongo, "How to Explain Work History Gaps in the Interview," *The Pongo Blog*, https://www.pongoresume.com/blogPosts/372/how-to-explain-work-history-gaps-in-the-interview.cfm (accessed February 16, 2016).

Regis University Career Services, "Interviewing Strategies for CPS Students and Alumni," Regis University, http://www.regis.edu/About-Regis-University/University-Offices-and-Services/Career-Services/Student-and-Alumni/Interviewing-Strategies.aspx (accessed June 19, 2015).

Safani, "Tell a Story."

See also, Simpson, Cheryl, 10 Healthy Ways to Cope with Job Search Rejection, https://www.linkedin.com/pulse/10-healthy-ways-cope-job-search-rejection-chery. March 27, 2017 (accessed March 29, 2017).

Smith, Jacquelyn. "How to Ace the 50 Most Common Interview Questions," *Forbes*, January 11, 2013, http://www.forbes.com/sites/jacquelynsmith/2013/01/11/how-to-ace-the-50-most-common-interviewquestions/ (accessed June 9, 2015); Thad Peterson, "100 Potential Interview Questions," Monster, http://career-advice.monster.com/job-interview/interview-questions/100-potential-interview-questions/article.aspx (accessed June 11, 2015).

Sutton, Robert I., PhD. *The No Asshole Rule: Building a Civilized Workplace and Surviving One That Isn't.* (New York: Warner Business Books, 2007), quoted in Kurtzberg and Naquin, *Essentials*, p. 18.

"Understanding the Employer's Perspective," Internships.com, http://www.internships. com/student/resources/interview/prep/getting-ready/understand-employer (accessed July 10, 2015).

U.S. Department of Labor, "Soft Skill #2: Enthusiasm and Attitude," Skills to Pay the Bills, http://www.dol.gov/odep/topics/youth/softskills/Enthusiasm.pdf (accessed June 19, 2015); Adams, Susan. "How to Ace Your Job Interview," *Forbes*, March 1, 2013, http:// www.forbes.com/sites/susanadams/2013/03/01/how-to-ace-your-job-interview-2/ (accessed June 15, 2015).

Weber, Lauren, and Rachel Feintzeig. "Why Companies Are Taking Longer to Hire," *Wall Street Journal*, September 1, 2014, http://www.wsj.com/article_email/companies-are-taking-longer-to-hire-1409612937-lMyQjAxMTA1MDIwMjEyNDIyWj (accessed February 16, 2016).

"What is Solution Selling?" Sales Performance International, http://solutionselling.learn. com/learncenter.asp?id=178455 (accessed June 8, 2015).

Whitcomb, *Job Search Magic*, p. 274.

Woods, Jennifer. "Working Longer—Whether You Want to or Not," CNBC.com, December 23, 2014, http://cached.newslookup.com/cached.php?ref_id=105&siteid=2098&id=10359 558&t=1419339600 (accessed June 9, 2015).

Zolfagharifard, Ellie. "First Impressions Really DO Count: Employers Make Decisions About Job Applicants in Under Seven Minutes," *Daily Mail*, June 18, 2014, http://www.dailymail. co.uk/sciencetech/article-2661474/First-impressions-really-DO-count-Employers-make-decisions-job-applicants-seven minutes.html (accessed June 5, 2015).

Chapter 12: Unique Tactics That Create Differentiation

See also, "The Best Website Builders 2016," Top10WebsiteBuilders, http://www. top10webbuilders.com/?s1-google/s2-us-search/s3-website-builder-p (accessed February 17, 2016).

Matt, "Brag Book."

Tracy, Brian. *Eat That Frog!: 21 Great Ways to Stop Procrastinating and Get More Done in Less Time*, 2nd ed. (Buchanan, NY: ReadHowYouWant, 2008), p. 84.

Safani, "Tell a Story."

Smith, Jacquelyn. "Why Every Job Seeker Should Have a Personal Website, and What It Should Include," *Forbes*, April 26, 2013, http://www.forbes.com/sites/jacquelynsmith/2013/04/26/why-every-job-seekershould-have-a-personal-website-and-what-it-should-include/#73ae8b8a902e (accessed February 17, 2016).

Skillings, Pamela, "The Ultimate Infographic Resume Guide," *Big Interview* (blog), June 18, 2013, http://biginterview.com/blog/2013/06/infographic-resumes.html (accessed February 17, 2016).

Strankowski, Donald J. "Your License to Brag: The Brag Book," Ascend Career and Life Strategies, LLC, April 2005, http://www.ascendcareers.net/newsletters/April2005.html (accessed February 17, 2016).

Chapter 13: References

Frederick, Carl, "Carl Frederick Quotes," World of Quotes, http://www.worldofquotes.com/author/Carl+Frederick/1/index.html (accessed June 10, 2015).

Chapter 14: Evaluating and Negotiating a Job Offer

CareerBuilder, "Forty-Nine Percent of Workers Do Not Negotiate."

Carnegie, Dale. *How to Win Friends and Influence People.* (New York: Simon and Schuster, 2010), p. 134.

Honck, Alan, with Gordon Orians. "Are We Born With a Sense of Fairness?" *Pacific Standard*, December 26, 2012, https://psmag.com/are-we-born-with-a-sense-of-fairness-edd2d2680c10#.ce304fxbb (accessed April 18, 2016).

LinkedIn Talent Solutions, "2015 Talent Trends," p. 30.

Portions of this chapter adapted from Claycomb and Dinse, *Career Pathways*, Part 9.

McLeod, Lisa Earle, "The Big Mistake People Make When They Negotiate," *Life on Purpose* (blog), *McLeod & More, Inc.*, March 26, 2014, http://www.mcleodandmore.com/2014/03/26/the-big-mistake-people-makewhen-they-negotiate-2/ (accessed June 19, 2015).

Whitcomb, *Job Search Magic*, p. 274.

Chapter 15: Resignation and Counter Offers

"Counter Offers," Cybercoders, http://www.cybercoders.com/home/counteroffer/ (accessed June 11, 2015).

Green, "Counteroffer."

Green, Alison "How to Resign Your Job Gracefully," *On Careers Blog, U.S. News & World Report*, July 28, 2008, money.usnews.com/money/blogs/outside-voices-careers/2008/07/28/how-to-resign-your-jobgracefully (accessed February 17, 2016).

Love, "Should I Entertain"; Lankford, Kim. "Should You Take That Counteroffer?" Monster, http://careeradvice.monster.com/in-the-office/leaving-a-job/should-you-take-that-counteroffer/article.aspx (accessed June 11, 2015); Alison Green, "Why You Shouldn't Take a Counteroffer," *On Careers Blog, U.S. News & World Report*, March 26, 2012, http://money.usnews.com/money/blogs/outside-voices-careers/2012/03/26/why-you-shouldnt-take-a-counteroffer (accessed June 11, 2015).

Love, Scott. "Counteroffer—Should I Entertain a Counteroffer?" The Vet Recruiter, http://thevetrecruiter.com/important-information-about-recruiters-for-job-seekers/counteroffer-should-i-entertain-acounteroffer/ (accessed June 11, 2015).

Smiles, Samuel. *Character*, new ed. (London: John Murray, 1876), p. 350.

Sun, Calvin, "10+ Things You Should Do When You Resign," *10 Things* (blog), TechRepublic, March 17, 2008, www.techrepublic.com/blog/10-things/10-plus-things-you-should-do-when-you-resign/ (accessed February 17, 2016).

"Thomas Fowell Buxton Quotable Quote," Goodreads, http://www.goodreads.com/quotes/891186-the-longer-i-live-the-more-i-am-certain-that (accessed June 10, 2015).

Chapter 16: Covenants-Not-to-Compete and Non-Solicitation Agreements

Broadcasting and the Law, Inc. "Employment contracts—'blue line' rule." Abstract. *Broadcasting and the Law* (1997). http://www.readabstracts.com/Mass-communications/Employment-contracts-blue-line-rule-Noncommercial-stations-underwriting-announcements.html (accessed June 11, 2015).

Izzi, Matthew. "California Ban on Covenants Not to Compete," LegalMatch, http://www.legalmatch.com/law-library/article/california-ban-on-covenants-not-to-compete.html (accessed June 11, 2015).

Non-Compete Agreement—Art Technology Group Inc. and Joseph Chung, http://contracts.onecle.com/art/chung.noncomp.1998.08.18.shtml (accessed March 16, 2016).

"William Shakespeare Quotes Measure for Measure," http://www.william-shakespeare.info/quotes quotations-play-measure-for-measure.htm (accessed June 11, 2015).

Chapter 17: How to Relaunch a Stagnant Job Search

Dougherty, "16 Tips to Optimize."

See also, Frasco, "11 Tips."

"Rocky Balboa Quotable Quote," Goodreads, http://www.goodreads.com/quotes/3228059-every champion-was-once-a-contender-that-refused-to-give (accessed April 12, 2016).

"Volunteering and its Surprising Benefits," HelpGuide.org, http://www.helpguide.org/articles/workcareer/volunteering-and-its-surprising-benefits.htm (accessed February 17, 2016).

Whitcomb, *Job Search Magic*, p. 273–274.

Chapter 18: Required Job-Search Skills for Long-Term Career Employment

Bureau of Labor Statistics, "Employee Tenure Summary," news release, September 18, 2014, http://www.bls.gov/news.release/tenure.nr0.htm (accessed May 29, 2015).

Bureau of Labor Statistics, "Number of Jobs Held, Labor Market Activity, and Earnings Growth Among the Youngest Baby Boomers: Results from a Longitudinal Survey," news release, March 31, 2015, http://www.bls.gov/news.release/pdf/nlsoy.pdf (accessed May 29, 2015).

"Wayne Gretzky Quotable Quote," Goodreads, http://www.goodreads.com/quotes/4798-you-miss one-hundred-percent-of-the-shots-you-don-t (accessed July 13, 2015).

Woods, "Working Longer."

Chapter 19: A Personal Letter to You about Career Management

ExecuNet, "Senior-Level Business Leaders Say Positive Attitude is the Key to Getting the Job," news release, March 25, 2013, http://www.execunet.com/m_releases_content.cfm?id=4812 (accessed June 11, 2015).

Maxwell, John C. *The Maxwell Daily Reader: 365 Days of Insight to Develop the Leader Within You and Influence Those Around You*. (Nashville, TN: Thomas Nelson, 2011), p. 227.

"Napoleon Hill Quotable Quote," Goodreads, http://www.goodreads.com/quotes/244859-a-goal-is-a dream-with-a-deadline (accessed June 11, 2015).

Vlooten, "The Seven Laws."

Appendix A: Success Story Worksheet and Sample

Durable medical equipment; see "Durable Medical Equipment (DME) Center," Centers for Medicare & Medicaid Services, http://www.cms.gov/Center/Provider-Type/Durable-Medical-Equipment-DME Center.html (accessed July 13, 2015).